Text copyright © 1982 Parts 1 & 2, Paul and Tessa Clowney
Text copyright © 1993 Part 3, captions to photographs (excluding London), Patricia Aithie
Text copyright © 1993 Part 3, captions to London photographs, Robert H. Baylis
Text copyright © 1986 Part 3, non-caption text, Alan Whitworth

This edition copyright © 1993 Lion Publishing

The authors assert the moral right
to be identified as the authors of this work

Published by
Lion Publishing plc
Sandy Lane West, Oxford, England
ISBN 0 7459 2771 8

First edition 1982
Enlarged paperback edition 1986
This edition 1993

A catalogue record for this book is available
from the British Library

Printed and bound in Slovenia

EXPLORING CHURCHES

PAUL AND TESSA CLOWNEY

Full Colour Guide to British Churches
Photography by Charles and Patricia Aithie

A LION BOOK

Contents

INTRODUCTION

The word 'church' can mean two different things: a building – or people. First and foremost, in fact, it means a group of people who have been called together by God to form the 'body' of those who share new life through Jesus Christ. A group of Russian Christians meeting in secret in a home is just as much a 'church' as a massive cathedral congregation.

But the word has also come to be used of the buildings in which the church meets. And so the buildings can help us to understand something of the motives of the original builders, the way the building has been used, and the beliefs it expresses.

Churches and cathedrals often form the peak of an age's architectural output. Whether built for the glory of God or of men, they represent a staggering commitment of time, skill and money, and were built by the foremost craftsmen of the day, often employing the most up-to-date building techniques. So simply as buildings, the heritage of churches and cathedrals is awe-inspiring. Exploring churches means enjoying centuries of cultural history. And sometimes the smallest church can be just as fascinating as the biggest cathedral.

But as well as being architecturally fascinating, each church reveals maybe hundreds of years of Christian history. Succeeding generations have used the building in different ways, in keeping with their changing understanding of the Christian faith. And each generation has left its mark on the building. An eleventh-century building, for example, might have been expanded in the Middle Ages, with the clergy's chancel entirely separate from the people's nave; in the Reformation screens, statues and paintings would have been cleared out; in the eighteenth century a new organ might have been fitted and a hundred years later new floors and heating; in the last twenty years all the pews might have been replaced by chairs and the altar moved from the east end to the

centre of the building. All these changes can be read in the fabric of building.

The second section of this book, The Story of Church Building, examines why different styles of building developed. In most cases the design of a church is a reflection of the way the people of the time understood God and their fellow men, and the way in which services of worship were conducted – whether the clergy said all the words, or the congregation took part, whether there was a procession or not, where the communion table was placed, and so on.

Churches were usually designed with a particular form of service or 'liturgy' in mind. An Eastern Orthodox church separates the priest from the people behind a solid screen. A Quaker meeting-house consists of simple benches facing each other – for there is no 'priest' at all. If the liturgy changed, the building sometimes had to be changed, too. The building itself could also affect the liturgy. Cavernous medieval churches had peculiar acoustics, for example, and to cope with them, it became customary to chant the service.

The first part, the Fieldguide, is intended to be a practical guide to the building and its use. It concentrates mainly on ancient churches as being of most interest to tourists. But many of the same features will be found in different forms of church buildings generally. The section also helps in dating the building and understanding its various parts.

It is worth having a good look at the outside of the building first. The architect will have given a great deal of thought to the overall impression the building gives. If it is an old town church, you may have to 'think away' the surrounding buildings before you can appreciate the church as it first was – with fresh clean stone.

Going inside, first impressions are of great importance. Was the church designed to evoke awe, or mystery? How do the people who meet here week by week feel in the building? Colour, light and acoustics all go to make up this emotional impact of the building. As you explore the inside of the building, it pays to be systematic, 'understanding' first the nave, then the transepts and finally the choir and chancel. Compare the different parts of the building with each other. Are they all of the same period? How does the building compare with the last one you visited?

Then look at the details: the windows, the columns, the doorways, the furnishings. Are there the tell-tale hints of changes in belief or practice, for instance – statues defaced, chapels added, arches filled in?

It is instructive to notice how the church building is used today. Is it a museum or a meeting place? Some seem to be little more than showcases of religious history, full of exhibits, postcards and money-boxes. Others demonstrate a faith that is as alive today as ever.

Exploring churches is a pastime which becomes more and more intriguing. The variety is inexhaustible. This book is a guide to help you see and ask questions. Perhaps it will help you touch, smell, hear and imagine history as you enjoy the design of places of worship. Perhaps too it will help take you beyond the building to a better understanding of the faith that the building was designed to express.

PART 1
FIELDGUIDE

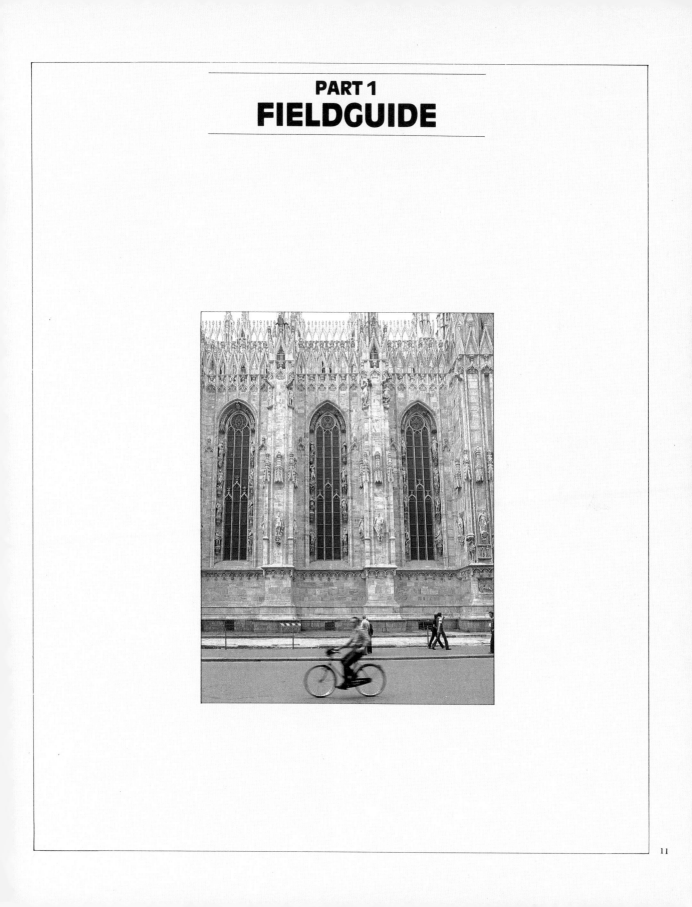

Outside the Building

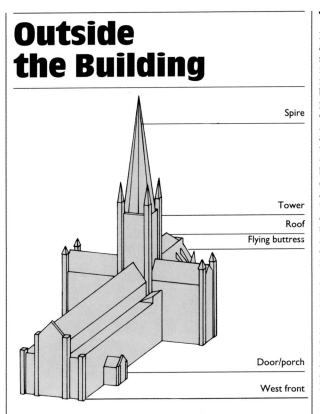

- Spire
- Tower
- Roof
- Flying buttress
- Door/porch
- West front

Towers

Building towers is not easy, as anyone who has tried to build sand castles knows. Towers require carefully-positioned foundations, a good deal of bracing, and well-fitted components. Sometimes they still collapse. In the late Middle Ages when tower building was almost a community competition, towers often fell. Considerable ingenuity has been applied through the centuries to propping up towers and spires. Iron bands, internal truss rods, strainer arches, additional flying buttresses – some towers have them all. And there are some remarkably crooked towers which do still manage to stand.

The obvious functions of a tower are to extend the range from which the church is visible and to support bells. Cathedrals have as many as nine towers, but the two most common arrangements are a single tower at the west end, and two towers on either side of the west front with a third large tower at the crossing. This

The huge tower of the church at Widecombe in the west of England.

central tower represents the church's contact between heaven and earth. Every effort has been made to keep the tower as light as possible; large windows and arches serve to reduce the weight. Towers have often been rebuilt or extended in later periods – not always with a happy marriage of styles.

West Fronts

The most considered exterior feature of larger churches and cathedrals is generally the west front. Medieval builders thought of this façade, incorporating the large entrance doors, as a symbol of the gate to heaven. As such it was more elaborately designed than any part of the building save the altar screen. The structure of the west front sometimes emphasizes the shape of the building behind it; sometimes it disguises it. The twin-tower façade which became the norm in the eleventh century divides the west end into three vertical sections, echoing the internal division of two aisles and a nave. A large window almost always fills the upper central part, sometimes balanced by openings in the flanking towers.

Because it was normal practice to begin building a church at the east end, the west is often dated later than the rest of the church. At times this difference is visible in a marked

The west front of Salisbury cathedral is dominated by the massive spire behind.

change in style. For example, west-end towers were regularly carried higher in later centuries. A Romanesque pediment surmounted by a Gothic tower and Baroque spire is not uncommon.

Norwich Cathedral, though bigger than any parish church, shows the typical cross-shaped plan of European Gothic churches. On the south side are the shaded cloisters: from its beginning, the cathedral had a monastery attached.

Spires

Not all churches have spires. Sometimes this is intentional design. In other cases the spire has been removed, has collapsed or has burnt after being struck by lightning. The spire has often been seen as a symbol of man's aspiration to be united with his creator. It was also a symbol of local pride, and a signpost for travellers. The building of a tall spire made tremendous demands on the finances and skills of a church. The easiest method was to build in timber and then clad with lead or copper; the wind stresses on such a construction are enormous, however, and so this sort of spire had to be drawn tightly down against the tower. If the foundations could take the weight, a spire could be built of stone, but this was expensive, dangerous and difficult. Each stone had to be carefully cut in compound angles, carried up the scaffolding, supported by templates and finally mortared into place.

The small spires or pinnacles at the base of the main central spire of a cathedral were more than decoration. By their extra weight they secured the base of the spire against the outward thrust.

Sites

Churches were often built on an important site – the grave of a martyr, or the site of a previous church. Not all of these locations were really ideal. The churches of Ravenna, Winchester and Ely were all built on marshland. Amsterdam required foundation piles driven as deep as the churches are tall. Subsidence in Ravenna has amounted to more than three feet (one metre) in places. Modern city life poses a serious threat to many old buildings; exhaust fumes erode the stone, vibrations from heavy traffic loosen the joints, excavations in the vicinity can affect foundations.

Many churches are built on hillsides, naturally dominating the area around.

Roofs

Roofs are often covered in lead plate, sometimes as much as a quarter of an inch (almost a centimetre) thick. The considerable weight of such a roof prevents it from being blown away but adds substantially to the stress on the walls. A carefully cross-braced beam structure lies between the roof cladding and the vault of the ceiling, and this forest of wood always adds to the hazard of fire. There are terrifying accounts of cathedral fires in which molten lead poured from the guttering like water.

The massive cathedral of Milan is roofed in great slabs of marble – sloping gently enough for people to walk on with ease.

Gargoyles

On a large roof, rain-water can pose problems. Simply getting rid of all the water from a cloudburst calls for careful design. If water overflows onto the walls or the vault it can cause rot or even collapse. The simplest way of getting rid of the water quickly was to fix great projecting spouts to the guttering so that the water could fall clear of the walls. These spouts commonly assumed the form of fantastic beasts called gargoyles.

Doors/Porches

The entrance doors of the west front of cathedrals were reserved for processions, state occasions and religious festivals. Day-to-day traffic entered in most cases through a doorway on the north-west aisle. This doorway was protected from the weather by a porch. The porch itself acquired a certain significance. Marriages were sometimes conducted there, and it was a common place to seal business agreements – 'by church door'.

There is some noteworthy sculpture in these porches, with two themes being particularly popular. The first is the baptism of Christ, for baptism is the symbol of entry into God's family, the church. The second theme is the changing seasons and their respective labours; this serves to remind the faithful that Christ is involved in all parts of human life.

As well as providing shelter at the door, the porch was used in medieval times for weddings and for trade.

Buttresses

Churches often have thickened sections of wall or even what look like small walls running out from the main building. The one purpose of these 'buttresses' is to give greater rigidity to the whole structure. The greater the weight of a buttress, the more it pushes down and the greater the lateral forces it can withstand.

The massive buttresses of Romanesque churches strengthened the fabric of the building but left little room for large windows. The Gothic builders, by contrast, placed buttresses only at key structural points. The further a buttress is from the wall it supports, the greater its efficiency. The best-constructed buttresses (and interior piers) are solid throughout. But it was simpler and cheaper to make them hollow and to fill the interior with rubble.

The structural strength of tall towers and walls is provided by carefully-placed buttresses.

Flying Buttresses

Flying buttresses are strengthening arches which reach from a vertical buttress to a wall, generally to the upper wall of the nave. These counteract the outward thrust of the roof against the comparatively thin upper nave wall.

The aisle, with its low roof, has a thick buttress outside it. On top of this are two levels of flying buttress which support the nave wall and bear outwards on a pinnacled column.

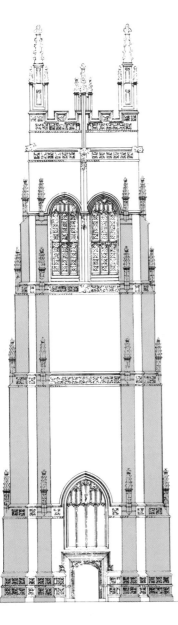

Bells

A full 'peal' of bells can weigh several tonnes, considerably adding to the weight of the tower. In the seventeenth century much ingenuity went into designing mechanical contrivances such as 'carillons' which could chime the bells. These are still used widely on the continent of Europe. In Britain 'change ringing' is more popular; the six or more bells are rung in intricately varying sequences.

Inside the Building

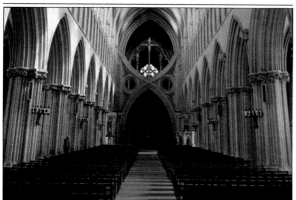

The Nave

The nave (from 'navis' = ship) is the main area for the congregation. In medieval times it was a popular meeting-place, even for trading. The length of the nave is divided into bays by 'piers' or columns. Shafts which extend up the surface of the wall from the piers or columns are called 'half shafts' because of their semicircular cross section. These vertical divisions are almost always stressed in Gothic architecture to emphasize height. (If they run from vault to floor in an unbroken line they will emphasize the vertical more than if they stop at the top of the arcade; if the piers are composed of 'bundles' of shafts this also contributes to a vertical stress.)

The Aisles

Aisles run parallel with the nave, often separated from it by the main columns. Generally the roof is lower over the aisles; the nave walls above the level of the aisle roofs are pierced with the clerestory windows. Aisles are mainly used for seating, but there may also be memorial tombs, as well as bookstalls and displays showing the work of the church and the missionary outreach it supports.

The Crossing

The intersection of the nave and the transept, the crossing, is a natural centre for a church. It is also the structural kingpin of the building. Here the space opens out in all directions and light from the nave mixes with light from the transept. In some larger churches there is a 'triforium', sometimes a passage-way which runs right round the transept. Get up into this space to look down on the crossing if you can possibly do so. The four corner piers of the crossing are thicker than the piers of the nave arcade. Occasionally arches are partially or completely blocked in to give the crossing greater strength. In some cases 'strainer arches' have been built in. But despite all the bracing and strainer arches, crossing towers and spires have some-times still fallen through the roof.

The Transept

The transept crosses the nave at right angles. It gives the church the form of a cross. Some bigger churches have several transepts, some-times diminishing in length towards the eastern end. The end walls of the transepts can be treated in many ways, but the most common is to have a 'blind arcading' – arches built nearly flush with the wall – sometimes with a large rose window above.

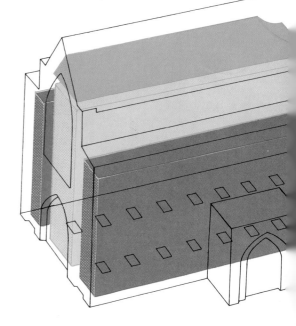

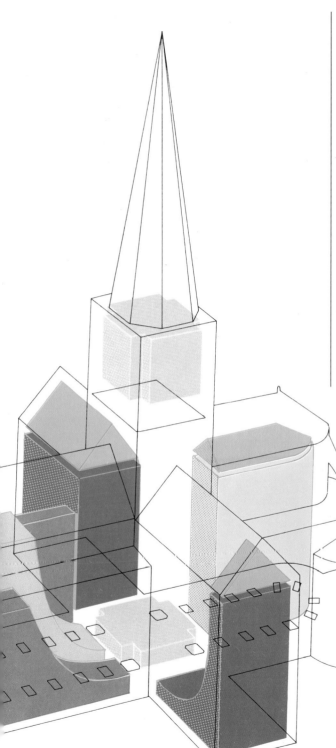

The Chancel/ Choir

The choir or chancel is where services are sung or said. To emphasize the mystery and holiness of the service in Catholic churches, the choir was often separated from the people by a screen. These screens are sometimes beautifully carved – the wood carver's flamboyant challenge to the stone worker. In addition to the screens the choir is also distinguished from the nave by a raised floor; in cases where churches were built over crypts, the level of the choir floor could be six to ten feet (two to three metres) higher than the nave. In the Middle Ages some choirs would be opened at stated times to allow pilgrims to view relics.

The Vault

The vault or ceiling is always one of the more spectacular interior elements. From the crudely-hewn tunnel vaults of early Romanesque to the bizarre and gravity-defying pendulum vaults of the seventeenth century, these stone ceilings are always fascinating. The first rib vaults in the twelfth century were a functional solution to the roofing problem. It was not long before ribs were being used for a decorative effect as well as for structural purposes. Short rib sections spread from the tops of half shafts like a net over the nave, each intersection embellished by a carved and painted boss. Vaults were often added later; it was common practice to roof first in timber. Sometimes a later vault does not fit in neatly with the clerestory.

When they were built, medieval churches reflected the belief that clergy in the chancel and congregation in the nave should be separate. Today the space is often used far more flexibly.

Nave Levels

Naves are often built in three 'layers'; at the bottom the large arched arcade; then the middle level of arches, the triforium. Above this is the clerestory – windows over the aisle roof which let light into the **nave.** Sometimes a fourth division called a **tribune** is added. The proportions of the different levels were the subject of extensive discussion. If the span of the arches in the triforium is too broad compared to their height, the middle section of the wall can seem a bit squashed!

Capitals

The capitals, or tops of the columns, are usually carved with foliage, figures, patterns, or all three. Note the way in which the shape of the capital is harmonized with the figures. Such carving required experience – if the chisel broke a bit off there was no option but to change the design or to start again.

Chapels

Small chapels are often built off the eastern wall of transepts and on side-aisles. Many of these were 'chantry chapels'; they were commissioned in the Middle Ages by the wealthy for the 'chanting' of daily mass on behalf of the souls of members of their family who had died, in the belief that prayers could reduce their time in purgatory. Today they are used for private prayer, for smaller services, or as places for people to come to 'confession', unburdening their sins with a spiritual adviser.

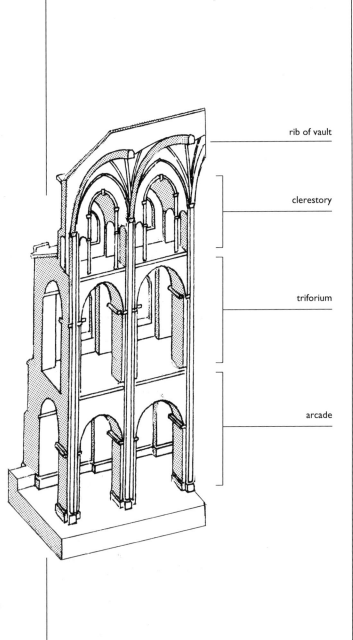

rib of vault

clerestory

triforium

arcade

In this example, the triforium forms a passage right round the building, almost the size of the aisle below it. The round-headed arches show that the nave was built in the Norman period. The pointed windows in the chancel date from the fifteenth century.

The Ambulatory

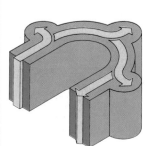

The passage which runs around and behind the choir is known as the ambulatory, for 'walking round'. In the more prestigious plans twin ambulatories were popular; it was a particularly suitable arrangement for pilgrim churches. The usual treatment of the eastern end of the building in Europe was the chevet or half circle of chapels opening off the bays of a rounded apse. In England there is sometimes a 'Lady Chapel' – usually in the form of a highly decorated extension to the east end of the choir, dedicated to the Virgin Mary.

Moulding

Moulding is sometimes cut from contrasting stone. The horizontal divisions are usually stressed with thin stone mouldings known as stringing. Compare cross-sections of the piers, window mullions (the vertical dividers) with half-shafts, stringing, ribs, and so on. These stones were cut from 'profile templates', so looking at cross-sections shows how the architect achieved his goal.

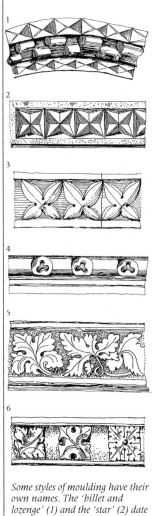

Some styles of moulding have their own names. The 'billet and lozenge' (1) and the 'star' (2) date from the eleventh century, the 'ballflower' (4) and 'vine' (5) from the high Gothic period. (3) also dates from this period, and (6) from the late Gothic.

The Building in Use

The activities of a particular church are represented in the building that has been developed over the years to serve its various purposes.

The local church or chapel is usually built as the meeting place of a local congregation, used for services for worship Sunday by Sunday, for festivals such as Christmas and Easter, for Sunday schools for children and many other purposes. There is plenty of seating for the congregation.

Festivals

Festivals such as Christmas and Easter are celebrated in local churches and cathedrals. **Christmas** celebrates the birth of Jesus; card services, candle-lit services and other traditions make it a joyful festival, often involving the children. **Easter** recalls the death and resurrection of Jesus: Good Friday is an opportunity for repentance and renewed forgiveness; Easter Day the triumphant celebration of the rising again of Jesus to new life as the first of a new creation. **Whitsun** remembers the coming of the Spirit of God to the church. Other festivals such as **Harvest** bring thanksgiving to God; all are opportunities for decorating the church in imaginative and appropriate ways.

Cathedrals

The Cathedral, usually in a city centre, is the central building of a diocese – the church's 'area headquarters', led by the bishop. Often it is used for more formal and civic occasions. Particularly if there is a choir school, there is stress on services being sung or said on behalf of the community rather than with the involvement of the congregation.

Congregation ①

The congregation sits in pews or seats usually facing one end; or in modern churches and those stressing communal fellowship they may be gathered round a central communion table.

Private Chapels ②

Private chapels were often built at the end of the medieval period or in the nineteenth century to say masses on behalf of a wealthy individual, not for congregational use at all. Side-chapels in cathedrals sometimes represent the same belief and practice. Reformed churches discontinued the practice, as it undermined their teaching that salvation is by trust in the work of Jesus, not anything we can do for ourselves.

THIS PAGE, LEFT *In this packed Baptist church at Christmas the gallery gives a good view of the children's nativity play.* ABOVE *The cathedral is used not just for services but also for events such as this international gathering of young people.* OPPOSITE, ABOVE LEFT *Baptism in this church is by 'total immersion'.* BELOW RIGHT *In an Anglican church, the minister leading the service gives bread and wine to the congregation.*

Baptism ③

Baptism is a vivid visual demonstration of becoming a Christian. The person 'dies' to his old sinful life by going down into water, and 'rises again with Jesus' in newness of life. Some churches practise this quite literally with a large 'baptistry' which allows people to go right into the water. In other churches a stone 'font' fulfils the same function more symbolically, and the water is sprinkled. In the case of children, promises are made by parents or god-parents on behalf of the child which are later 'confirmed' if the person comes to full belief.

Choirs ⑤

The choir lead the singing from the chancel or choir-stalls, usually accompanied by an **organ**. Hymns and psalms are a major part of services. In some churches the whole service is sung: in medieval times the voice would carry to a very large congregation if the service was intoned or sung.

Priory, convent or monastery churches are designed for the daily services of a community of Christians who live together. Sometimes they require only the 'chancel' or choir part of the church, as there is no other congregation, so no need for the main nave at all – except for churches at a place of pilgrimage.

Communion ⑥

The **Communion service, Mass, Eucharist, Lord's Supper** (varying names for the same service) is usually a main event in the church's life. It is a 'visual aid' of the death and rising again of Jesus: just as bread and wine are shared, believers share in forgiveness for their sins by the death of Jesus, and in new life by his rising again. It is celebrated from a communion table; sometimes a simple wooden table, or in churches which stress the service as a re-enactment of Jesus' sacrifice a stone or marble altar. In some churches different coloured altar-cloths are used at different times in the church's year.

Sunday Schools ④

A Sunday school often has a corner or room in a church: children are taught in classes appropriate to their age-group.

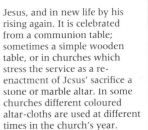

Main Periods of Church Architecture

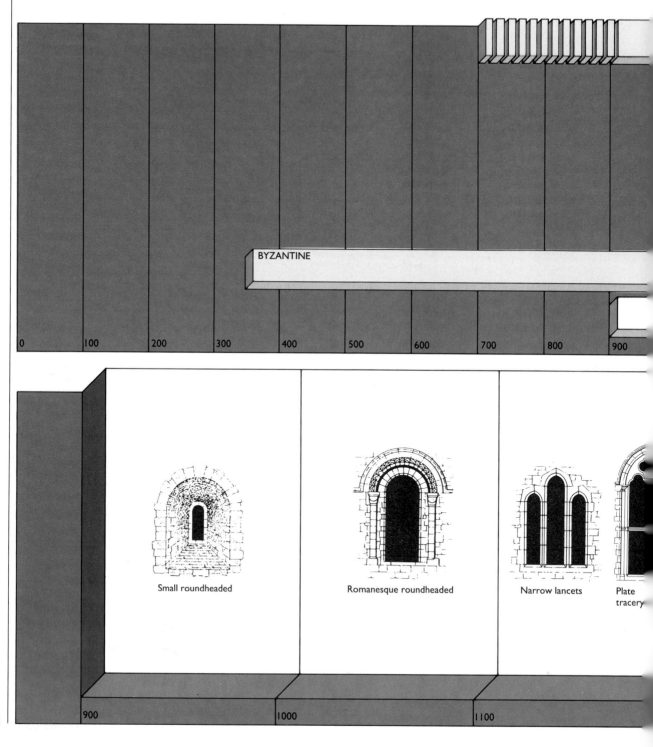

BYZANTINE

0   100   200   300   400   500   600   700   800   900

Small roundheaded

Romanesque roundheaded

Narrow lancets

Plate tracery

900   1000   1100

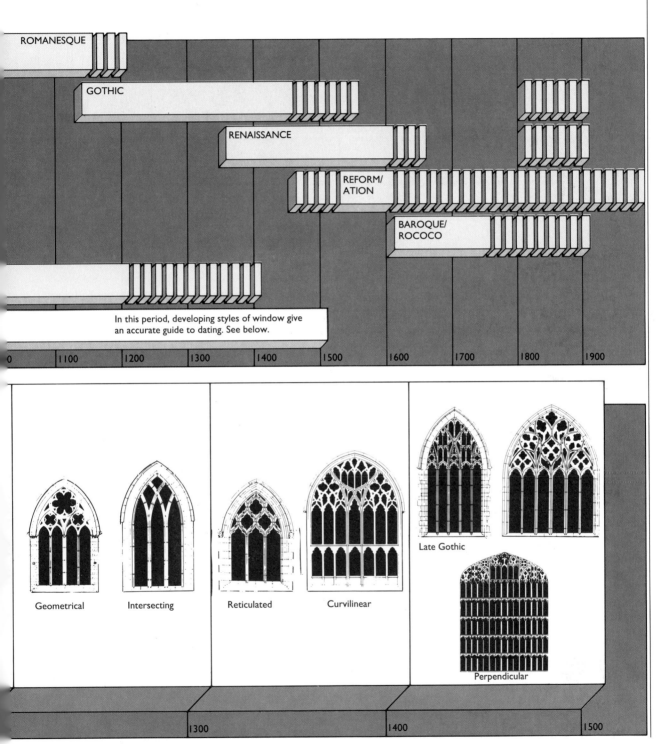

ROMANESQUE

GOTHIC

RENAISSANCE

REFORM/ATION

BAROQUE/ROCOCO

In this period, developing styles of window give an accurate guide to dating. See below.

| 1100 | 1200 | 1300 | 1400 | 1500 | 1600 | 1700 | 1800 | 1900 |

Geometrical

Intersecting

Reticulated

Curvilinear

Late Gothic

Perpendicular

| 1300 | 1400 | 1500 |

Arches and Vaults

THIS PAGE, RIGHT. *Sturdy, undecorated round-headed vaults in the crypt of Canterbury Cathedral.* OPPOSITE, LEFT *Gothic vaulting, decorated with delicate ribs and bosses.* RIGHT *Lace-like fan vaulting dates from the English 'Perpendicular' period.*

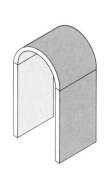

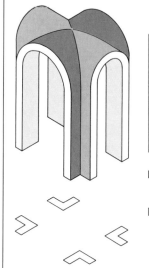

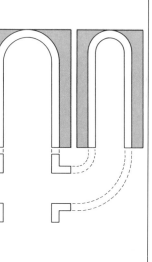

The problem of building doors and windows has been solved in a variety of ways. The structural strength of the building must not be lost because of these openings. The simplest solution is a flat stone or wood lintel which sits on top of the supporting columns.

After the Romanesque period rectangular windows were rare in churches. One reason was strength. The load on a lintel could easily crack it. An arch spreads the thrust and is inherently stronger. The natural strength of arches is such that they often remain in place after surrounding walls have collapsed.

A Romanesque arch is very similar to the arches used by the Romans in their vast building programme. Yet making round-headed arches on a large scale creates problems. The width of the archway is determined by the radius of the arch.

This causes particular problems where a narrow transept meets a wide nave: the different widths of arch have to meet at the same height and so the narrower transept arch has to begin its curvature higher than the nave arch.

The solution to this was the invention of the pointed arch. This enabled a much expanded variety of building forms. Unequal widths of arch can still reach the same height, for the angle of the curve can vary as needed. A pointed arch can be tall or broad and still retain its strength.

The top of the arch can come within a few degrees of horizontal before it becomes weak. This style of flattened or depressed arch was very popular in the sixteenth century English style known as Perpendicular.

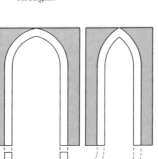

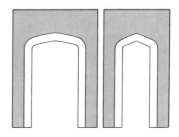

The principles of the arch are true of the vault as well. Vaults are simply a lattice of arches with some kind of infill between the ribs.

Vaults were a fashionable challenge to the architect and because of the expense incurred in their construction they were often built after the basic building was complete.

Fittings and Furnishings

By looking at some of the furnishings of the building we can see not only what it is used for, but also what sort of life and beliefs are expressed.

In many churches there has been a centuries-old tradition, dating back to the Old Testament of the Bible, to stress quality, artistry and craftsmanship: nothing but the best would do for the house of God.

This tended to shift the emphasis, however, from the church as people to the church as a building. So in 'Reformed' churches there was a return to a simpler style, emphasizing the building as a meeting-place rather than 'temple'.

Fonts

The font is used for baptizing people: the children or adults are sprinkled with water as a symbol of the washing away of their sin. In medieval churches the font was almost always positioned near the entrance to the church, symbolizing the entry into the family of God. In Baptist and some other free churches baptism is carried out by 'total immersion'. A baptismal pool at the front of the church is generally covered over when not in use.

ABOVE *An elaborate font cover.* BELOW *Designs drawn from pre-Christian Viking legends.*

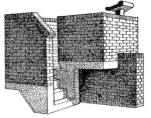

Pulpits

The pulpit is the other main focal point: in churches and chapels emphasizing preaching it is often the main one. The teaching and preaching of the 'Word of God', the Bible, was re-instated at the time of the sixteenth-century Reformation, and the centrality of preaching is also reflected in other churches built at a time of revival and renewal.

When the new emphasis on

preaching led to the development of the galleried church, pulpits rose to great heights so the preacher could address the gallery as well as the floor level. Stairs led up to the pulpit, which in some instances was double or treble tiered – the lower levels used for announcement and readings, the uppermost level for preaching. The pulpit was normally placed against one side of the arcade.

Made just after the Reformation, this pulpit is built into the 'box' pews. Above is a sounding board or 'tester'.

Lecterns

The lectern often balances the pulpit on the other side of the nave. From here the service may be conducted, or at least the Bible 'lessons' read; but the preaching is from the pulpit.

Medieval brass lecterns are often in the form of an eagle, with spread wings supporting the Bible.

Choir Screens

Choir screens are often among the more ornate furnishings in the church. In Eastern Orthodox churches, the screens are covered with painted icons – images which are used to focus meditation and worship. By the end of the Middle Ages, with the stress on the 'priestly' function of the clergy and the mass as 'sacrifice' most churches were divided in two, the eastern end for the clergy and the west for the people. The choir screen marked the boundary, emphasizing the mystery of the service in the chancel. The screen had at least one door in the centre for processions to pass through, and was often surmounted by a **rood** – a crucifix attached to a horizontal beam. The choir screen is sometimes referred to as the rood screen. After the Reformation the choir screens were either removed or altered as a demonstration of the Reformers' teaching that all people could have direct access to God through Christ. There was no need for priests or sacrifice. In England the screens unfortunately became the most convenient place to put the organ pipes – in many churches the organ appears as an ungainly intrusion. Many screens were again built in the nineteenth century, with the revival of sacrificial ideas of Communion and the new interest in Gothic architecture.

Choir Stalls

The choir stalls are often the most impressive seating in a church. In monastic churches, the monks would use these tiered walled seats in saying their daily 'offices' – prayers and services said up to seven times a day. As this involved hours of standing in prayer, a narrow shelf-like ledge on the underside of a raised seat provided the monk with something to lean against. Called **misericords**, these props were customarily carved in a whimsical fashion.

In large churches elaborately carved seating was provided for the choir.

Tables/Altars

The communion table or 'altar' is often the focal point of the building. Where it is a simple wooden table this is a reminder of its use as a table for a memorial meal: at the Communion service it is used for the bread and the wine. A stone or marble altar may reflect a belief in the Communion or Mass as re-enactment of the sacrifice of Jesus (see previous section).

BELOW *In this church a modern communion table is placed closer to the congregation than the old one.*

Pews

Pews are today a dominant feature in many church buildings. It was not common to sit in church until the fifteenth century. At first the weary and laden had to bring their own chairs, but eventually the more far-sighted churches decided that it would be easier to provide seating. With the Reformation came the first regular appearance of pews in Protestant churches, when preaching became the central component of the service. Seats were arranged in a semi-circle around the pulpit. Later they were fixed to the floor. By the eighteenth century pews were often 'sold' to families in the community. In some instances they were considered private property and decorated according to the owner's (sometimes peculiar) taste. In some churches there are box pews which date from this time, these were occasionally equipped with padded armchairs and fireplaces!

Wooden pews, in this case 'box' pews, traditionally provide seating for the congregation. However, their arrangement is inflexible, so some churches now prefer chairs.

Memorial Tombs

Memorial tombs are a feature of many old church buildings. The early church's practice of burying the more famous or influential within the church building continued until the present century. The monuments, shrines and plaques in churches make an illuminating study in themselves. The various stages of church patronage can often be worked out. In some cases the monuments themselves came to be the church's most important asset.

Carved stone tombs and decorated 'brasses' mark the place where wealthy or prominent members of the community were buried.

Confessionals

Confessionals or confession boxes are common in most Roman Catholic churches. The priest sits to listen to those who make their confession. The box serves the purpose of focussing attention on the words of the priest rather than on his person. Confessionals usually have a small window or aperture to speak through.

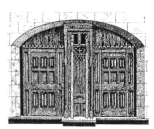

Candles

Candles begin to appear after about AD 1100. Gigantic candlesticks in some churches show the difficulty of trying to illuminate them by candlelight! Special lighters and snuffers soon followed.

PART 2
THE STORY OF CHURCH BUILDING

The last great medieval Gothic cathedral was built in Milan, Italy. Its entire construction was based on an elaborate geometrical grid of intersecting circles and equilateral triangles, which had a metaphysical meaning as well as a satisfying form.

The First Christians

In Jerusalem in the year 30AD, Jesus of Nazareth was crucified and his followers fled in despair. Three days later their lives had changed: Jesus had been raised to new life. As the weeks went by, they came to understand what this meant, and at last, Jesus left them for the final time. What were the disciples to do now? Jesus had told them that they were to go into all the world to spread the good news of new life – but first they were to wait for him to send them his Holy Spirit. Ten days later, on the feast of Pentecost, the Spirit came. This was the explosive birth of the Christian church.

As the first Christians were predominantly Jewish, the natural place to meet was the Temple or synagogue. The Temple in Jerusalem was an impressive building, the religious centre of Judaism, but it was not the right building for the new faith. The Christians believed that the daily ritual of sacrifice, the central part of Jewish ceremony, was no longer necessary. The death of Jesus on the cross was a once-for-all sacrifice for human sin.

A better 'model' for the Christian gatherings was the Jewish synagogue. The synagogue had been developed to maintain the Jewish faith when the Jews were in exile. By this time it had become the meeting-place of the local community.

The tension between the idea of a church-building as 'temple', to re-enact the sacrifice of Jesus, or simply as 'meeting-place', has remained with the Christian churches since those early days. As the story unfolds, as we shall see, different groups have emphasized one side or the other, with profound implications for the style and architecture of the buildings they have used.

At the heart of the Christian faith is the belief that Christ's followers belong together. Early references to the Christians often mention their communal life and support. At first the common meeting-place was the home, and because the primary part of Christian worship was the celebration of the Lord's Supper, or Eucharist ('thanksgiving'), most of their meetings were held in the dining-room.

Houses in Palestine often had three or four stories and the dining-room was usually on the top floor (hence the 'upper room' described in the Gospels where the Last Supper took place). Christians would come together for an ordinary meal, probably prepared by the women of the group. Sitting around a large table on couches or benches the congregation would exchange news, study and pray together and review the work they were involved in. The supper would be concluded with a communal sharing of bread and wine in remembrance of Christ's death.

A meeting like this took place at Troas once, when the apostle Paul was the special guest. The book of Acts records how, during the long meeting in a crowded room, a young man perched on the windowsill literally dropped off!

Other meeting-places would be determined by circumstances or planning. Informal public meetings in the market-place might be organized for preaching. Meetings in the Temple precincts might be arranged to continue the dialogue with the Jews about who Jesus was. For a special visitor a large hall might be hired to accommodate the extra numbers, as when Paul spoke at Ephesus.

Small groups of Christians sprang up in the cities throughout Asia Minor and grew to become sizable communities. Because of the restrictions on domestic space, large churches often would be spread between homes. The first 'purpose-built' church buildings were generally similar to ordinary houses. Inside, the rooms equivalent to sleeping and living quarters would have been used as classrooms and for storing the

Jerusalem was the spring-board of the Christian faith. In the first century it was dominated by the Temple, centre of the Jewish sacrificial system. In AD 70 this was destroyed by the Romans. The new Christians needed not a temple, for Jesus had died as a once-for-all sacrifice for sin, but a meeting-place. Their model was not the Temple but the Jewish synogogue.

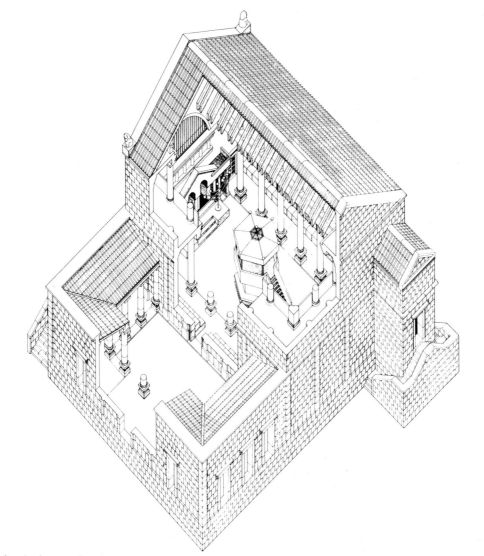

goods which were distributed to the poor. The large upper room would still have been the assembly areas.

The Christian population continued to swell in the second and third centuries. By the year 250 two-thirds of Asia Minor was Christian, and in Rome the community numbered between thirty and fifty thousand. Although the house-church would still have been an important place for worship, larger church buildings were constructed, patterned on the usual form for large halls, the basilica.

But building churches was not simple. Not only was there Roman red tape and crushing taxation, there was also constant uncertainty about the attitude of the Roman state to the church. The political wind could change overnight.

To begin with, the Roman Empire regarded the Christians as a Jewish sect.

They did not much care what people believed so long as they paid their taxes and treated officials with respect. But by the end of the first century the Eastern idea of ruler-worship had been imported to Rome. When it was applied as a test of loyalty to the regime, the Christians usually refused to venerate the emperor. Often this led to persecution and church property was confiscated or destroyed.

Yet the church continued to grow. Even the Roman persecutors were impressed with the Christians' fortitude in the face of torture and death. The tribulations may have dispersed the church, but far from destroying it, they toughened it. And as Christianity became more acceptable it attracted people in prominent positions, until eventually it was even adopted by its former enemy – the Roman Emperor.

The meeting-place for every Jewish community was the local synagogue. It was a simple hall with seats and a raised reading desk. Next to it there might be a room used as school or library.

The Official Church

The Emperor Constantine was converted to Christianity by a vision. He was instructed to put the sign of the cross on his soldiers' uniforms before a crucial battle. When the battle was won Constantine became the first powerful political leader to embrace Christianity.

Now, in the Edict of Milan in 313, the faith was recognized and granted official status. Though Constantine himself was not baptized until he was on his death-bed, he regarded himself as the thirteenth apostle, God's appointed 'vicar'. He asserted himself in church affairs by mediating in doctrinal disputes and presiding over church councils and he applied the leverage of the state to ensure that the decisions of those councils were upheld.

State patronage changed almost everything in the church. Simple house-groups gave way to larger congregations managed by full-time professional clergy. The participation of ordinary 'lay' people decreased, and ceremony became more pronounced in church services. Bishops and other church 'officials' took to wearing insignia of rank on their vestments in imitation of the status symbols of the imperial court.

These changes in the social profile of the church naturally affected church building. The domestic model was no longer adequate to accommodate the expanding needs of both clergy and congregation. One end of the church became the seat of the clergy, who were separated from the people by means of a screen and a raised floor. The simple wooden communion table was replaced by a more substantial and ornate one, becoming an altar, sometimes covered with precious metals and jewels.

Now that the dignity of the church was assured by imperial patronage, there was demand for buildings of the highest order. The model for these came from the architectural forms of public buildings – palaces, forums and temples. Yet it was clear to Christians that the pagan religious architecture of antiquity was not a suitable pattern. Temples in particular had unsavoury associations. Also the form was impractical, for temples were designed as a place for individuals to adore an image, not for large congregations to meet together.

So it was the official state architecture which was adopted. The most common form of public building was the basilica. In its simplest form this was a long timber-roofed hall ending in a semi-circular 'apse', with windows in the side walls. Such buildings could serve a variety of functions: audience hall, trading market, banquet hall, imperial forum.

Groups of Christians adapted the basilica to meet their own special needs or the wishes of a patron. Christianity was now socially acceptable, so there were funds enough for construction. Differences came from circumstances; a commemorative chapel sponsored by a wealthy patron would be more lavish and intimate than a basilica designed for a congregation of five thousand. Because there was no precedent for public church building, a great variety of experimental forms appeared.

Many small chapels were built as monuments to martyrs because of the growing veneration of those who had died under persecution. The 'martyria' often acquired porches, wings and rooms to accommodate those who wished to be buried near the martyr – almost as a superstitious way of guaranteeing salvation. Many of these memorials gradually became churches for the local community, and often required further rebuilding. This has been a common process: some Italian churches today are built on sites known to have been occupied by at least a dozen previous buildings.

Other churches were purpose-built to honour a saint or martyr and to accommodate a congregation. The old St Peter's basilica in Rome (replaced by the present building in the sixteenth century) was designed with a large 'transept' (or 'cross-piece') at the east end to permit pilgrims to circulate in front of the shrine. There was no seating. The service was conducted with the whole of the large congregation standing. Celebration of the Eucharist, the Mass, became a dramatic re-enactment of Christ's sacrifice: the action was now round the altar, and worshippers would be able to move around to view the pattern of service, the liturgy, more clearly.

By the end of the fifth century it was common to orientate churches so that as one faced the altar one was also facing east – toward Jerusalem. This became required

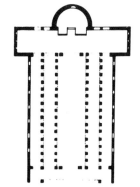

The style of building known as the basilica was common amongst wealthy Romans. Big basilicas were very suitable for larger Christian groups; there was plenty of space for the congregation and a natural focal point for ministers leading the service.

practice by the Middle Ages.

As the church consolidated its power, in Europe a more uniform architectural policy resulted. The nave and aisles of the early basilica developed into the classic form of the medieval cathedral. The pattern of service, the liturgy, influenced by the manners of the imperial court, was handed down to the medieval church.

The early alliance of the church and state clearly assisted the spread of Christianity. But the very expansion of the church's power brought difficulties with it. Some Christians were greatly alarmed by the indentification with secular powers, particularly when emperors made decisions about church doctrine. The elevated position of secular rulers in the church hierarchy was intended to reflect the cooperation of a Christian society, but more often led to power struggles. The question of the nature of the church's authority in society was to become one of the recurring themes of medieval history.

THE BASILICA

The basilica of Santa Sabina in Rome is remarkably well preserved. It gives a good idea of the spacious interior, decorated simply with patterning on the marble surfaces.

The original form of the basilica was a long shoe-box-shaped building.

The interior of the building was generally brighter than secular basilicas and was often decorated with paintings of Christian symbols, geometric designs, words from the Bible and creeds.

②
The form of service (or 'liturgy') varied. The elders or clergy might be seated in front of the altar table or behind it. The bishop's throne or cathedra might be raised on a platform. An extension of this platform into the nave called an ambo would serve as a place for the reading of lessons.

①
The timber roof was supported by two internal rows of columns.

Secondary lowered roofs often covered the aisles and had windows above them onto the central nave.

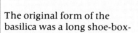

③
The eastern end of the building, where the service was conducted, was usually rounded into an apse.

⑤
Those under instruction for baptism ('catechumens') had a separate building or a foyer-like division in the west part of the church.

④
The side aisle and a clear space in front of the apse were used for processions, and so came to be known as the ambulatory.

The Eastern Church

Over the centuries the Eastern Church has developed separately from the West. In the Soviet Union the Russian Orthodox church is active (BELOW). In Greece there are tens of thousands of tiny chapels (OPPOSITE).

While the churches near Rome naturally developed the Roman style of building, the basilica, in the Eastern part of the Roman Empire rather different needs and emphases were developing. The great city on the Bosphorus, Constantinople (now Istanbul) became the centre of the Eastern Orthodox faith which continues its own traditions to this day.

The Eastern Church placed great stress on symbol and ritual. The clergy dominated the liturgy even more than in the West: services became priestly actions carried out on behalf of the people. The ritual celebration of the Eucharist was carried out in a 'chancel', a holy of holies separated from the gaze of the common people by screens.

The nave had become the place of the congregation in churches in the West: in the East the people were squeezed out still further, as the nave was used for processions and the congregation was relegated to the side aisles.

The solemn performance of the Eucharist in the East did not easily fit into the limits imposed by the basilica type of building. The basilica has no natural centre. A new type of building was required to accommodate the shift in doctrinal viewpoint.

One particularly well-known church reflects this new emphasis: Saint Sophia in Constantinople. Now an Islamic mosque, it was built by the Emperor Justinian in the early sixth century at staggering cost. Tradition has it that on the day of the church's consecration, referring to the Jewish Temple, Justinian exclaimed, 'Solomon, I have surpassed you!'

The centrality of the ritual was reflected in a central-plan building covered by a massive dome. The technical challenge required architects versed in structural dynamics, physics and mathematics. The dome had to be light enough to be carried by the walls, yet resilient enough to withstand the stresses of wind, weather and earthquake. Placing a dome on a square obviously limits the points of attachment, so it was necessary to design 'squinches' for the corners to distribute the weight evenly, so giving the interior of the building its characteristic octagonal shape.

The resulting building is enormous: full of mystery yet light and airy. Solid masses are made soft by tinted stone, cut and polished to show its patterned 'figure'. Silver, gold and acres of mosaics splinter the light from the windows in the rim of the dome and create a resonant sense of mystery. It is easy to imagine how the mystery of the building would have been heightened during its use. The congregation in the side aisles only catch glimpses of the processions. First comes the bishop in his robes, followed by the clergy bearing the bread and wine to the altar. Light from the dome falls in long rays in the mixture of

dust and the smoke of incense. The procession halts, then to the sound of bells and Greek chants slowly passes through the altar screen to the sanctuary beyond. The actual celebration of the Eucharist takes place out of sight in the screened-off chancel.

The rituals that were visible often were those reflecting the belief that the Emperor and the Patriarch were representatives of 'the halves of God'. Their ritual 'kiss of peace' under the great dome was a symbol of the religious and secular cooperation in the Christian state. This fusion of politics, theology and acting is difficult for us to grasp. For the man of the sixth century, the church building was a model of heaven on earth, a kind of preview of the presence of God in the company of the saints. The

clergy were the entrusted agents of communication with God. The radiance of the gilded dome of the church was a reminder to all in the city of the power of God and his representatives, and of the fact that God's ways can never be fully understood by men.

The mystical conception of Christian worship points toward the undefinable character of God's majesty. In the architecture of the Eastern church there is a pervading sense of those words the Bible uses to describe God - light, breath, and fire.

Often plain outside, Greek Orthodox churches are richly decorated inside – reflecting the fact that God is not simply concerned with external appearances. The atmosphere inside is also a reminder of the splendour and mystery of God. Often icons – images of saints – are used as an aid to worship.

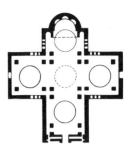

Many Eastern churches are built on the plan of the 'Greek cross', with four arms of equal length.

Commissioned by the Emperor Justinian as the greatest church of the Byzantine Empire, Santa Sophia in present-day Istanbul, Turkey, was the most ambitious building that had ever been undertaken. When the Turks took Constantinople in 1453 they turned it into a mosque, but even though they whitewashed over the mosaics and put up Islamic texts, the building still maintains much of its glory and mystery.

THE ART OF MOSAICS

Apart from the shape of the building, the most obvious innovation in the East was the splendour of the mosaics and other decoration. Some of the finest are to be seen in a city which lay on the border of the Eastern and Western Empires, the Aegean coast town of Ravenna in Italy.

Though the ground-plans in Ravenna are still mainly of the Roman basilica type, the decoration of the buildings from the fifth and sixth century is Eastern. Built for the imperial court when it had to remove from Rome in the fifth century because of barbarian invasions, most of the dozen buildings have been scarcely altered since their construction. In S. Apollinare Nuovo, for

instance, the lavish decoration transforms the piers and walls by an infusion of colour, making the large areas of stonework 'melt away'. There are horizontal bands of contrasting masonry, and the light filtering in illuminates the rich texture of the incised capitals and glittering mosaics.

The decorations are not just wallpaper. They reflect the meaning of the church and the history of God's acts of salvation. Kings, elders, prophets and saints are a reminder of the past and an aid to reflection and meditation.

This gold mosaic from the church of San Vitale in Ravenna is a portrait of the emperor Justinian who commissioned the building.

Christian Communities: the Monasteries

For all its splendour and status, the secularized church of Constantine's empire repelled some Christians because of its pomp and worldliness. Many of the dissatisfied joined monsteries – communities devoted to the disciplines of study, work and regular prayer. When barbarian invasions upset the secular foundations of the official church it was the monasteries which proved most hardy. Located in remote and often inhospitable places, the monasteries lived out the dark ages like seed pods awaiting a change in climate.

With Islamic invaders threatening Europe from the south and barbarian raiders attacking from the north, there were few places which afforded security. Many sought refuge in the desert. In the sixth and seventh centuries groups of monks left the Mediterranean by boat for the rugged coasts of Cornwall, Ireland or the Hebrides. Using dry stone-wall construction, the immigrant scholars built tiny fortress-like churches. Eventually these coastal monasteries so grew in size and strength that they sponsored missionaries to Britain, and took over the running of the Irish church from the bishops. The Irish church, perched on the edge of the known world, survived with vigour. For churches on the European continent, the climate was harsh until the ninth century when the migrations had slowed down and a greater political stability permitted the growth of monasticism.

The Italian monk Benedict was to become the most influential designer of patterns of monastic life. He upgraded the image of the monk and paved the way to the belief that gifts to monks were 'damnation-deductible'. As a result, landowners, knights and princes liberally endowed the monasteries. They became formidable institutions. Eventually the rigours of vows became incompatible with the extravagence of financial management. The history of monasticism is a constant pendulum swing from reform to excess.

Contemplation, the disciplined attitude to work and (in most orders) access to books helped the monasteries develop the arts. The monastery of Cluny, founded in the tenth century, became for a time the artistic centre of Europe. It is not unreasonable to suppose that the architecture of the great abbey was the product of the minds of monks if not their hands. As Cluny grew in power and fostered satellite monasteries, its artisans and style spread too. Cluny supported pilgrimages and so its influence led to the construction of similarly-styled monasteries right along the pilgrim routes.

Monastery churches were commonly built in the form of basilicas with a number of transepts, often with towers. Because an active monastery would have over 400 monks, a great deal of space was required for them to say their daily offices, the seven set liturgies. If a monastic church did not also serve a local secular community, choir stalls might fill the entire nave – indeed some churches were constructed without naves. Theoretically, decoration was sparse. But St Bernard, the most famous of all medieval monks, had Cluny itself in mind when he asked other monks, 'Tell me, you professors of Poverty, what is gold doing in a holy place?'

It was around the year 300 that groups of Christians in Egypt first set up communities 'away from the world' where they could live out in rigorous asceticism the demands of piety and self-denial. The remote monastery of St Catherine (OPPOSITE) at the foot of Mount Sinai was begun in the sixth century.

Other groups of monks live in greater contact with the outside world, in service and worship.

The construction of monastic churches in remote locations taxed the skill and imagination of the builders. Built on mountain tops, into cliff faces or in the desolate emptiness of the wilderness, the structures posed immense logistical problems.

After the Reformation, the ascetic life lost much of its popularity and many monastic foundations were converted for other uses. New orders continued to be instituted until well into the nineteenth century, but the scale of monastic building never again equalled the scope of the eleventh and twelfth centuries.

Down the centuries, monasteries have been important centres of learning, teaching, medical work, missionary outreach and cultural life. Santo Domingo de Silos in Spain (RIGHT) dates from the eleventh century. Its peaceful cloisters are decorated with delicate sculpture of New Testament stories.

Foundations of Western Society: Romanesque

The development of the Romanesque style between about 1050 and 1200 has long puzzled historians. Buildings of this period all over Europe show a remarkable similarity – but no clear source. The term 'Romanesque' indicates the most obvious influence: late Roman building. Roman ruins abound in Europe today and there would have been many more in the eleventh century, but why would church builders suddenly begin to copy Roman architecture?

Close inspection of Romanesque architecture reveals many 'un-Roman' details - rugged 'chevron' ornament, fantastic carved figures and patterning which is almost like calligraphy. Scholars have traced some of these elements to Byzantine, Islamic and Celtic sources, an indication of the importance of medieval trade and pilgrimage routes.

One key factor leading to the upsurge of building in the eleventh century was the fact that the world had not ended! Christians believe that Christ will return to earth to bring this world to its conclusion. There had been a widespread belief that this

The five centuries following Rome's collapse in AD 476 gave rise to hardly any sizeable building in Europe except in the reign of the emperor Charlemagne. The chapel of his great palace at Aachen, Germany, (Aix-la-Chapelle) still stands. Octagonal in plan, it is built in Roman style.

In England, stone churches were built to replace former wooden buildings which have not survived. Windows were small (ABOVE), giving very sombre interiors (BELOW).

Even with their tall columns and more spacious interiors (OPPOSITE), churches of the Romanesque period were still dark. Extraordinary carving, for example at Souillac in France (INSERT), was common.

'Second Coming' would be in the year 1000. When Christ did not return, it was as if people waited for a while and then got back to work. By the mid-eleventh century a new enthusiasm for building had replaced the preparations for the Second Coming. Trade, commerce and pilgrimage blossomed. Cities sprang up along the busiest commercial thoroughfares. At the same time, new monasteries were set up along the trade routes. At first simple retreats, they became influential power-centres, wealthy enough to support lavish building programmes. Churches of hewn stone replaced wooden ones. They were larger, longer and more complex structures, many with timber or stone spires. Such churches would have been the most prominent buildings in the community, for virtually all domestic buildings were built of timber. So the local church was a matter of considerable civic pride. It was a landmark which could be seen from afar, and a cultural marvel to be examined at close range. On Sundays the whole town would meet there and a fair volume of trade would be conducted around it through the week.

Romanesque churches display a delightful variety of regional detail. In their basic structure and form, however, all are very similar. They are really modified basilicas. The main change was to the roof: timber roofs were replaced by tunnel vaults of massive masonry. Eventually the 'rib vault' – crossed semi-circular arches of stone spanning the nave – was developed. Stone ribs are stronger and more fire-resistant than timber, but far more complex to construct. Each stone had to be precisely cut. Timber forms called 'centering' held the stones in place until the mortar set. The spaces between the ribs were then filled in with a mixture of mortar and rubble on a woven lattice of willow branches. Later,

OPPOSITE *Romanesque churches in Germany are sturdy and solid, often with several towers. The monastery church of Maria Laach (ABOVE) and the cathedral at Speyer are typical. Inside, too, such as Mainz (BELOW), they are simple and dark.*

Across Europe, styles and details were similar, whether in a French cathedral (Poitiers, BELOW) or an English parish church (Stewkley, RIGHT). English architecture of the period is known as Norman, since it was the Norman conquerors who brought it with them from France.

vaults were built entirely from stone.

The extra weight of the ribbed vault and the stone walls of the nave meant that the arcade, aisle walls and buttressing had to be stronger. To the eleventh-century builder strength meant mass. Columns in Romanesque churches sometimes have the girth of a small elephant and walls often spread to fifteen feet thick. Round-headed

Sweden has some delightful variants of Romanesque building at Vitaby (ABOVE) and Hagby (BELOW). Dalby (RIGHT) is the oldest stone church in the country.

arches linked the arcade to the aisle, and the windows echoed the shape. The weight, the simplicity of form and the logic of this system make these churches very attractive to us today (though to the Gothic architect they seemed 'childish'). The earliest Romanesque churches make up for any elegance they may lack by their great, solemn strength. The forms were extensively copied in the Romantic revival of the nineteenth century.

It was natural that changes occurred quickly in such an intensive period of building. The rough-and-ready masonry of the early Romanesque churches was soon replaced with more sophisticated work.

Later, columns were made of cylindrical blocks rather than stones laid like brick.

More complex elevations evolved. 'Blind arcading' emphasized the wall surfaces and linked the bays together.

Eventually the massive single column in the nave arcade gave way to the 'compound pier', a cluster of shafts bearing several different directions of thrust together at one strategic point.

The ground-plan of these churches anticipate the Gothic plans, with staggered apses, ambulatories and radiating chapels.

The nave bays are usually square in plan, and the aisles together take a quarter of the total width. These dimensions were determined by the restrictions of round arches. The outside of the church reflected the interior structure. Simple buttresses divided the side into bays and 'blind arcading' was the principle form of ornament.

One Romanesque invention was the twin western facade; an idea which was developed by the Gothic builders and has become the norm for church building ever since.

Perhaps the most notable legacy of the

Romanesque is its carving. Scenes on columns in the nave and cloisters were visual aids, with a dramatic scene around every corner. The artistic fashion of our own age makes us look at these rugged carvings as 'art' rather than as the lessons they were intended to be. Geometric carving was very popular, judging by the frequency of its appearance. Dog-tooth, chevron, ball-and-dagger, diaper, running dog – these are some of the names given to recurring designs; but many sculptors simply produced their own designs.

The riot of sculpture on the west front was intended to be an advertisement for the church and also a reminder of the seriousness of life. A common arrangement is that the major virtues and vices are portrayed on either side, with Christ on the Throne of Judgement between them. Considerable imagination goes into depicting the fate of the wicked. The society of the time was based on feudalism, with its underlying notions of obligation, duty, punishment and reward. So people readily believed that God 'kept score' just as they did. The sculpture on the front of the local church was an ever-present reminder of the

The doorway of Kilpeck church in the west of England (ABOVE) *shows how local sculptors mingled Romanesque styles with local influences.*

Churches on pilgrim routes in France are very large, with chapels around the apse so that pilgrims could see local relics.

The church of St Servatius in Maastricht, Holland, is built on the site of a sixth-century chapel. The Romanesque west end has been added to, over the centuries: the towers date from the nineteenth century.

Romanesque churches were built by itinerant craftsmen who took their designs with them. So there is an extraordinary similarity of style right across Europe. These three carvings showing Christ in glory come from church doorways in Moissac, France (RIGHT), Barfreston, England (ABOVE) and Soria, Spain (BELOW).

stakes of life, and of the need for the church, though the more basic Christian gospel of free forgiveness for the sinner was less clear.

The eleventh century marks the beginning of an all-embracing society. The church's authority and teaching extended beyond national boundaries. The solidity and imagination of Romanesque architecture reflects both the seriousness with which the church was viewed and also the magical world which medieval man saw all around him.

THE ART OF THE SCULPTOR

The earliest church buildings were quite plain. A community struggling to survive has little time for ornament and decoration. Image worship in surrounding pagan cultures also made some Christians strongly against religious sculpture at all.

As the church grew in size and power many members wanted to make the place of worship more prominent and more fitting. God is a God of beauty, they reasoned, and sculptural decoration can be used to express faith.

The use of sculpture in church architecture began to flourish in the Romanesque period. At first decoration consisted mainly of incised geometric patterns and floral ornaments, but the human figure (which has always attracted the artist) and other figurative sculpture followed. To illiterate people statuary and narrative scenes were a visual reminder of the serious truths of the Christian life.

Most of the Romanesque carving is not very naturalistic. By our standards their human forms are crude and stylized. But for the Romanesque artist and his patron these rough and ready figures rightly placed the emphasis of the carvings on the scene rather than the individual characters. Many of these carvings have an undeniable power, far in excess of smoother, more tastefully proportioned carvings from some later periods.

In Gothic art sculpture becomes more important in its own right. Figures are given a greater sense of weight and posture. They look at one another and gesture to the viewer with real feeling. The relationship between the sculptural groupings and the architecture as a whole also becomes more important. By the twelfth century sculpture was considered an essential part of a church and elaborate treatises were compiled about the proper arrangement of figures for each different part of the church.

Carvers working their way along the trade and pilgrim routes saw the work of other sculptors and engaged in a fruitful collaboration with other builders and masons. We know little of their actual working methods. There is some reference to the use of models, but the greatest emphasis seems to have been on theory. There were many attempts to discern underlying geometrical principles governing the human figure. Certain proportions were considered harmonious, and a vast lore of symbolic imagery was built up. Yet artists flexed these rules as much as they discussed them.

English sculpture in the Romanesque period was not as fine as French. Nonetheless, the work

In the fanciful details of many capitals and corbels we can see that the imaginative life of the sculptor was very rich.

Sculpture must have proved very popular, for in some churches it is hard to see the building for the decoration. In medieval English churches the west front is often wider than the building itself – making a

of some craftsmen was superb. This carving of six of the apostles is in the porch of Malmesbury Abbey.

kind of backdrop, much like that of the altar screen. This permitted a fuller display of statuary of biblical figures and saints (commonly painted in bright colours). In the cathedral at Wells, for example, the screen is so large that the doors scarcely rise above the level of the pediment. In France, by contrast, the doorways are much larger, with doorway arches often rising nearly to the full height of the church, and with many rows of statues carved into the moulding of the arch. The columns supporting the arch are often reserved for particularly notable figures – the archangel Michael or the apostle Peter standing guard with his set of keys.

The sculpture of west fronts is a study in itself. Romanesque churches tend to be covered with a writhing mass of people and mythical creatures with isolated clusters of the godly holding them at bay. The technical ability of the best of these carvings ranks them as important reference points for modern sculptors. Certainly the majestic pose of the 'kings' in the Chartres portal suggests an artist of sensitive humanity as well as commanding skill.

In modern churches taste and economics have severely curtailed the use of sculpture. There may be a few plaques or a small scene, but the modern world itself provides so much imagery through the media that sculptural portrayals have rather fallen into disfavour. Newer abstract experiments have not yet achieved the same universal language as sculpture did in the medieval world, and probably never will. Yet the attraction of carved things remains strong, and perhaps a greater use of sculpture in churches may be developed in the future.

Sculptors included charming detail in their work, even at points which are hardly visible to the human eye; this angel is from the cathedral at Rheims, France.

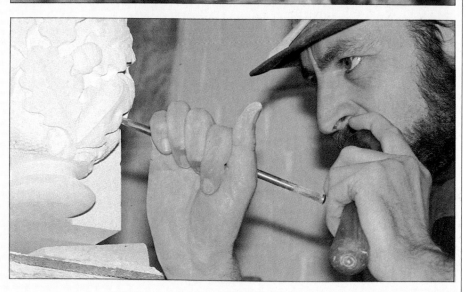

BELOW *Today sculptors are kept busy restoring old buildings.*

Pilgrims and Pilgrimage

Since the fourth century, the Holy Land has been a major destination for pilgrims. Sizeable churches have been built on the sites of Biblical events, for example the Church of the Nativity in Bethlehem.

The 'sites' of Christendom attract visitors by the tens of thousands today. Yet few modern tourists would think of spending two or three years on foot to reach their destination; fewer still would travel without money, maps or hotel reservations – all in the hope of ensuring salvation. But this was common in the eleventh and twelfth centuries.

It is hard to fathom the phenomenal magnetism the holy sites held. What we see is a host of churches which were important pilgrim sites, and a few seemingly superstitious objects which apparently made all the deprivation and hardship of pilgrimage worthwhile. The relics were of extraordinary importance. Without them there would have been no pilgrim routes, and probably no crusades either. Churches sprang up all along the pilgrimage roads, and it was those which had important relics which became the major stopping points.

There were three primary pilgrimage routes in the Middle Ages: to Jerusalem, to Rome and to Santiago de Compostella in Spain. Jerusalem was an important city for obvious reasons, for, as one early pilgrim wrote, what could be better than 'to put the finishing touch to virtue by adoring Christ in the very place where the gospel first shone forth from the cross'. Travellers could visit the Church of the Nativity, the Church of the Holy Sepulchre, see the place where Christ was put on trial before Pilate and revere countless relics. This was an

The long business of pilgrimage was for some an entertaining social event as well as a spiritual exercise.

expensive and time-consuming journey (up to seven years), made even more difficult since Palestine was occupied by the Moorish 'infidel'. Pilgrims to Jerusalem often travelled in armed bands; some of these journeys were little different from crusades.

Rome was important for two reasons. It was the seat of the Western church, and it was steeped in the history of the martyrs. It became customary for newly-appointed bishops to make the pilgrimage to Rome. A certain degree of confusion between ancient Roman statues and memorials to Christian martyrs added to the impression of the Christian heritage of the city. The most important relics of the pilgrimage to Rome were held in the Lateran Basilica; they were the heads of the apostles Peter and Paul. The church also exhibited the ark of the covenant, the tablets on which Moses wrote the ten commandments, the rod of Moses' brother Aaron, an urn of manna, John the Baptist's hair shirt, the five loaves and two fishes, and the dining table used at the Last Supper!

Despite this impressive catalogue, the most popular route was not to Rome, but to Spain, to Santiago de Compostella and the remains of the apostle James. At the peak of his popularity more than half-a-million pilgrims made the tiring trek over the Pyrenees to Santiago every year. They came primarily from France, but also from England, Germany, and Italy. Not all were devout volunteers seeking spiritual improvement. Many walked the road as punishment. Pilgrimage was prescribed as a means of penance. It was also a convenient way to banish trouble-makers; in thirteenth-century England, for example, the penalty for killing a relative was to go on pilgrimage in chains until they wore off!

The five major routes to Spain were dotted with churches, monasteries and hostels for the pilgrim. Among them are some of the most exquisite churches ever built. Vézelay on its commanding yet serene hilltop site was a marvel then and still is today. Poitiers, with one of the liveliest west fronts in France; Aulnay, with a carved portal showing the influence of Moorish artists, and Le Puy, where the whole church is somewhat Arabic; St Sernin at Toulouse with its immense interior . . . these are only a few. Thousands of architectural remains attest the vitality of the period, and any traveller in France will see them, restored, or in odd new uses: incorporated into the side of a barn or as a bicycle repair shop!

The major pilgrim churches all have a similar architectural form. All are spacious, with a long nave, aisles and gallery. All have wide transepts to hold the crowd of pilgrims and chapels to house the relics. The churches could get very crowded, particularly near the time of St James's day on 25 July. As a contemporary account said, 'No one among the countless thousands of people because of their very destiny could move a foot. No one could do anything but stand like a marble statue, stay benumbed, or, as a last resort, scream . . . The brethren, who were showing the tokens to the visitors . . . having no place to turn, escaped with the relics through the window.'

Some of the later pilgrim churches were designed with practicality in mind. The floor of Chartres cathedral is gently sloped and gutters round the walls allowed the floor to be washed after the crowds had left. The windows were designed to unlatch so that the building could be aired.

The pilgrim routes were important links in a primitive system of communications, and it is not surprising to find that they served as channels for architectural styles. French churches along the route to Spain show many Islamic details such as horseshoe arches and decorative arabesques, which came from Spain.

The tremendous flurry of building along the pilgrim routes in the twelfth century gradually subsided. Festivities and commerce began to obscure any spiritual goals. The Renaissance and the Reformation then undermined the pilgrim spirit. But pilgrimages continued until well into the eighteenth century.

Perhaps the most striking observation to make today is that the art and architecture of the period was thoroughly integrated. The sculpture of the portals, capitals and screens was part of an all-embracing scheme aimed to encourage and teach the traveller. There are different styles and different artistic treatments sometimes drawing on local folklore, but they all tell the same stories. The artist and architect were in no doubt about what their work should communicate.

Tombs of martyrs have been popular pilgrim sites. At Canterbury, pilgrims visited the shrine of Thomas à Becket who was assassinated in 1170 after refusing to allow the state to limit the church's action.

The church of Sainte Foy at Conques in south-west France is typical of churches on the pilgrimage routes to Santiago de Compostella in Spain.

RELICS

The lists of relics are both fascinating and macabre: Peter's tooth, the blood of Jesus, a piece of the head of John the Baptist, bones of Mary Magdalen, a finger of the apostle Thomas, a phial of Mary's milk . . . and all of these were part of one church's collection!

The natural liking for souvenirs and superstition are two of the reasons behind the medieval fascination with religious relics. Originally intended as an aid to devotion, the relics soon seem to have been worshipped in their own right. They were traded, collected, taken on tour. People took oaths on them, and built churches over them.

RIGHT *Relics were often stored in ornate cases which themselves became the object of veneration.*

BELOW *St Ambrose was the influential adviser of Emperor Theodosius in the fourth century. After his death his body was put in a specially-built basilica in Milan, where he had been bishop.*

It was Helena, mother of the Emperor Constantine, who first actually hunted for relics. Visiting the Holy Land in 326 at the age of sixty-nine she unearthed what she believed to be Christ's cross. This she shipped back to Constantinople. From there over the years it was disseminated in splinters as gifts to the worthy.

By the eleventh century overt worship of relics was commonplace. The church taught that the martyr's example of sacrifice should be followed by the faithful, and therefore took great stock in relics as visual aids. The crusades swelled the number of these mementos in currency.

There is no doubt that virtually all of these relics were spurious – either intentional swindles or innocent mistakes. Cynics have speculated that there are enough relics of 'the true cross' to construct the Spanish Armada! But notions of 'truth' in the Middle Ages were vastly different from our own bias for empirical 'proof'. The relics were considered 'true' because they had the power to aid worship, even to bring healing, and above all to provide an emotional insurance policy.

They were certainly powerful. The relic bones of St Foy were acquired by the monastery of Conques in France by outright theft. A monk infiltrated the neighbouring monastery at Agen and waited ten years for his chance to make off with them in the night. Conques quickly shot to prominence and Agen folded.

Such was the worth of relics that complex procedures were devised to safeguard them. Workmen excavating the site of a monastery in Reading, England, found a mummified hand built into the old foundations – surely the monastery's prized hand of St James, hidden before the building was destroyed. As the church's most important asset, relics were prominently placed in the building. The small chapels off the apse which were so common in the twelfth century were built to display reliquaries. Caskets were fashioned in gold, silver, enamel and jewels to house the remnants, often with small glass windows through which the object could be revered. These caskets themselves were fitted with handled carrying cases so that they could be taken on ceremonial processions.

Artists were hired to paint pictures of the relics, usually surrounded by scenes from the life of the saint. These paintings themselves commonly became objects of veneration in their own right. Martin Luther, for example (before he began to question such practices), hired Lucas Cranach the Elder to paint some of the 9,000 relics in the collection of the local archbishop as a kind of medieval promotional brochure.

By the early sixteenth century the mania for relics had subsided. The confident humanism of the Renaissance dispelled much of the general fear and insecurity of life and death. The Reformation attacked relics as flagrant idolatry; the violent rampages associated with the Reformation destroyed many of the prominent relics, as well as statues and church furnishings.

THE CRUSADES

Some crusaders marched out of genuine trust that it was 'the will of God' to liberate the Holy Land from the Muslims. But there were other factors. The prospect of winning new lands, coupled with the promise of religious merit, had a great appeal.

There were four major crusades. The first in 1097, reasonably well organized and highly motivated, managed to capture a number of key cities, including Jerusalem. But subsequent crusades foundered for lack of enthusiasm, funds, and above all, strategists. At last the fourth crusade, detoured from its original plan in an effort to pay its transport debts to the city of Venice, attacked the capital of the Eastern Church, Constantinople. Thus one of the more bizzare architectural effects of the crusades was the dispersal of the spoils of Constantinople.

RIGHT *During their occupation of the Holy Land, the crusaders built churches at important sites. The church of St Anne, Jerusalem, is a beautifully preserved example of crusader architecture.*

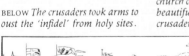

BELOW *The crusaders took arms to oust the 'infidel' from holy sites.*

The Viking Craftsmen: Stave Churches

Some of the most intriguing churches ever built grace the rugged Norwegian woodlands. Built in the eleventh to thirteenth centuries, these all-wooden buildings are called 'stave churches' because the timbers used in their construction are like the staves of a barrel.

They are among the earliest churches built in Norway. Christianity came to the region through the Vikings' contact with Christians in England and Ireland. The churches built by these returning sailors are clearly inspired by their familiarity with ship-building. Shipwrights techniques were used throughout; a keel beam ran down the centre of the roof; there were trusses, elbow joints and brackets virtually the same as those of a Viking longboat.

Stave churches were constructed on a sub-frame of massive hewn and notched tree trunks, raised off the ground by boulders. Great masts were mortised into these beams to support the stacked roofs. Working with axe, auger, plane and chisel (saws were an expensive rarity), Norse builders fitted the walls into slots in the beams and locked the joints with well-seasoned wooden nails. The close tolerances they achieved are attested by the fact that, after centuries of storms, some of the churches still stand – their joints still tight.

One unusual feature was an outer 'ambulatory' right round the building. This provided a porch where the people could stamp off the snow – and deposit their weapons! It also helped to protect the foundations of the church.

The interior of the church was dim. A few small windows high in the walls were augmented by candles; many of the initial 800 churches must have collapsed in flames. The chancel was built as an annexe and decorated with large hanging tapestries. Some interiors were painted, but the real decorative forte was wood carving. The writhing, interlocking patterns of the carvings combine the mythical beasts of Norse legends with Christian symbols. The predominant theme of the exterior carving is the adventures of the Norse hero Sigurd. Like others in Norse mythology, he is eternally condemned to endure the effects of his mistakes. These pagan narratives may have been a kind of ready-made local 'Old Testament' for the Norwegians – a prefiguring of Jesus.

The Viking trade routes led to a fertile artistic exchange: the style of the carving is very like Celtic work. It is also possible that the small wooden 'stock' churches of Ireland provided inspiration to the builders of stave churches.

Some of the most delightful decoration occurs in the only metal-work in the building – the doorlock. Iron was painstakingly gathered from the bottom of bogs where sediment from decaying upstream deposits had settled. It was smelted in a highly romantic and difficult procedure and shaped with hammer, tongs and anvil to a finish which would impress the most demanding smith.

Viking converts to Christianity merged some of their old beliefs into their new faith. The dragon-heads on the shingle roofs of stave churches are ancient Viking symbols. This church is at Vik in Norway.

THE ART OF THE CARPENTER

Wood has always been an attractive building material. In some climates well-chosen timber can last almost indefinitely. The stave churches of Scandinavia are a delightful example of both the solidity and warmth of totally wooden structures.

Stone buildings require the use of wood as well, and the carpenter was an essential member of the master builder's army. In the medieval period the master builder himself was expected to be a proficient woodworker.

Timber was usually felled while the foundations for the church were under construction. The trees were chocked up off the ground and left to lie for six months or a year. This seasoning made the timber more stable when cut, and also lightened the load to be transported.

The two most favoured woods were oak and pine, the former for structural work and the latter for scaffolding, centering forms for arches and ceilings, windlasses and general purposes. At the building site timber would be cleft or sawn to rough shape and then prepared with adze and planes. Drawings were made on the shop floor and the carpenter worked with ruler and dividers to transfer these measurements to his work.

Almost all the work was done prior to installing the piece in place. Large beams were awkward to manoeuvre, so there was no point in 'trial and error' fitting. Completed components were numbered and stored until they were needed. For a major construction such as the internal bracing for a tower or steeple, this meant that the carpenter had to have a grasp of the whole construction as well as the parts. During construction pieces would be hoisted up in order and secured with wooden 'tree nails' or trunnels. The holes for these pegs were precisely misaligned so that as the peg was driven in it would pull the joint tight.

The carpenter was also required to make the ladders and scaffolding for the masons. Some of these were ingeniously designed modules which could be easily dismantled and reassembled. During construction of the walls the masons left square holes in the stone work at regular intervals. The scaffolding fitted into these and was held fast by means of wedges.

When the walls were in place, the carpenter could begin assembly of his most important contribution – the roof. The construction of a roof was planned to ensure that the outward thrust against the

BELOW LEFT *Tree trunks would be roughly cut to shape where the tree had been felled.* RIGHT *The finished article, such as this bench end, would not be carved until the wood was fully seasoned.*

supporting walls was kept to a minimum. This meant that the roof had to be extensively cross-braced. Each brace had to be fitted to its respective rafters and tie beams. Today these units would be assembled on the ground and then hoisted into position by means of a crane. For the medieval builder it had to be done piece by piece. Obviously the joints had to be made with great precision or the roof would not fit together. It was exhausting and dangerous work.

When the basic structure was complete and the building was watertight the carpenter could begin on the furnishings. There were doors to be made and hung, choir screens to be designed, carved and fitted, and a variety of smaller woodworking tasks. Here the carpenter had the opportunity to show his skills in carving and joinery. Oak was the preferred timber. A large choir screen or reredos (the backing screen over an altar) would again be made in hundreds of pieces and pegged together. The carpenter knew how to position the grain to facilitate carving and cutting mouldings, yet maintain strength. As most churches were unheated the wood tended not to warp or split (until heating was installed in modern times!).

The delicacy of some of this work draws admiration from even the most skilled woodworkers today. The work is infused with a spirit of dedication and good humour. The carpenter may or may not have seen his work as a service to the glory of God, but he clearly felt that only the best was good enough. There is little sign that he used inferior short cuts. In our machine age tools have brought speed and accuracy to woodworking, but these techniques have also bred a dependence on the machines. As a result many of the traditional skills of the carpenter are now near extinction.

Wood was vital both for structural work, such as roof vaults, and for the furnishing of the church, such as the choir screen.

An elaborate choir screen (BELOW) is made from hundreds of parts pegged together. This beautiful pulpit, in contrast, is carved from a single tree trunk!

In New Zealand, wood was plentiful when the cathedral in Auckland was first built; the structure could also resist earthquakes.

The Power and the Glory: Gothic

Grandeur and majesty are the key notes of the church of St Denis in Paris (OPPOSITE). The influential patron wanted the building to express the majesty of God. The result set the style for the whole Gothic style of building.
The 150-foot-high nave of Europe's largest cathedral at Cologne (RIGHT) and the filigree spire of Freiburg cathedral express this same emphasis, pointing upwards to God.

No programme of building in history expresses the conviction and common faith of a people as does the building of churches during the Gothic era. The statistics are astounding. During the twelfth and thirteenth centuries more stone was quarried in France than had been used in ancient Egypt. Foundations for church buildings dropped thirty feet, often with a mass as great as the building above. Spires soared to the height of a forty-storey skyscraper (Strasbourg cathedral) – often the result of plain competitiveness between builders. Amiens cathedral was so vast that the entire population of the city (10,000) could attend at once. Beauvais was built so tall that a fourteen-storey block of flats could fit inside. Winchester cathedral is 556 feet long – enough to fit one and a half football pitches in it.

In France from 1050 to 1350 over 500 large churches were built and tens of thousands of parish churches covered the countryside. There was a church or chapel for every 200 people, a ratio which has never been surpassed. The importance of the church in every sphere of human activity was paramount.

The cause for this dynamic period of building inventiveness cannot easily be isolated. The spread of monastic orders and their organizing influence certainly helped, as did the growth of the pilgrimage routes. By the early eleventh century cities were growing fast, and as the development of civilization is always allied with urban life, it is possible that the intellectual life of the cities spawned the new style.

But if causes are unclear, timing certainly is not. There are few watersheds in architectural history which can be pinpointed as accurately as the Gothic. The style originated in the east end of the Parisian church of St Denis. It was here that a powerful and ambitious church leader by the name of Abbot Suger sought to remodel his church in keeping with the religious thought of the day. A fifth-century Greek theologian called Dionysius was one of the prime contributors to twelfth-century thinking. (At the time he was confused with

Rich materials and textures inside medieval churches added to the majesty of the buildings. This silver chalice comes from Sweden.

a third-century Dionysius, the patron of Paris, and also with a Dionysius who was a contemporary of Paul!) His writings emphasized mystical enlightenment and stressed that the church should be patterned on the heirarchy (he perceived) in heaven. Numerology, the symbolic interpretation of numbers, figured prominently in his work and had already been influential in Byzantine worship. Other Greek philosophers were also read avidly, and their concepts of the 'divine proportions of the universe' seemed to have obvious implications for the building of churches.

Suger and his contemporaries sought to apply this mixture of Greek and Christian thinking to the requirements of the church. Suger also courted the patronage of the royalty and guided the king in the role of the 'apostle of France'. (Secular rulers commonly claimed divine authority, some even termed themselves 'vicars of Christ'.)

The buildings display a more sophisticated knowledge of structural dynamics than is evident in Romanesque work. In particular, the new pointed arches work 'differently' from the old rounded ones. But this feature in itself is not what makes the new style.

What is different is something less tangible – a sense of order, of lightness in materials and lightness in illumination. Suger and his mastercraftsmen seemed to make the new choir in St Denis (St Dionysius) defy gravity. Gone are the ponderous piers and massive internal buttressing. The walls are thin, the windows large. The ambulatory and radiating chapels are not just mortared together but flow in a harmonious rhythm of pointed arches and slender shafts. All the components have been considered together. Suger was a keen collector and believed that the beauty of God could only be understood through the effect of beautiful things on the senses – quite a radical idea in the Middle Ages!

The effect on kings, peasants and churchmen must have been stunning. Here was a building which transported the visitor in a kind of mystical levitation. It was rational, elegant and mysterious, full of light and opulently decorated.

Suger's builders achieved this effect by some subtle means. The buttresses on the outside of the choir are carefully positioned to be as invisible as possible from inside.

A unique drawing of the west front of Strasbourg cathedral shows something of the craftsmanship that went into every part of the great Gothic churches. A comparison of the plan with the result (RIGHT) shows very few differences.

Pointed arches permit flexibility in the placing of the piers. By carefully positioning supports to receive stress, the architect could use tall thin piers in the place of the ponderous columns of the Romanesque. The result is a space with the three features which were to become the hallmarks of the Gothic style; verticality, achieved through height and visual stress on vertical lines; lightness, created by large windows and slender buttressing; and unity, with all the architectural details integrated into one whole.

The Gothic style quickly spread through western Europe. Itinerant architects carried it to England, Germany, Italy and Spain. There is even a 'French' Gothic cathedral in Upsalla, Sweden. The style changed in

Twin spires are common. The church at Deventer in Holland (ABOVE LEFT) *and the great Gothic cathedral at Uppsala in Sweden both have simple and striking spires.*

Even small village churches had grand towers. English churches (BELOW) *are often decorated with crenellated tops.*

OPPOSITE *The late Gothic ('Perpendicular') college chapel of King's College, Cambridge. Universities were originally guilds of students attached to cathedrals. The college chapels of Oxford and Cambridge have no naves: like the chapels of other communities no space was required for a congregation.*

Thousands of churches were built in France. Even the most out of the way were often superb buildings. This one, for example, is complete with rose windows and flying buttresses.

contact with local traditions and taste. Where the French had sought great height in the nave, the English produced naves of monumental length. The Italians preferred extensive use of arcading on the exterior, and the Germans became masters of the tower and spire. Though 'high gothic' was primarily a French invention, the many regional interpretations co-mingled. And all shared the same symbolic interpretation.

The burst of building in the twelfth and thirteenth centuries has left lasting monuments not only to the ingenuity and sensitivity of those charged with construction, but also to the elaborate attention given to the clergy. The layman could not participate in the services. It was thought that God was too holy to be approached by untrained people. So the

people merely watched the rituals conducted on their behalf.

Because of their education and the authority of church offices, the clergy became a powerful class. Though their role was to be servants of God, the all-too-human temptations of power caused problems. By the late Middle Ages the elite position of the clergy was becoming excessive – and so, too, was their wealth. One particular excess was the sale of spiritual privileges'. Wealthy families would pay large sums to have mass said for them and their deceased relatives in chapels within the church. Charges were also levied for the viewing of relics, for blessings and for special masses. The proliferation of ritual and magic did neither the clergy nor the layman much good. When the authority of the Pope at the top of the pyramid was questioned, tremors were felt right down to the local parish. The great age of Gothic building was only possible because of a total belief in the security and authority of the church. The church in Gothic times was relatively more powerful and influential than government is in our age. There was no shortage of wealthy patrons to finance church building – and there was a considerable degree of competition which also fired the efforts of builders and patrons.

Attempts to revive the Gothic style in the nineteenth century produced many buildings with a superficial resemblance to the great Gothic cathedrals. But the similarity was only superficial. The understanding of the church, of the world, of God's requirements of men had changed in the intervening centuries.

The term 'gothic' was first used in the seventeenth century. Goth-ic meant 'like the uncultured Goths'. It was not meant to be complimentary. 'The external appearance of an old cathedral cannot but be displeasing to the eye of every man who has any idea of propriety and proportion,' says Tobias Smollett in 'Humphry Clinker' (1770). 'Natural imbecility,' complained Sir Henry Wotton in his 'Elements of Architecture'. 'It ought to be exiled from judicious eyes.' Another critic termed Gothic architecture a 'congestion of dark, monkish piles without any just proportion, use or beauty'. Needless to say that negative verdict has been reversed today.

CHARTRES CATHEDRAL

The cathedral of Chartres has been extravagantly praised as the most splendid architectural space in the world. Anyone who has spent a sunny day in its garden of coloured glass and soaring stone stems would probably agree.

In the twelfth century Chartres was a respected intellectual centre, with a monastery, universities, libraries and churches. It had connections with royalty and was essentially a twin capital with Paris. Churches had occupied the town's hilltop site since the eighth century. Though Chartres was not directly on the pilgrimage route, it was itself an object of pilgrimage. The church possessed a highly venerated relic, the tunic of the Virgin Mary. Worship of Mary, rare in the early church, had become very popular by the twelfth century (almost all the major French Gothic cathedrals are dedicated to her) and Chartres considered itself specially favoured in being protected by the Virgin.

In 1194 the old cathedral burnt down. All that remained were the western towers. While the building was still in flames the dean of the cathedral found an architect to undertake the rebuilding. Work started the same year. The dean and the other church officials volunteered three years of their own substantial salaries (the dean's salary alone would have been equivalent to £250,000/ $450,000 a year!). Further financing was assured when the Virgin's tunic was discovered unharmed in the rubble-filled crypt. The enthusiasm of the building project is virtually impossible for us to understand: our civilization has no comparable centre'. Townsfolk from far and wide brought building materials and provisions. A semi-permanent town-within-a-town was erected to cater for the builders.

Everyone agreed that the new structure was to be far more glorious than the old. Indeed many believed that the Virgin had willed the fire, in order to clear space for a more impressive edifice. But the architectural problems were immense. The existing Romanesque foundations were strong, but the walls were very far apart for a roof as high as the one proposed. The solution was daring. The upper reaches of the nave walls were pierced and lightened by huge windows, and the outward thrust of the roof was supported by a system recently developed in Paris – the flying buttress. The result was in interior space larger, lighter and brighter than any other of the time.

Inside, the architect simplified the nave by eliminating the tribune gallery, which traditionally had been used as a kind of balcony for worshippers. There was liturgical reason for this departure. As the celebration of the Mass had become increasingly important, so a great emphasis had been placed on the viewing of the bread and wine – the 'elements'. Many contemporary accounts tell of worshippers having visions of Christ at the instant when the bread and wine were held aloft. It must be remembered that these were thought to be the actual presence of Christ himself. Doing away with the gallery meant that the whole congregation was united in the nave at this key moment in the service. The simpler nave design also created a greater sense of spatial unity in the sanctuary. This solution was subsequently copied in all the classic cathedrals of France.

The riches of Chartres' decoration are virtually inexhaustible. There are more than 10,000 figures in the

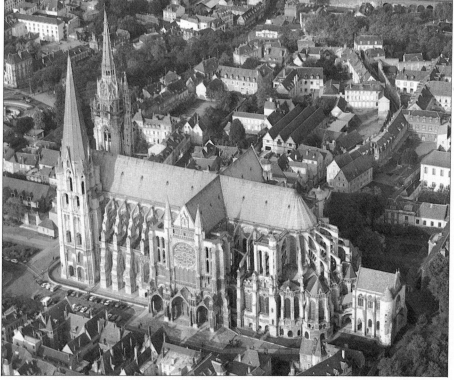

With its weathered copper roof and twin spires, the north one built three hundred years after the simpler south one, the cathedral dominates the town.

Serene figures of kings guard the Royal Portal – the great west door.

sculpture and stained glass. Some scholars have spent more than fifteen years studying the themes in the building! The pictures and story cycles are not merely ornamentation: they are a recitation of the basics of Christian belief applied to every area of life. In an age when few people could read, the building itself told stories. The decoration was an attempt to embody all man's knowledge of the world, and to tell the story of God's action in history. There was a sense that any further learning could only be a refinement of what was already known.

The visible church building was both a symbol and a model for the invisible or 'spiritual' church. The cruciform shape of the church represents both the cross, with the altar as 'head', and the four points of the compass, signifying the extended community of all believers. The church was considered to be a tangible expression of a host of images and ideas expressed in the Bible. It was the body of Christ, a city of refuge, the New Jerusalem, God's presence among men. Some people carried this symbolism to every detail of the building and saw the roof tiles as soldiers of Christ and the steps to the altar as the apostles.

Most of this complex allegory would have been lost on the layman. Indeed even with binoculars it is difficult to make out the figures in the clerestory windows. No matter. Just as the learned theologians could always understand more, so too the cathedral embodied more analogy, allegory and moral symbolism than could ever be grapsed by one person. The very richness of its composition was a symbol for the wealth of God's grace.

The tall columns of the nave reach up elegantly. On the left is the triforium of the south transept.

THE ART OF STAINED GLASS

Glass is as old as the Egyptians, though the glazed window was not developed until Roman times. Cast glass has been found built into the walls of the ruined cities of Pompeii and Herculaneum. Glazed windows were particularly valued in the colder northern climates, but curiously until the tenth century most European glass was imported from Greece. The art of stained glass manufacture began in earnest in the twelfth century.

Coloured glass was produced by adding various metallic oxides (gold, copper, cobalt, manganese and so on) to a molten mixture of sand and potash. (The red produced by this process was of such intensity that it had to be laminated to clear glass so as not to be too dark.) When the right consistency had been achieved, the glass was blown into a cylinder, and unfolded to make a 'sheet'.

The construction of a thirty or forty-foot window was a time consuming craft. This was

French artist Gabriel Loire puts the final leading into a window which shows the story of Noah.

especially true of the early twelfth century windows, when the average size of the fragments was less than two square inches! First the glazier would whitewash a long bench. On this was drawn the placement of the iron bars to support the window. (The joints between lead and glass are very fragile and a large window would collapse from its own weight if it were not wired to this support.)

The design would then be drawn and glass cut to fit. Glass was cut by slowly drawing the tip of a hot iron over the glass – a method which produces a high percentage of rejects. Doubtless these scraps were incorporated into other designs.

When all the glass was cut for a particular part of a design the glazier would then paint the glass with a mixture of iron oxide and a low-melt glaze. The purpose of the painting was not only to treat details too small for glass and lead, but also to control the flow of light through each part of the window. When we look at a bright light in a dark place, we see around it a kind of 'halo' which makes it seem a good deal larger than it really is. So in a stained-glass window the light from each piece of glass tends to 'etch' into the opaque line of the lead strip around it. The glazier often painted the edge of the glass darker where it met the lead to soften the

contrast so that the brightness of each fragment could be controlled. This is an astonishing feat. The unfired glaze looks nothing like it will after the glass has been refired in order to fuse the 'paint' to the surface. The glazier could never really know what a window would look like until it was finished and installed. Working with a small team he proceeded from figure to figure, drawing and copying, squinting and imagining.

The stained glass of the twelfth and thirteenth centuries has rarely been equalled in quality and beauty. The crude manufacturing process produced glass with imperfections which greatly enhance the quality of light. These early windows have a mosaic-like evenness and the jewel-like fragments splinter the light into a rich texture. Later glass, though technically 'better', is often artistically worse, for two reasons. First, improved fabrication produced glass which was uniform in quality – and quite characterless. Second, artists tried to copy the fast-growing techniques of painting. They spent lifetimes trying to reproduce in stained glass effects which can really work only on canvas. The results are rarely as pleasing as the simple mosaics of earlier windows.

If the style of medieval windows was simple, the content was certainly not. They often show complex allegories. A common variety is the 'type–antitype' where an image on the left side of the window is 'explained' by another on the right. The 'Good Samaritan' window from the cathedral of Sens in France is a good example. (It is also interesting because two identical windows were made. The second was originally at Canterbury. There was a fruitful exchange of ideas between English and French glaziers in the twelfth and thirteenth centuries.) The man 'going down from Jerusalem' is compared to Adam leaving

Architects today make use of stained glass to create a particular mood. This is the lantern of the Catholic cathedral in Liverpool, England.

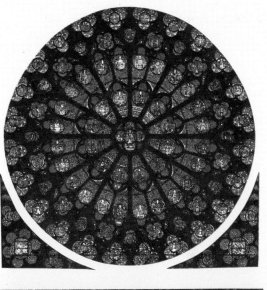

Paradise. He is fallen upon by thieves (the seven deadly sins). The priest and the Levite (the Old Testament Law) pass by and at last the poor man is cared for by the good Samaritan (Christ).

Such riddles were very common. One can almost imagine an earnest prelate explaining the significance of a metaphor to the bemused glazier, tongs in hand. Saints were also popular subject-matter. In the renowned 'tradesmen's windows' at Chartres each of the windows donated by a guild advertises both their craft and their patron saint.

In the late thirteenth century another type of window was developed, the 'grissaille'. This was predominantly white glass cut in small diamond-shaped panes and decorated with small sections of colour. This had the advantage of letting more light into the church. Indeed a nave illuminated by old glass could be so dark as to make reading impossible on a dull day.

Stained glass windows have

The great south rose window of Notre Dame in Paris, 42 feet/14 metres across, is a collection of Bible stories in glass.

had their enemies. After the Reformation thousands were shattered. In the eighteenth century the English architect Wyatt removed the old glass from Salisbury cathedral to make the nave lighter. He sold the lead for scrap and used the glass to make drainage for the cathedral precincts! Nineteenth-century 'restorers' often made copies of the old windows which to our eyes look characteristically 'nineteenth-century'. Bombs during the two World Wars blew many fine old windows apart. Today the greatest enemy is probably pollution; the old glass is gradually wearing away, eaten by the acidity of the air.

The Church Builders

The great churches and cathedrals were built by professionals. The architect or master mason was familiar with all the various skills which went into the construction of a building. He asked a substantial fee, and got it. Travelling with a team of trusted workers he supervised every aspect of the work. Groups of masons even organized conferences to discuss building techniques – attracting masons from many countries. Each mason had his own drawings and cloth rolls containing essential measurements, angles, and means of calculating stress, which were his reference book. He often actually owned quarries.

After drawings were accepted by the patron, the first task was to organize delivery of materials. Anyone building in the twentieth century knows how difficult and aggravating this job can be; it used to be worse. Until the nineteenth century it was common to transport building materials by ox-cart and barge; the former meant that roads had to be built and the latter not uncommonly meant diverting rivers! River transport was preferred because of cost and load capacity. Stone would sometimes be finish-cut in the quarry and given a mark to indicate its final position in the building. Another mark would show who had cut it, since the workers were paid per block.

Supplies were often given to building projects, but this generosity could be subject to abuse. One benefactor gave a bishop permission to cut 'as much timber as his men could remove in four days and nights'. Imagine his fury when the bishop brought 'an innumerable troop' and denuded a large part of his forest!

Facilities set up on site would include a host of stone-cutters' workshops, kilns for burning lime to make mortar, saw pits for cutting timber, forges for making metalwork, other kilns for glaziers and store houses for materials and tools. The basic tools of the stone-cutter were mallets, bow drills and chisels. Perhaps the most interesting tools were those used for measuring and 'machines' for lifting heavy

Lifting materials into place was one of the difficulties the builders face. Elaborate machinery was designed to do the job.

weights. Measuring tools were simple, but in expert hands could produce work to extremely fine tolerances. To find a right angle for reference the builder would lay out a triangle with sides three, four and five units long; the two shorter sides joined at 90°. The architect could check the accuracy of the strings stretched out for foundations, and other angles could be derived from the right angle. Two sets of footing walls were built, one to carry the arcades and the other to support the exterior buttresses.

After the foundations had set and settled (a year or two) the first courses of stone would be laid at the east end of the building. Mirrors and water-filled wooden troughs were used to check horizontal levels, and plumb-lines to check the verticals. Working from east to west the builders would first raise the internal arcade and then the walls and buttressing. To lift the cut stones into place a variety of windlasses were used, often large man-powered 'squirrel cages' with a rope wound round one shaft. Smaller loads of stone and mortar were carried with hods or wooden buckets. Scaffolding was usually erected by leaving holes in the walls where horizontal beams could be inserted and roped to vertical supports.

The construction of vaults required experience. First the shape of the ribs would be drawn on a 'tracing floor' – a large white-washed or plaster-covered floor. Templates were made from these drawings so that the cutting of the stone could be checked continually. A wooden centering form was then built to the inside dimensions of the arch and this was secured to a movable scaffolding under the first bay to be vaulted. The stones were laid along the centering from alternate sides until at last the keystone was put in place. When both ribs were in place the centering would be moved to the next bay and so on down the nave. Additional forms were used to support the infill between the ribs – though in some churches this is only rubble, straw and plaster.

The main difficulty in the construction of church towers was the problem of height. Scaffolding had to be constructed on site, so that heavy components could be brought up in stages. But the difficulties did not deter the craftsmen from showing real care.

Few large churches or cathedrals were built in a generation. Most were constructed over centuries, with later styles superimposed on the earlier. In some places, such as the transept of Winchester

Cathedral, evidence of the improvement in construction technique during the period of building can be seen; the later joints are thinner and the surfaces more precisely worked. Standards for measurement might also change. At one time in England the basic unit was the rod, which was determined by marking out the length of sixteen grown men's feet! A later mason might very well arrive with another standard – for there was no efficient co-ordination of measurement until well into the seventeenth century.

Because of the time such a building required to construct, it was generally put to use for services well before completion. A temporary wooden 'west end' closed the building off, and oil-soaked linen filled the window spaces. The sound of chisels, the creak of wooden gears and the shuffle of feet on boards high overhead must have made a curious accompaniment to the chanting of the mass. One can understand the great ceremonies which attended the consecration of each completed section of the building.

THE ART OF THE BUILDERS AND MASONS

Many do-it-yourself enthusiasts have worked with wood at some time or other, but few have attempted to cut stone. The specialist stone-cutters today rely on tools such as diamond-edged power-saws, pneumatic chisels and high-speed engraving tools, and use protective goggles. To cut flowing organic forms from stone with a mallet and chisels thus seems even more of a feat.

Just as it is easier to carve lime wood than ash, so too each type of stone has its own 'grain' and other characteristics. Certain types of stone have always been pre-ferred for carving ornate capitals; others are better for constructing walls. The master builder therefore had to have a good eye for stone. He had to evaluate the qualities of local stone, and work out the quantities required.

The first job at the quarry was to free large chunks of rock so that it could be cut into the required shapes. This was done in several ways. Holes were drilled into the stone during the winter and filled with water. When the water froze it would expand, splitting the rock. Another method was to light fires which would heat the rock and then to cool the rock suddenly by pouring water on it to make it split.

Once the boulders had been freed the masons could go to

work. The master builder would supply the dimensions, and each mason would have his own ruler, square, and calipers. Lines would be drawn on the surface with chalk. Chisels were coarsely serrated edges were used to rough out the work. Final shaping and polishing were sometimes accomplished by rubbing the stones on another hard flat stone. Most of the basic build-ing stones would be cut and shaped in the quarry and given the mark of the workman (workmen were generally paid per stone). These dressed stones are called ashlar.

Pieces destined to become capitals or moulded sections were usually transported to the mason's lodge at the building site. Here there was a drawing floor covered with chalk or plaster. Using a combination of flat drawings and wooden templates, the master carver made the more complex com-ponents. Important carvings such as capitals and statues were roughed out in the lodge and then installed before finishing. This eliminated the risk of damaging fragile under-cuttings during installation.

Stone carving is very laborious, and bits which break off cannot easily be 'glued' on. The master carver needed to be a patient sort, but efficient and fast. In addition he needed to be sensitive to the wishes of the patron and aware of the latest stylistic developments. The secrets of the craft were carefully guarded among the masons.

The next time you look at stone carving try to imagine what it would be like to carve some of those intricate shapes. Imagine the steady tapping of

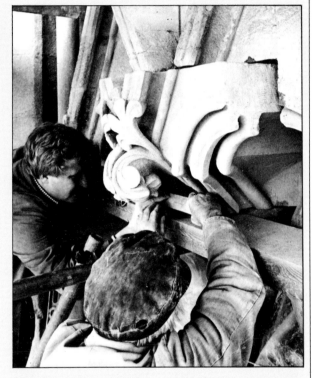

the mallet, the flying chips of stone, the dust and the constant measuring. Try to envisage the atmosphere of the workshop, the stories, the comments made by other stone cutters, the long hours and the cold feet. It was hard work, a labour which placed an emphasis on time and accomplishment which it is difficult for us to understand today.

A piece of stone is precisely cut to size and carved.

The Ascent of Man: the Renaissance

The Italian architect Alberti was a prototype of what was to become in the late Renaissance the ideal man. He built churches and public buildings; he was an accomplished horesman and athlete; he studied law, physics and mathematics; he painted, wrote plays, poems, music and a treatise on economy, and was renowned for his dazzling wit.

Alberti and the other great architects of the Renaissance – Bramante, Raphael and Michelangelo – enjoyed a new type of artistic prestige. Rather than being skilled tradesmen building churches for the needs of the Christian community, they were artists, expressing their insights. Fifteenth-century Italy was quite prepared to acknowledge earthly as well as heavenly brilliance. Even before the Renaissance the architect had been highly regarded, but now the artist's vision was regarded as sacred. And over the centuries, this shift from tradesman to visionary has had a profound affect on the role of the artist.

A dramatic change in ideas about man in the fifteenth and early sixteenth century brought about a revision of cultural, political, economic and church life. The new thinking began in Florence, spread throughout Italy and then followed the trade routes north.

Already in the late Gothic period the combination of Greek thought with Christian concepts had gradually focussed thinking men's attention on the nature of man himself. Art of the time shows this. Portrayals of Christ began to stress his human nature, for example; representation of saints were less concerned with symbolism and more with anatomy. In all walks of life, the nobility of man was becoming the key theme. In Italy this humanism grew with the development of a merchant class. Independent traders and bankers seemed to fare quite well without an unduly subservient attitude to the church. New commentaries on Greek philosophy emphasized the nobility of man and the individual's need to take his potential into his own hands. Artists became more highly regarded, too, and found a new source of patronage in the merchants to supplement their reliance on the church.

The church, of course, was still a powerful institution. Indeed, the Renaissance popes readily adopted the manners and pretensions of secular rulers. In the cultivated self-awareness of the age, they sought to modernize the church in keeping with their own confidence.

Church building was often sponsored by princes and merchants as well as the clergy, so the requirements of services were not usually the main concern. This can be seen simply by looking at the ground plans of most Renaissance churches. The chancel is smaller, the crossing larger. The dome over the crossing has become the true focus of the church. The scale of the buildings has also changed radically. The soaring height of a Gothic nave made a person feel dwarfed, humble and contrite. Now the Renaissance churches are scaled to a more 'human' level.

The vertical stress of the High Gothic has been replaced by a careful balance of proportions. The mystical space of a Gothic church is gone, and the tangible mass of walls and sculpture have once more been emphasized. For example, the standard arrangement of side aisles is altered by making each bay a separate chapel, slowing down the speed at which the eye can 'take in' the building.

In the Middle Ages it was generally acknowledged that construction of a church took more than a lifetime. Like an ancient tree, a cathedral would sprout new branches from generation to generation. But the Renaissance was concerned with wholeness, and so it was unthinkable that a church should be altered after it had been built. When Pope Pius II had a cathedral built in his home town of Pienza he decreed that no one should ever add or remove anything, or even alter the colour scheme of the interior.

The church architecture of the Renaissance is rather like entries in a competition, with each new building trying to be more perfectly proportioned and detailed than the last. New methods of construction were developed, and there was an excited dialogue among the architects and intellectuals. But the life of the church does not always move at the same pace as the building. The same ideas which produced Renaissance churches eroded the faith that the buildings were supposed to serve.

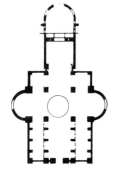

Renaissance architects drew their inspiration from classical forms. Church plans were far more compact than Gothic ones.

Commissioned by Pope Julius II in the early 1500s, the monumental new St Peter's in Rome (OPPOSITE) was worked on by all the famous architects of the time. The result was a triumphal statement of the institutional church's power and the builders' genius.

BELOW *The sculpted gold doors of the great Florence baptistry. Portrayals of biblical scenes were now not 'other worldly' but lifelike.*

Back to Basics: the Reformation

By the late fifteenth century the church knew it was in trouble. Laxity and corruption was wide-spread amongst the clergy and authorities seemed deaf to the pleading for a crackdown to save the church. Rome dragged its feet. Running the ecclesiastical bureaucracy was costly and reforms would certainly reduce revenue.

While the church dithered Europe exploded. Movements of protest and reform had already prepared people for the inevitable revolt against a corrupt and oppressive system. Renaissance learning and a new class of literate activists questioned both the doctrine and policy of the church. The development of cheap printing encouraged people to read, compare and draw their own conclusions. By 1500 over 30,000 titles were in circulation in Europe – most of them religious works. So when Martin Luther in Germany publicly protested against the practice of 'selling tickets to heaven' to raise money for St Peter's Church in Rome, there were plenty of others to support him. The issue of course went deeper. Can we earn our way to heaven by good works, or is it, as Luther discovered for himself in the New Testament, a matter of trusting in God's grace alone?

Changes to churches after the Reformation show dramatically how beliefs are expressed in church buildings. Zwingh's church at Zürich, Switzerland is typical of churches throughout Protestant Europe: the altar for the celebration of the mass, high in the chancel was removed; seats were put in its place. The focus was now the pulpit half-way down the nave.

Luther in Germany, Calvin in Geneva, Zwingli in Zurich thrashed out the theology of the issues. The response from the church authorities was defensive. Popular support was enormous: the new message was a liberating one.

But one response to the teaching of Luther and the other reformers' was a wave of idol-smashing iconoclasm. The reformers rejected many traditional church practices: confession, pilgrimage, relics, prayers for the dead, clerical celibacy and ecclesiastical wealth. These had no foundation in the Bible and undermined the gospel of faith in Jesus Christ as being all that is necessary to approach God. Rowdy crowds tore down monasteries, smashed statues and stained glass – and displayed none of the virtues of spiritual enlightenment. The reformers tried to restrain them, but the church was an easy target, rich and soft.

'Protestantism', as it was to be called, took hold. By the mid-sixteenth century Western Europe was firmly divided between Catholics and Protestants. The Catholic church did eventually institute far-reaching reforms, but the breach was too wide to be closed.

It was one thing to throw bricks through stained-glass windows and quite another to develop alternatives to the medieval pattern of worship. The kernel of Reformation thought was that people could not enter into a relationship with God, or grow in that relationship, without hearing the gospel preached. The focus of worship shifted from the ritual re-enactment of Christ's death at the altar to the preaching of God's word from the pulpit. The cavernous old churches, well suited to creating a sense of mystery, were acoustically dreadful for preaching. This became even worse after the removal of the rejected choir-screens, icons and altars which symbolized the separation of priest from people.

How could the building, then, be made to suit the people's needs? The reformers did not eliminate the communion table, but gave it a position of less prominence. The pulpit was moved into the nave, generally attached to one of the pillars. A large sounding-board behind it helped combat echo. The sermon became a fixed part of the service, and so benches were provided for the congregation to sit in a semi-circle beneath the pulpit. Sometimes an additional reading desk or lectern was built on the opposite side of the nave. The whole idea of what the communion service meant

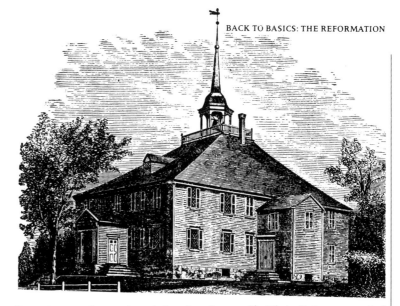

changed. The reformers considered that it was not a re-enactment of Christ's sacrifice, but a celebration of what that sacrifice meant. The people were now to take part in it. In some churches, the table was moved from the position of 'altar' at the east end of the church down to the chancel steps. Simple wooden tables were used instead of stone altars.

Chantry chapels, no longer used to say mass for the deceased, were sometimes converted to libraries or teaching rooms or used for wedding services. The multi-coloured medieval wall paintings were painted out.

The resulting space was cool, bright and large. The seventeeth-century Dutch painter Pieter Saenredam gives us a good idea what Dutch Reformed churches looked like in the 1600s. The nave remained open through the week and was a popular meeting place.

The austerity of the all-white interior was softened by the gradual accumulation of monuments, plaques with creeds and the like. But the biggest introduction was generally the organ.

The early stages of Protestantism did not require new church buildings; the Protestants took over the existing church buildings and adapted them for their own use. But as old buildings fell into disrepair and as congregations grew, new facilities for worship were required. The new buildings reflected the doctrinal shift from altar to pulpit. There was much experimentation with the shape of the church in an effort to permit the preacher to use a normal speaking voice. 'L' form, 'T' form, cross,

The Pilgrim Fathers were radical Protestants who sought a new start, away from repressive European state churches. This church built in 1686 shows how their building style reflected their 'clean sweep' attitude.

St Andrew's, Holborn Circus (LEFT) was one of the churches Sir Christopher Wren built in London after the Great Fire of 1666. With its gallery, dominant organ and pulpit and classical style it is an elegant expression of formalized post-Reformation protestantism.

BELOW *The artist Pieter Saenredam recorded what Dutch churches looked like in the seventeenth century when they had been cleared out after the Reformation.*

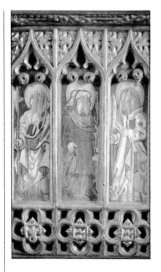

The Reformation had its destructive side. All over Europe, beautiful carvings were defaced and stained glass smashed as people revolted against medieval abuses.

A meeting of Quakers (RIGHT) *typifies the radical Reformation groups. Most, such as the Anabaptists, stressed the sole authority of the Bible without the need for church hierarchies. They were the forerunners of Baptist churches today. Congregational and other churches also date from these 'gathered churches' which stressed the 'priesthood of all believers'.*

round, oval, polygon – virtually everything was tried. They all attempted to concentrate on the principle liturgical centres of pulpit, communion table and font.

Later, a major innovation was the introduction of the gallery, which made it possible to fit a larger congregation into a smaller space. The English architect, Wren, even conducted experiments to determine the maximum permissible distance from the pulpit in all directions before 'clarity' was lost. Hearing the preacher became the main consideration in church design. With the advent of galleries, pulpits grew taller to reach up to them. In the Frauenkirche in Dresden (1738) there were five tiered galleries and the pulpit was at the second-storey level! Many free church buildings still used today are built with galleries, no chancel, but impressive positions for preacher and organ.

In the New World, architects had a clean slate. America in the seventeenth and eighteenth centuries was full of architectural experiment. Traditional English church styles were reinterpreted in the most abundant local material – wood. The Anglicans (Episcopalians) tended to build rather nostalgic imitations of medieval English parish churches, complete with carved chancel screens. Puritan building, on the other hand, tried half-a-dozen different liturgical arrangements, all of which stressed the position of the pulpit. The form of the parish church devised by Wren and Gibbs became rooted in America in the nineteenth century, and produced some of the most attractive 'post colonial' buildings.

The Reformation could not instantaneously produce its own architecture. By trial and error it settled on a variety of 'hall-church' types. Reformed churches tend to emphasize clarity, order and solemnity, features which can produce elegant architecture, but can also be quite plain and boring. The desire to make these church interiors more 'spiritual' was one of the key motivations behind the nineteenth century revival of 'ancient styles'.

LEFT *The reformers realized that through new hymns with popular music, it would be possible to 'sing the Reformation into the hearts of the people.' The organ soon became an important feature in churches.*

The Drama of Religion: Baroque

The style known as Baroque was both new and a continuation of the elaborate sculptural building of the High Renaissance. It received impetus from several sources.

The Protestant Reformation (which coincided with the High Renaissance) presented a frightening challenge to the Roman church. At the Council of Trent in the mid-sixteenth century the Catholic church set about putting its house in order. Reforms in church doctrine and practice were easier now because by the time of the Council virtually all the dissenters had left. The founding of the missionary and teaching order, the Society of Jesus (the Jesuits) was part of the same aim – to reunite the church under the papacy. The restored authority was used to organize the church both administratively and liturgically, and as a result of these efforts the Catholic church regained many areas lost to the Protestants in the Reformation. By the seventeenth century national boundaries, governments and religions were more clearly defined than ever before. Northern Germany, Scandinavia, the Netherlands and England remained predominantly Protestant. France was Catholic but less dependent on the papacy than Italy, Spain and Portugal.

The Baroque style developed most quickly in these southern areas, but was not limited to them. Neither was it purely a Catholic style – though later it was thought to be so. The missionary excursions to Central and South America in the eighteenth century helped fortify the Roman church and the Baroque style soon took root there, blending with the local forms of decoration to produce churches of astonishing complexity.

The early Baroque churches in Italy are characterized by a sense of drama and mystical religious feelings. The cool experiments of the Renaissance yield to the urge for more emotional experience. Catholic theology placed great importance on the mass as a dramatic re-enactment of Christ's death, on savouring the mysteries of the gospel and on feeling the wounds of Christ suffered on one's behalf. As a result, everything about the churches has emotional and symbolic meaning. Through

The church at Wies in Bavaria is a lavish example of the Baroque style. The almost overwhelming ornamentation is designed to exalt the worshipper, emphasising the drama and mystery of religion.

Details such as sculpture (BELOW) and metalwork all contributed to the overall effect.

The Baroque style began in Italy. The church of Sant'Ignazio in Rome (CENTRE) dates from the 1690s. Its extraordinary ceiling was designed to appear like the gate of heaven itself.

The style of European Baroque churches, such as the church of Vierzehnheiligen in South Germany (LEFT) was taken by Jesuit missionaries to other parts of the world, such as Mexico (RIGHT).

the lavish texture of the interior the worshipper is to be caught up into the realm of the infinite. Led by the senses, he is intended to transcend them.

In essence Baroque church architecture returns to the medieval spirit. But the means used are quite different. The medieval cathedral focussed on the sacramental elements; the Baroque church was an all-encompassing totality. The skills of orchestrating sensual experience, refined in the Renaissance, were put to full use in the Baroque.

The church buildings were metaphors for the gates of heaven itself. In many churches this is almost literally true. The ceiling is a painted illusion of the heavens; the whole roof of the building dissolves into the glorious realms above. Theatrical means are employed throughout the building, and these relate to the events taking place over the altar – the ascension of the Virgin, St Michael and the Dragon or the vision of a saint. These churches work like cinema: they have plot, sustained drama and conclusion. Ingeniously placed windows spotlight the dramatic groups.

Compared to the writhing interiors, Baroque exteriors are relatively plain.

Straight lines are often modulated with curves and the sheer bulk of the church is emphasized. The Baroque churches of South America are an exception in that they are rarely plain, and when there is abundant ornament it is richly coloured.

The magnificent church of Vierzehnheiligen ('The Fourteen Saints') in Northern Bavaria, Germany, is a good example of late Baroque at its most sophisticated. The west front is calm and stately. The interior is so complex that it is impossible to 'understand' it without referring to a ground plan. In fact the nave is comprised of four interlocking ovals, with circular transept arms. The oval plan became popular in the second half of the seventeenth century and seems to epitomize the builders' urge to make the church a symbol of the union of heaven and earth.

The refinement of the Baroque style, lighter and less frenzied, is known as Rococo. Rococo ornamentation is more abstract and 'frothy' than the Baroque, and less obviously theatrical. By the late eighteenth century several other stylistic currents were blending with the Baroque and Rococo. In particular, the world of ancient Greece and Rome was once again a key influence.

The Baroque church is an exuberant chorus of sensory experience designed to foster spiritual vision. This direct effect on the senses has proved to have a continuing appeal; indeed there are few Baroque churches which are not still in use today, and Baròque forms of decoration still sell well in our machine age.

Every part of the building was richly decorated. This door is from a church in Spain.

THE EXPORTED CHURCH

People take their beliefs with them when they travel. European commerce in the sixteenth and seventeenth centuries opened trade routes to Asia, Africa and the New World.

The most vigorous exporters of the church were the Jesuits who combined trade with missions in South America, India and the Philippines. They supervised church construction and trained locals in building techniques. Invariably their churches have a pronounced regional style. The elaborate Mexican churches, for instance, owe as much to the local Indian style of convoluted carving as they do to the Spanish Baroque tradition.

Missionaries had a difficult decision: should they 'christianize' the local religious architecture, or should they import Western forms which would be free of misleading associations with the old religions? They usually chose the latter. Today the balance has shifted. New churches often follow local forms.

The cultural cross-currents of the exported church have generated many mixed styles – but also some beautiful buildings.

Many churches in 'mission areas', such as this chapel in Fiji, were built in imitation of traditional European styles. Today there is greater emphasis on reflecting local styles and culture.

In the eighteenth century Central America was an important missionary area.

Missionaries taking their faith to other cultures have realized that there is nothing particularly sacred about their own forms of worship, let alone buildings. This simple meeting place is in East Malaysia.

The Birth of the Modern Age

In the mid-eighteenth century the established church was in decline. Science and philosophy were growing fast, and the idea of Progress captured the minds of the people as religion had done in earlier ages. The brash new philosophers not only attacked the bureaucracy of religion but even dared to question the existence of God.

What began as an intellectual ferment soon became a revolutionary political action. The American Revolution delivered a blow to the old order. Then the Enlightenment, born in the drawing room of aristocratic French idealists, became a revolution which shook the foundations of Europe. The Industrial Revolution, though not overtly religious or political, ensured that the old order would never return. In France, part of the violence was directed against the established church. Many beautiful buildings including St Denis and Cluny were badly damaged, and it was proposed that Chartres should be pulled down and replaced with a 'temple of wisdom'.

Yet curiously this turbulent century was also a period of religious revival. In America, England, the Netherlands and Germany itinerant preachers revitalized churches. The Moravians and Methodists particularly had a strong missionary outlook. Preaching in the open air, tents, houses or wherever they could, they brought a spirit of conviction to their testimony of God's love. Waves of revival swept the Protestant nations.

One result was that scores of churches were built by new groups of Christians. It is hardly surprising that the building was sporadic and stylistically varied. By and large, the Rococo style was rejected as being unsuitably frivolous. The simple functional style was Neo-classic, yet another return to the source of Roman antiquity. Neo-classicism differed from earlier classical revivals in being both more consistent and more austere. New revelations about classical styles came through excavations of the Roman town of Pompeii and caught the imagination of architects and people alike.

By this time the position of the professional architect had been firmly established and architectural practices had been set up. The Roman styles were carefully analyzed and measured drawings of columns, capitals and pediments were

American churches of the eighteenth century (LEFT) have a simple, graceful style. The layout, with no lower side aisles, is known as a 'hall church', reflecting the hall-type meeting-places of the radical Reformation.

In England, the aristocracy sometimes built churches in their own estates. This private church shows the influence of Italian architecture.

circulated. Wren's famous church of St Paul's in London marks the transition between the Baroque and the classical. The staggering variety of churches he built after the great London fire of 1666 shows both his own ingenuity and the desire to make churches more rational, orderly and usable. In France the earliest Neo-classical church, Ste Geneviève (1755) was converted into a 'temple of reason' during the French revolution.

The calm, stately orders of Neo-classicism had a great influence on even the most modest of church buildings. Methodist meeting halls were fronted with graceful pilasters and columns, and 'classic' Georgian architecture enhanced many of the new churches of the Atlantic seaboard. Besides the imposing columns, stressed

quoins and heavy cornices, Neo-classical designers favoured the central plan, surmounted when possible with a dome. Neo-classicism was to have its greatest effect on civic architecture, as can be seen in virtually any capital in Europe.

Generally Neo-classical styles had the widest distribution in countries most affected by the thinking of the Enlightenment – England, France, Germany and the then young United States. In Scandinavia the change was less pronounced and the traditional local forms persisted. Spain apparently found it difficult to relinquish the love of ornament and the austerity of Neo-classical architecture made few inroads there.

Alongside Neo-classicism, another architectural current was also strong –

St Paul's Cathedral in London is the finest church built by Sir Christopher Wren. It is Baroque in its feeling, but the techniques are neo-Classical.

The exciting revival of faith which was begun by itinerant preachers such as the Wesleys led to the building of many small chapels – often in quiet agricultural communities!

Romanticism. Some architects and artists disliked the emphasis on the cold light of reason and longed for an architecture that was mysterious and (that most important eighteenth-century word) 'sublime'. In particular, the Romantics admired the Gothic cathedrals. Goethe was rapturous about their emotive effect and the German artist Casper David Friedrich made the ruined Gothic cathedral the symbol of his own mystical pantheism. The nineteenth century, popularizing eighteenth-century Romantic theory, was to see in the once-despised 'Gothick' the only 'true Christian architecture'.

The clean lines of neo-classicism are clear in this American church.

Forwards or Backwards? The Nineteenth Century

In 1800 most of western Europe was dominated politically by Napoleon's France and intellectually by the ideals of the Enlightenment. Science, industry and philosophy appeared to be making great strides and there was a romantic optimism about the future of mankind, an optimism which was decidedly secular.

This hope for a bright future coupled with a new interest in the order and beauty of Greek culture gave birth to an architectural style called Romantic Classicism. Arcades of Ionic columns sprang up on public buildings, shopping arcades and church façades. Until this time, Christians had rejected the Greek temple as an architectural model because of its pagan associations. But this was no barrier to the nineteenth-century designers who saw in the temple not paganism but order.

The interest in classical antiquity was matched by an enthusiasm for the Middle Ages. In both France and England there was revived interest in Catholic liturgy. The Anglo-Catholic movement of nineteenth-century England was a conscious effort to recapture the mystery, beauty and intensity of worship. An idealized view of medieval life led to conscious attempts to imitate Romanesque and Gothic buildings. These styles seemed to have an inherent 'spiritual' quality about them, a quality which more and more people were beginning to miss in the new 'machine age'. By mid-century it was becoming apparent that the 'triumph of reason' was making much of the social fabric quite unreasonable. Devout revivalists hoped to provide an alternative by rediscovering the lost essence of religion.

Yet the attempts to infuse church buildings with devotion were not particularly successful. The best-informed architects of the period, such as England's Pugin and France's Viollet le Duc studied ancient building in detail. The majority, unfortunately, simply copied things from books or from other architects. Their productions are uniformly boring. Why? For one thing, there was little sensitivity to the past periods of architecture. Components were selected from each, almost at random. The beginnings of the communication era meant that most architects could be aware of the work of others. Shared information brought with it uniformity. Nineteenth-century churches throughout Europe are quite similar. The prime model for most nineteenth-century architects was the French Gothic cathedral. Countless style-books circulated and similar forms were pasted onto buildings almost at random.

The latest technical advances also brought problems. Constructional short cuts eliminated the need for that logic of design which had determined the form of the great medieval cathedrals. It was possible to make steel pillars to hold the church up and then to box them in with machine-cut stone. The effect somehow is not 'right'.

The biggest problem with the revival of old styles is really a philosophical one. Why do we try to express ourselves with someone else's words, or make suitable places for worship with the style of another age? The uncomfortable answer, of course, is that we do not know what style is appropriate for our own age. The nineteenth century's frenetic pace of life sent traditional values tumbling in a

What are the nineteenth-century church builders trying to achieve? St Patrick's cathedral in the heart of New York (RIGHT) harks back to the fourteenth-century rather than relating to the tower blocks which now surround it.

As well as building new churches, architects carefully renovated old buildings. The Dutchman P. J. H. Cuijpers rebuilt this Romanesque church.

maelstrom of change. There was nothing to fill the void except imports from the past. But the imported style was stranded without its most essential support – the social and religious base on which cathedrals were built. It is for this reason that many nineteenth-century Neo-gothic, Neo-classical, or Neo-romanesque churches were never a happy experiment.

Revivalism continues in the twentieth century. There are still 'Gothic' cathedrals under construction (though very few recent commissions). The cost of completing them is now astronomical. If nothing else, they are a testament to the enduring success of their ancestors: when we think of a glorious church, the Gothic cathedral naturally comes to mind.

Despite its attempt to turn back the clock, the nineteenth century did make its own contributions to the development of church architecture. The restoration of old buildings, though over-zealous, saved many structures from dilapidation and collapse.

As the secular philosophies of the Enlightenment threatened the church, some groups responded by trying to define their doctrine more specifically. Some believed that the church should be organized differently – for example, with a group of 'non-professional' leaders rather than one full-time paid clergyman. Here the Enlightenment's emphasis on freedom had another effect; many Christians felt that if they were unhappy with existing church structures and organizations there was no reason why they should not start another church more to their liking. But these 'non-conformist' churches were not just a reaction against the established state churches. They were also a response to the renewed spiritual life that the new emphasis on evangelism was bringing to the churches.

New religious groupings produced many variations on the galleried hall-church, using iron pillars in place of stone. Some of the churches have great charm as well as a practical layout designed for the needs of the congregation. Invariably these buildings are of greater interest than the many revivalist attempts. The proliferation of small churches and chapels provided for the needs of a growing population. The multiplication of church buildings in the nineteenth century rivalled the building surge of the twelfth century. But the church itself was under attack, and putting up buildings could not shore up a crumbling institution.

Cuijpers' church of St Agatha and St Barbara at Oudenbosch (LEFT) *is a direct copy of St Peter's in Rome.*

In England and France, the nineteenth century was a time of revived interest in medieval life. Architects such as Pugin used modern techniques to recreate the atmosphere of medieval churches. This rich, dark chapel at Cheadle in England (BELOW) *gives a real sense of mystical religion.*

ODDITIES OF CHURCH DESIGN

Escaping from persecution, Christians in Göreme, Turkey, hollowed out volcanic rocks to make tiny churches and monasteries.

Every age has its dissidents, visionaries and nuts. Some start political parties or art movements; some perform feats of endurance or set out to walk around the world backwards; some build churches. They can become cult heroes or outcasts – sometimes both. History periodically reviews their achievements and decides whether they are due for revival or ridicule. The church builders either believe that they are providing for an as yet unrealized need – for example a floating church – or simply do what seems appropriate to them.

Only occasionally are their extreme forms backed by groups of Christians who actually mean to use the building. Most often these maverick buildings are the pet projects of an architect or a determined and wealthy individual. The bizarre schemes often call for unusual materials or techniques.

The Floating Church of the Redeemer for Seamen at Philadelphia was built in New York in 1851. It floated on the twin hulls of two clipper ships; its exterior was painted to resemble brown stone and inside it was complete with groined vault and bishop's throne.

At Lalibela in Ethiopia are some extraordinary seven-hundred-year-old churches built vertically downwards. They are carved out of the solid rock.

Temples or Meeting Places? Church Building Today

A group of Christians meeting today to discuss plans for a new church building has a difficult task. It is awkward enough to agree on delicate matters of budget, but it is virtually impossible to be in accord about 'style'. In a sense, there are too many options.

Regrettably, many contemporary churches seem to have been constructed primarily to look impressive – and indeed they do – rather than to meet the actual requirements of an actual worshipping congregation. Churches have been built in the shape of a fish or a crown of thorns, but these symbolic forms in no way relate to the actual practical use of the space.

Part of the problem stems from a conception of worship which makes going to church like going to the theatre or lecture hall. The word 'auditorium' is often used in reference to churches, and the personality of a preacher is too often the prime element in the service. Passive worship becomes the norm, though in fact passive worship is a contradiction in terms. The most extreme example of this is the American 'television church'. Broadcast services in America are followed by millions of viewers, many of whom would otherwise be unlikely to make the effort physically to attend church. The movements of the television camera and the studio-mixed sound of the organ can undoubtedly communicate, but these services lack the active personal contact which is so crucial to the church as a 'body of believers'.

Yet building practical and attractive churches in the modern style is possible – and preferable to attempts to cling to Gothic imitations. Invariably the modern church building which 'works' is the result of a careful review by the congregation of what the 'church' means and what elements of their life together are important. By consultation with an architect, various methods of achieving those ends can be compared. The technical possibilities of building in our century are greater than ever before. Reinforced concrete components can be made at a factory and bolted together on site. The strength of modern components means that walls no longer have to be massive. Modern building techniques are now similar to furniture making: the strength of the joints is the most critical calculation. With an internal frame of steel or pre-stressed concrete the outside of the building need not be load-bearing. It is possible to make a roof which holds up curtain-like walls of shimmering glass.

But the technical ability and the personal enthusiasm of architects has not guaranteed success. Looked at from the point of view of architecture, one reason why there is no distinctive twentieth-century 'church style' is simply that there is no distinctive twentieth-century architectural style. After the immense shock of the First World War, architects were among the most prominent voices clamouring for change. Many honestly believed that only a renewed and reconstituted environment could establish values and bring about peace. The choice, said the famous French architect Le Corbusier, is 'architecture or revolution'. It has taken us a long time to realize that their visionary utopias of architecture are only possible in a totalitarian state, and that

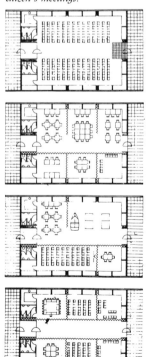

Today church buildings are designed to be used not just for use one day a week. This simple hall in the new city of Milton Keynes in England can be used for worship for 224 people, for children's activities, for film shows, a boat-building club and senior citizen's meetings.

In Asia and South America
church-building has a special
problem – the phenomenal rate of
church growth. This church in
Seoul, South Korea (LEFT) is
doubling its membership every
eighteen months. The main
auditorium holds 11,000: six
Sunday services are telecast to
dozens of other buildings.

Le Corbusier's chapel of Notre
Dame du Haut, one of the most
famous buildings in this century,
was not built for a congregation of
Christians at all. It is a pilgrimage
church. Inside, it seats only fifty
people. The occasional vast group
of pilgrims stay outside – a pulpit
and altar are built on the outside
wall specially for them.

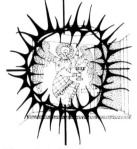

The cathedral in Coventry, England, was destroyed in the Second World War. The new cathedral contains works of art by leading British artists, such as this huge crown of thorns.

living in orderly ranks of tower blocks can be numbing and degrading.

After the Second World War there was a building spree of unprecedented proportions. About three-quarters of the buildings were utilitarian blocks with no pretensions to being 'architecture'. This energetic sprawl relied on the new techniques of construction, but made it painfully obvious that technical advances alone do not make for better buildings. In this period many churches were built as a kind of 'religious art' by architects who did not understand the beliefs of the congregation or the uses of the building.

The architecture of the twentieth century has no unifying style, but rather a plurality of styles. The modern freedom of choice allows a wide range of possible forms for

churches and many congregations are quite baffled when faced with the prospect of building a new church. Yet it would seem better to brave the tangles of congregational dispute than to settle for a compromise which causes no one offense but pleases no one either. Modern architecture provides scope for reinterpreting the church building as a tool for the congregation and as an emblem for the community.

The role of the church in the community is changing, too. Whilst the church is exploding in South America, Africa and South-East Asia, in the West no one is likely to call the twentieth century a particularly Christian era. But there is remarkable renewal taking place – often in unexpected ways. This renewal is bringing two things to the fore in many churches – informality

A small, simple Baptist church in Stockholm, Sweden.

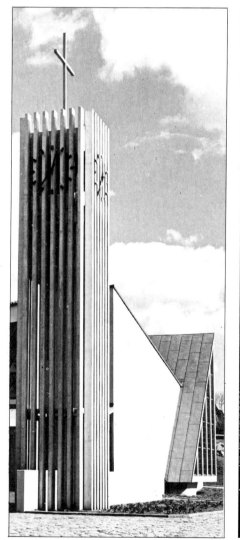

OPPOSITE, ABOVE *Christmas is celebrated at the Roman Catholic cathedral in Bristol, England. The large, low area for the congregation can be used in a variety of ways.*

No less than in other periods, today churches are built for many reasons. The Taivallahti church in Helsinki, Finland (BELOW) was designed for a competition in 1960. But as well as being an exciting construction, sunk in a rock crater, it is also an imaginatively designed meeting-place.

in worship, and a sense of community. (Interestingly these seem to have been the hallmark of the earliest Christian churches.)

Both these factors have had a direct effect on church building. The boundary between nave and chancel is now generally more symbolic than physical. Open spaces are often used for informal worship – even including dance. Many congregations also use their buildings for more than just housing the weekly worship service. Some function as community centres and schools during the week, others provide libraries, study rooms, lounges and space for regular communal meals. The policy of some congregations is that if the church grows larger than two hundred people, another church is begun so that close personal contact can be maintained. Such a young

congregation might meet in a home, a school hall or a converted shop until it outgrows them.

Church building today is characterized by its great variety. Basilica types, ovals, cross plans, free form – there are few 'rules'. This willingness to experiement with form has been particularly significant for church building in the Third World. Here the traditional 'Western' forms have no roots, but local building methods and styles offer many new possibilities.

A church building is not 'the church'. But an imaginative and considered architecture can be a useful and attractive tool for the work of the church. The history of church building demonstrates that the urge to express faith through architecture is basic. The quality of church architecture depends on many factors, not least the sensitivity and dedication of the congregation concerned in assessing its role in the community. As society changes the church needs to apply the gifts and skills of its members to finding new means of expressing its life. It needs to listen, look and learn. The exploration of churches past and present can not only give pleasure but also help cultivate an alertness of what the church is called to be.

The spectacular Crystal Cathedral in California is a product of the US 'electronic church', built from $20 million donations received from vast TV audiences. It is designed in the shape of a four-cornered star to make an impressive backdrop for the TV messages delivered each Sunday from the marble pulpit.

Christians meet together to worship God in a variety of ways (CENTRE). Purpose-designed buildings help, but they are not indispensible, as the persecuted church in the Soviet Union (BELOW) has shown.

Places illustrated in England, Wales and Scotland

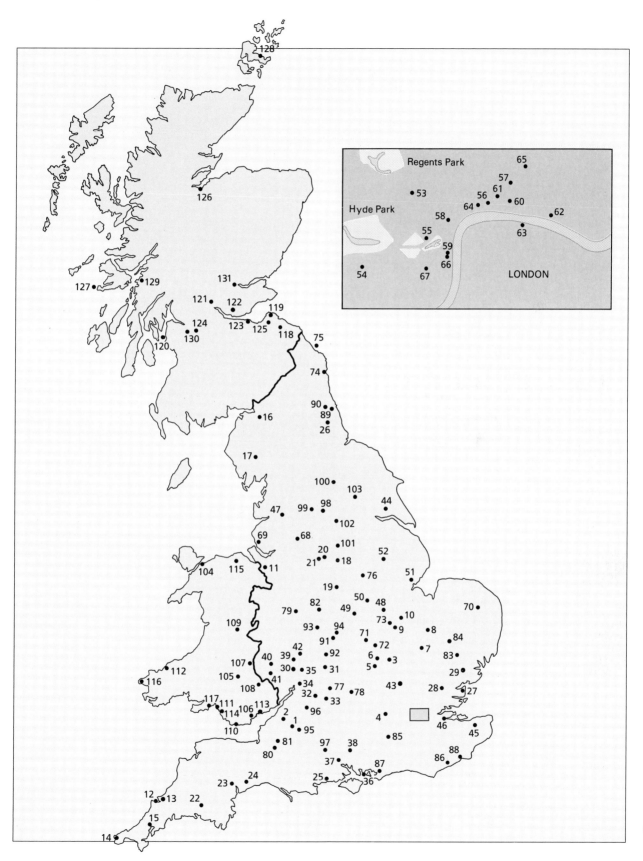

Regents Park

Hyde Park

53

57
65

56
61
64 60
62
58
55
59
63
66
54 67

LONDON

128

126

131

121
122
123 124 125 118 119
130
120
127 129

75

74

90
89
26

16

17

100
103

47 99 98 44
102
69 68
20 101
21 18 52
104 115 11 76 51
19
50 48 70
79 82 49 73 10
109 93 94 71 9
91 72 8 84
42 92 6 3 83
107 40 39 30 35 31 5 29
105 34 77 43 28 27
108 41 32 33 78 46
117 111 2 96 4 45
114 106 113 1 95 85
110 81 97 38 87 88
80 37 86
36
23 24 25
112
116
12 13 22
15
14

93

England

Avon

BATH
Bath Abbey

Bath Abbey has one of the most original frontages in the country, with splendid carved angels climbing up and down ladders that lead to heaven. It was part of a grand design by King Oliver, Bishop of Bath and Wells (and chief secretary to Henry VII), who had had a dream in which he was told a 'King' must rebuild the crumbling Norman abbey!

The work began in 1499. The grand Perpendicular building with huge clear glass windows makes the interior full of light, earning the abbey the name 'Lantern of the West'. Elegant slim columns, and beautiful fan vaulting designed by William Vertue, Henry VII's architect, are the abbey's most outstanding features.

The marvellous east window is a triumph and classic of the Perpendicular style. Basically a rectangle with an inset arch, it depicts 56 scenes of Jesus' life. More than 600 memorial wall tablets grace the walls of the church (only Westminster Abbey has more).

The abbey is probably the third church to stand on this spot; Christians had been working in the town for some considerable time, and there is evidence that some Romans were converted here. We know that Augustine passed through here in 630, after being sent by Pope Gregory the Great to convert the English.

The first monastery, known as 'Hat bathu', founded by Abbess Bertana and a group of nuns, was given its first royal endowment from King Hwicce of Osric (a sub-kingdom of Mercia). Later, land was given by King Offa. Contemporary chronicles tell of the magnificent craftsmanship at the Saxon abbey, probably using material from a nearby ruined Roman temple, and of how it became one of England's most important churches, where Edgar was crowned King of the English in 937.

BITTON
St Mary
Built on a Roman site, Saxon in origin, the church has a long Saxon nave, a late 14th C chancel, a chantry of c.1300 and probably the finest Perpendicular-style tower in the region.

BRISTOL
Bristol Cathedral (above)
The art historian, Nikolaus Pevsner, said that in spatial imagination, Bristol's early 13th C work was superior to any other contemporary building in Europe. It is Britain's only 'hall' church, with its nave, choir and aisles all the same height. The choir's 50-ft arches are also the tallest in the country. The Elder Lady Chapel, off the north transept, is a particularly wonderful example of 13th C Early English architecture.

Remarkable Romanesque work can be seen in the heavily ornamented Norman chapter house, dating from 1140, and the 14th C chancel features the earliest lierne vault in England. This became one of the six abbey churches raised to cathedral status by Henry VIII in 1552, and by the 17th C, due to the prosperity of the city, it had also become superbly furnished, with a good deal of fine silver.

The cathedral holds one of Britain's finest Saxon stones, probably a coffin lid, depicting Christ at the harrowing of Hell. The oldest candelabrum in the country is also here—a medieval brass work of the Madonna and child with St George slaying the dragon.

New Room Chapel (Methodist)
This is the oldest licensed Methodist place of worship in England (1739), frequently visited by John Wesley. It is a superb example of a preaching hall in classical style, and the octagonal lantern which provides light to the interior echoes the later tradition of octagonal chapels. It is galleried, with 19th C box pews. There is a museum collection, with furnished rooms where visiting preachers would have lived and worked.

Redland Parish Church (below)
Redland is a fine Georgian church, opened in 1743 as a private chapel for a

wealthy London grocer who had retired nearby.

Elegant and English Baroque in style, it is very much a post-Reformation building. There is a communion table rather than an altar, a single area of worship rather than a separating screen, and a forward positioning of the original three-decker pulpit. When it was opened, there were no statues, no stained glass and the interior was whitewashed.

The Victorians made several alterations. The pulpit was relocated and reduced to just one tier, and a new vestry was built in the south-east corner of the building. Two arches were added below the gallery, and the nave was extended to provide extra seating space. The high-box pews with doors at the aisle were also adapted to the form in which we find them today.

Outside and across the churchyard, the top of the cupola is visible—the dome above the belfry containing an orb and the cross. The orb symbolizes our world yesterday and today, while the cross speaks of the death of Jesus nearly 2,000 years ago.

St Mary Redcliffe (*below left*)
Originally built on the site of a Norman church, St Mary Redcliffe is of Early English, Decorated and Perpendicular styles. It is positioned above the docks and has close links with seafarers; Admiral Sir William Penn, whose son William founded Pennsylvania in 1681, is buried in the south transept.

The spire of St Mary's is 292 ft tall, and is surrounded by pinnacles and flying buttresses, towering over what has been called 'a wall of glass with a roof of stone'.

Inside, the ribbed roof vaulting of the nave is decorated with more than 1,200 carved stone bosses, and the outer north porch is one of the loveliest in England. The east window in the north choir aisle commemorates the composer Handel, who cried over his work, *The Messiah*, believing himself to have been totally inspired by God.

The churchyard holds the grave of the church cat, a stray tabby, found by a former verger, Eli Richards.

YATTON
St Mary
One of the most impressive churches in Avon, surmounted with a central tower crowned with a truncated stone spire. Inside there are some notable 14th and 15th C monuments, and a rare treasure—a pall (coffin drape) made up from a late 15th C dalmatic, or open-sided ecclesiastical vestment.

Bedfordshire

COCKAYNE HATLEY
St John the Baptist
Medieval exterior, containing inside some of the most impressive woodwork in England, brought from Belgium in the early 19th C (except for French stalls of 1689, brought from Aulne Abbey). Other features include brasses and fine 13th–18th C stained glass windows.

ELSTOW
The Moot Hall (*above*)

This 16th C hall was once the meeting place for the followers of the preacher and novelist, John Bunyan. Born in Elstow in 1628, Bunyan grew up an uneducated tinker. After years of inner turmoil, he found peace with God and began to preach. His preaching was rated more highly than that of the most learned men of the day.

The Elstow parish church—the Abbey of St Mary and St Helena—is also famous for its association with Bunyan. He was both christened and, in 1649, married there. The building has several references to him, and the stained-glass windows in the north and south chapels depict the 'Holy war' and 'Pilgrim's Progress'. The famous Bunyan window, of which a postcard was sent to the hostage and Archbishop's envoy, Terry Waite, while in captivity in Lebanon, is in the nearby Baptist Church.

PAVENHAM
St Peter

Predominantly a 14th C exterior. Inside, there is a triumph of woodwork from different periods, consisting of every technique from marquetry to high relief.

WILLINGTON
St Lawrence

Historically important late Perpendicular church built, like the huge dovecote nearby, by Cardinal Wolsey's Master of Horse.

Berkshire

ASHAMPSTEAD
St Clement

Essentially a church of the Early English period, the chief feature is an important series of 13th C wall-paintings. These were the visual aids of the medieval church, and illustrated the stories of the Bible for the largely uneducated population.

COOKHAM
Holy Trinity

Cookham Church is best known for its painting by Stanley Spencer, who was born in the village. Spencer's experience of both World Wars provided many themes for his paintings. His largest work, 'Resurrection', is set in Cookham churchyard and shows a serene 'state of rest and contentment', which Spencer believed would come with resurrection.

Inside the church is a facsimile of one of Spencer's most well-known paintings, 'The Last Supper', also set in Cookham—this time in the local malthouse. It shows Christ breaking bread, with St John asleep on his shoulder.

A succession of different church

developments and alterations between 750 and 1500 have resulted in several architectural styles. Before 700, the church would have been made of wood and thatch. At the time of the Domesday Book, however, there was a 40-ft stone church here; in addition, an anchoress lived at the church, and was paid a halfpenny a day by Henry II from 1171 until she died in 1181. The Lady Chapel was later built on the site of her cell.

LANGLEY MARSH
St Mary
St Mary's is a picture-book country church containing many fine points of interest. Most notable are the early 17th C Kederminster and Seymour transept, pew and library, which still remind us of the importance of the church as a centre of culture and learning. The library is practically

unaltered, with books, painted panelling and a heraldic over-mantel to the fireplace.

SHOTESBROOKE
St John the Baptist
Both inside and out, a singularly complete 14th C cruciform-plan church surmounted by a lofty elegant spire. Undoubtedly the work of one master mason with a profound sense of proportion. The interior is full of fine, carved, period details, including a nice sedilia, or priest's seat.

WICKHAM
St Swithin
The Victorians built this 'decorated-style' church of knapped flint with stone dressings, adding it to the original Saxon Tower. This hides an eccentric interior, complete with life-size papier-mâché elephant heads

supporting the north aisle roof, wooden angels, and red and purple stained glass windows.

WINDSOR
St George's Chapel (*above*)
This magnificent building at Windsor Castle is dedicated to the patron saint of the Knights of the Garter. It ranks with Henry VII's Chapel in Westminster Abbey and Kings College Chapel at Cambridge as the finest example of Perpendicular Gothic architecture in Britain.

Built between 1478 and 1528, it is made up of two sections—the nave and the choir—separated by a Gothic screen. Buried here are Henry VIII, Queen Jane Seymour, King Charles I (centre aisle of the choir), and most of the sovereigns from George II onward.

The choir, with its exquisite fan vaulting and intricately carved stalls, is where the present queen attends divine services while in residence at Windsor. Above the stalls hang the banners, swords and helmets of the present Knights of the Garter. At the back of each stall are ancient enamelled plates telling in Norman French the arms and titles of the first knights of the order who occupied the seat. The beautiful stained glass of the great west window is 16th C.

Fortunately, St George's chapel was unharmed by the fire which gutted parts of the castle in 1992. The chapel is open to the public most days except during services.

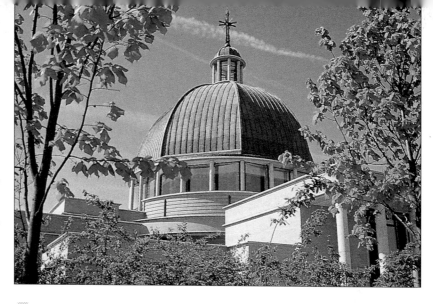

Buckinghamshire

AYLESBURY
St Mary
Mainly 13th C, large and noble with a complex plan which is actually cruciform. Much restored in the 19th C, but it has managed to retain a rare 15th C vestment press.

CHETWODE
St Mary and St Nicholas
Here, in a remote spot, is the remnant of a small 13th C Augustinian priory which became the parish church in 1480. Almost totally 13th C, it is the best example of this period in the county, enhanced by excellent 14th C glass.

DUNTON
St Martin
A largely Norman church. Inside there are box pews, and an 18th C west gallery (with texts and lists of church dignitaries inscribed on the front)—all giving the impression of rural calm.

LITTLE HAMPDEN
Little Hampden Church
Architecturally unpretentious; interior contains the earliest St Christopher wall-painting in England. The timber two-storey north porch is unique in Buckinghamshire.

MILTON KEYNES
Church of Christ the Cornerstone
(above)
In the centre of the new city of Milton Keynes stands one of the newest city centre churches, opened as recently as March 1992. The dedication is unusual, recalling a verse from Peter's first letter, where Jesus is called 'a cornerstone, chosen and precious'—he it is who holds the whole structure of life together.

This church is unusual in another way, too, in that it belongs not to one denomination but to five: Church of England, Baptist, Roman Catholic, Methodist and United Reformed. The services and the whole ministry are shared between these Christian communities.

This striking building is surmounted by a great dome, topped by a lantern. The worship area is circular, and round it, on two floors, are other areas, including a chapel for private prayer and a Guildhall. The round worship area is surrounded by a cloister, and below the dome is a stained glass 'collar' with panels by Alexander Beleshenko.

The overall effect is of a church peculiarly suited to its position at the heart of Britain's newest city.

NORTH MARSTON
St Mary
Historically interesting church, associated with Rector John Schorne. In late 13th–early 14th C, Schorne performed miraculous cures of the gout, succeeded in imprisoning the devil in a boot and became venerated as a saint. The remains of his elaborate 14th C shrine can be seen in the south aisle. His relics, however, were removed to Windsor. The church was restored in 1855 at Queen Victoria's expense, in memory of Neild.

OLNEY
St Peter and St Paul *(below)*
The importance of the village church is no more eloquently expressed than in the lovely town of Olney. It has a prominent spire and a peal of bells which 'undulates upon the listening ear', according to the 18th C poet

William Cowper, who spent 19 productive years here.

Collaboration between Cowper and John Newton, curate at the church, produced the famous 'Olney hymns' (1779). A large, spacious church, St Peter and St Paul is in a perfect position on the River Ouse and is built in the Decorated style, with a 185-ft spire.

WEST WYCOMBE
St Laurence
An architectural jigsaw with fantastical overtones. Sited within Iron Age earthworks alongside a flint Dashwood mausoleum. Partly medieval. Some inspirational features, and unholy associations with the 18th C 'Hell-fire Club'. The tower is surmounted by an 18th C folly—a huge golden ball which seats six people inside.

WING
All Saints
Architecturally, probably the most important Saxon church in England,

noted for its polygonal apse, vaulted crypt, aisles and for its sheer overall size. Also contains a number of good later fittings.

Cambridgeshire

CAMBRIDGE
King's College Chapel (above)
A major achievement of English medieval architecture, King's College Chapel is one of the greatest examples of Gothic architecture in Europe. The College itself was founded in 1441 by Henry VI, and five years later, on 25 July 1446, the foundation stone of its chapel was laid. It was completed in 1515.

It has one of the most spectacular fan-vaulted interiors anywhere— magnificent, clear and crisp—looking more like lace than stonework. The master mason John Wastell worked on it with master carver Thomas

Stockton. Sculptural decoration around the walls is breathtaking, with relief crowns that are almost detached from the wall, and with equally impressive portcullises and roses.

The screen and choir stalls are the purest work in Early Renaissance style in England. It is generally accepted that there is is no wood carving of this period north of the Alps that compares with its brilliance. Yet no one knows who made them or even exactly when.

The stained-glass windows are as important as the stalls, and the most complete set surviving from the time of Henry VIII. Flemish craftsmen spent 26 years making the stained glass with iconographical schemes in the medieval manner. Depictions from Old and New Testaments are juxtaposed to create parallels, and the Old Testament stories are chosen particularly to point towards the coming of Christ and the fulfilment of the Old Testament.

Rubens' masterpiece *Adoration of the Magi* (c.1634) stands behind the altar.

The Round Church (below)

Following the capture of Jerusalem for Christendom in 1099, pilgrimage to the Holy Places became easier, although still dangerous. The two main places of pilgrimage—the site of Jesus' crucifixion and of his resurrection—are both in the Church of the Holy Sepulchre in Jerusalem, whose most notable feature is the Rotunda.

It was this feature which was translated into the Round Churches of 12th C Europe. The Round Church in Cambridge is one of four round churches still in use in England. The others are at Northampton, Little Maplestead in Essex, and in the Inns-of-Court area of London.

The Church of the Holy Sepulchre—the Round Church, Cambridge—was built c.1130 and has the second oldest parish in Cambridge. It was built by a fraternity of monks and originally comprised only the circular nave and ambulatory (both of which survive), and a short chancel.

By the mid-13th C, however, the Round Church had become a parish church, and the patronage passed to Barnwell Priory. The chancel was apparently rebuilt, and a north aisle added in 'beautiful and highly-finished Early English work'.

A second structural remodelling of the church took place during the 15th C. The small Norman windows in the nave were replaced by larger Gothic

ones, and the angel rooks in the chancel and north aisle date from this time, as does the polygonal bell-storey of brick above the existing nave.

Further major repairs followed in the mid-1800s, removing the now dangerous bell-storey and replacing it with a domed roof similar to the original. The chancel arch was narrowed, and 15th C Gothic windows were replaced by smaller Norman ones modelled on one that had survived earlier alteration. As a result, the building is now close to the original form that its founders intended.

One beautiful feature is the stained-glass east window at the front of the building, showing Jesus with his crowned head raised up, looking straight out, very much alive. The wood of the cross is sprouting new green branches, and the whole is a metaphor for the new life possible for all.

ELY

Ely Cathedral (above)

In 673, St Ethelreda, Queen of Northumbria, founded a Saxon nunnery at Ely. It was probably a double monastery for monks and nuns but, like the two succeeding Abbesses (also Saxon queens), St Ethelreda would have ruled over both houses.

Today, only the Ovins stone, the base of a cross in the cathedral, remains from Saxon times.

The first stage of the present building was not completed until 1189. The choir and presbytery were rebuilt in 1252 while the octagon, Ely's most unique feature, was built during 1328–42. The octagon tells St Ethelreda's story in a series of eight carvings on the capitals of the great lantern pillars. Each pillar was cut from a massive oak tree, and the structure is unique in Europe and supports 400 tons of wood.

The octagon was conceived when the Bishop of Ely, Hugo de Northwold, initiated one of the earliest great surveys of woodlands in Britain, called *The Old Coucher Book of Ely* (1251). The octagon's inner timber tower sits on 16 struts, approximately 40 ft by 13 sq. in., and is thought to be a feat of engineering genius.

The nave is 250 ft long, and bosses on the ceiling often display oak leaves or acorns. The walls of Ely Cathedral are built from Barnack stone, the hardest limestone in England, taken from a quarry near Stamford. Its quality can best be seen in the Prior's door on the south side of the nave.

LITTLE GIDDING
Little Gidding Church (above)

An important event in the history of the English Church occurred in 1626 at Little Gidding. Nicholas Ferrar, having bought the manor house nearby, established a lay community with 30 other people, all committed to take on a simple rule of prayer and work. The Ferrars also renovated the church, reducing its size and creating the present stone west front.

In 1977, a new thriving community of 'Christ the Sower' was started, inspired by the Ferrars' example. Anglicans, Roman Catholics and Free Church members live, worship and work together, united with the old community by the 60-ft long church that lies next to them. A notice above the west door says, 'This is none other than the house of God, and this is the Gate of Heaven.'

The interior has unique, wooden panelling, with small areas of old text inscribed in gold. Brass panels of the Lord's Prayer, Creed and Commandments, date from 1625, and 17th and 18th C furnishings rest on black and white marble floor slabs, giving the whole church a Classical feel. There is also a 15th C eagle lectern, an hourglass, and a font with a 17th C crown top, believed to be one of the most unusual in Britain.

The poet T.S. Eliot founded a group called 'The Friends of Little Gidding' in 1947. Of Eliot's work, *The Four Quartets* (1944), possibly the most rewarding is 'Little Gidding'. Today, the community of 'Christ the Sower' runs a farm that contains some rare breeds of cattle, sheep, pigs and poultry. Like the old community, it is establishing a fine garden and, for the weary traveller, there are excellent cakes and coffee too.

NORTHBOROUGH
St Andrew

This is the surviving fragment of a much larger church. Mostly 12th and 13th C work. Historical association with Cromwell, whose wife is buried here, as is the wife of John Clare, Northamptonshire peasant-poet.

PEAKIRK
St Pega

Developed from the site of the cell of St Pega into a much-restored medieval chapel, and now part of a convent. It has a Norman bell tower and 14th C wall-paintings.

PETERBOROUGH
Peterborough Cathedral (below)

Peterborough Cathedral is one of

Britain's least altered Great Norman churches, and has a magnificent west front, with three huge arches, originally designed to be freestanding.

The first monastery established on the site was by Peada, King of Mercia, in 655. Its destruction by the Danes 200 years later led to the consecration of a second abbey c.970 in the presence of Dunstan (the Archbishop of Canterbury), Oswald (the Archbishop of York) and King Edgar. But in 1116 this one was also destroyed (by accidental fire), and the foundations of the present church were then set down.

Inside the cathedral, the first impression given by the bold Norman arches is of tremendous stability. The extraordinary painted ceiling (c.1220) is a unique feature, for it has the most important series of medieval figure studies in Britain, influenced by manuscript decoration and Romanesque art. It is possible to light up the whole ceiling and view bishops, kings and saints, alongside beasts and monsters.

Other features to look out for are the central tower, rebuilt in the 15th C, which has a splendid vaulted ceiling; the apse, perhaps the most complete of its period in England; and the Hedda, or Monk's stone, one of the most important Anglo-Saxon sculptures in Britain. There is also a rare 12th C watch-tower in the chapel dedicated to St Oswald.

The cathedral is the burial place of Catherine of Aragon, Henry VIII's first wife, over whose divorce the breach with Rome was caused. Mary Queen of Scots was also buried here in 1587, after her execution at Fotheringhay, but was later reinterred at Westminster Abbey by her son, James I of England and VI of Scotland. A memorial to Richard Scarlett, the grave-digger who buried both queens, can be seen on the west wall of the nave. He lived until the age of 98.

RAMSEY
St Thomas of Canterbury
Part of the monastic abbey, built originally as a 'hospitum' to care for the sick and infirm; the presence of a

13th C font indicates that it was probably always a parish church, too. Predominantly 12th C.

SWAFFHAM PRIOR
St Mary and St Cyriac
One of the few parishes in England where two churches coexist in one graveyard. Unfortunately one is partially ruined and both are in the care of the Redundant Church Fund.

Cheshire

BADDILEY
St Michael
A 'cosy' church with half-timbered chancel and 17th C brick nave encasing an earlier structure. Famous for its tympanum, one of the most interesting in England which is 20 ft square and painted with the Creed, Commandments, Lord's Prayer and heraldic arms, dated 1663.

CHESTER
Chester Cathedral (*above right*)
Chester was formerly the Roman town of 'Deva' or 'Casta Devana'—the 'camp' or 'station' of the Roman army's famous 20th legion. Later, in the time of Edward I, Chester was near the front line of the king's Welsh campaign and, as such, it is an important historic town.

Chester's Christian history starts with a nun and Abbotess called St Werburgh, daughter of the Mercian king, Wulfhere. St Werburgh died in Staffordshire in the early 8th C, and her remains were brought here in 907. The 10th C Anglo-Saxon church gave way to a Norman Benedictine abbey, which saw much rebuilding between the 13th and 16th centuries.

Since 1541, the great red sandstone church of Chester has been a cathedral. In the form of a great cross, it still retains a 13th C refectory and glassed-in cloisters, among the best preserved monastic buildings in Britain. But its soft sandstone material, susceptible to crumbling, led the

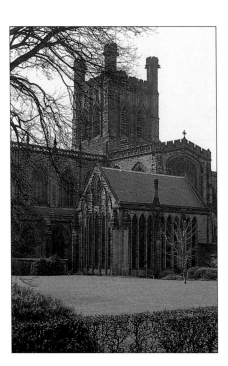

architect Sir Gilbert Scott to call the cathedral a 'mouldering sandstone cliff' when he first saw it in 1868. His major restoration of the 1870s brought the cathedral back to its present state.

The wooden, medieval choir stalls are a magnificent feature and were built by Richard of Chester, one of Edward I's military engineers in Wales. Each stall has a canopy to protect the monks from cold draughts, and a corbel showing one of a range of scenes from the birth of Christ to fantastic animals and beasts. Underneath the seats are a series of carved misericords with images of the virgin and child, angels, mythological and satirical subjects, animals and even domestic chores.

In the nave is a colourful stained-glass window (1961), designed by W.T. Carter Shapland. It portrays six northern saints beside Mary, Jesus and Joseph. Nearby, a series of mosaic panels on the north wall of the nave displays a number of Old Testament stories.

On the right-hand side of the second window from the east is the famous 'Chester imp', a figure of the devil in chains carved by a monk to scare away evil spirits.

103

CHOLMONDELEY
St Nicholas
A cruciform-plan, private chapel to the nearby castle. The family pew or state gallery has cushions made from robes worn at the coronation of William IV.

CONGLETON
St Peter
An 18th C town church with contemporary glass, galleries, brass candelabrum, font and altar rails. Unique to the county, the pulpit is centrally placed in front of the altar in order to satisfy the liturgical fashion of the period for lengthy sermons.

LOWER PEOVER
St Oswald
Despite restorations, an excellent example of a timber-built church, with a tower of stone. Inside, the atmosphere is still 'medieval' and some of the box pews have their lower halves fixed to retain the rushes— once the standard floor covering of parish churches and houses in certain parts of the country. The old church custom of 'rush bearing' stems from the annual changing of these reeds.

MOBBERLEY
St Wilfrid
A typical east Cheshire medieval church. Magnificent rood screen of 1500, over which is a ceiling painted and adorned to represent heaven above the great crucifix which once stood below.

Cleveland

KIRKLEATHAM
St Cuthbert
Perhaps the most interesting church building in the county. The church and attached mausoleum are predominantly 18th C. External details include a Chippendale Gothic door to the octagonal Baroque Turner mausoleum. The inside is dominated by rows of Tuscan columns on

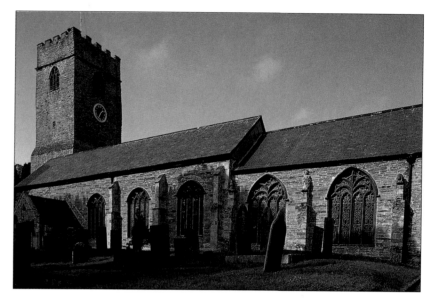

pedestals but, despite restoration, there is a wealth of original furniture, including a 14th C parish chest which would have housed all the important documents of the church.

MARTON
St Cuthbert
Historically important as the baptism church of Capt. James Cook, RN, although since then it has been totally rebuilt (1843).

STOCKTON-ON-TEES
St Thomas
Light in an otherwise drab landscape; a stately Classical building of 1710–12 in which Wren had a hand in the design. The imposing pulpit was once part of a three-decker, and in the fine woodwork note the 18th C altar and rails carved from the wood of Capt. Cook's ship, *Endeavour*.

UPLEATHAM
St Andrew
The surviving west section of the nave was originally part of a large Norman church and is often mistaken for a complete church. As such, St Andrew's is sometimes wrongly referred to as the smallest church in England. The tower is 17th C.

Cornwall

ALTARNUM
St Nonna
Shadowed by one of the loftiest towers in Cornwall, this Perpendicular church contains a fine display of medieval art, in particular the rood screen which spans the chancel and aisles. Early 17th C panels depict the Holy Communion and the Crucifixion.

LANLIVERY
St Brevita
As with many Cornish churches, an unusual dedication, here to St Brevita. One of the great churches of the county, refashioned in the 15th C. There is a nice ringers' rhyme board.

LINKINHORNE
St Melor
Built from local granite. Inside, there is a wagon roof typical of the south west, and a wall-painting showing the Works of Mercy. A holy well, of late medieval structure, stands in a nearby field.

PADSTOW
St Petroc at Padstow *(above)*
Although the present building at Padstow is 15th C, the first church

was built on this site in about 518 by Petroc, a Welshman. Two 'Lives of Petroc', written in the Middle Ages, were recently discovered in a Paris library, and it appears that his church grew into a monastery with a school, an infirmary, a library and a farm.

St Petroc made a considerable impact on the area. By 936, the church was granted privilege of sanctuary by Athelstan, first king of England. Only two other churches in Cornwall were accorded this privilege.

The three main features of the interior are an unusual 14th C font with carvings of the 12 apostles, a large memorial in the south-west corner to the 16th C builder, Nicholas Prideaux, and a notable wagon roof.

ST ENDELLION
St Endelienta
An isolated prebendal, or 'Chapter' church, surrounded by the low slate houses of the prebendaries, which seem to have survived all Reformations.

ST JUST
St Just-in-Roseland *(below)*
In in his book *In Search of England*, H.V. Morton describes St Just, snuggled between a bank and a small estuary, like this: 'I have blundered into a Garden of Eden that cannot be described by pen or paint. There is a degree of beauty that flies so high that no net of words nor snare of colour can hope to capture it . . . I would like to know if there is, in the whole of England, a churchyard more beautiful than this.'

St Just is surrounded by rich gardens, including bamboo and rhododendrons, and suggesting hotter climates and far-off places. Many of these were planted in Victorian times by John Garland Treseder, a Cornish traveller and gardener.

The church itself was once part of the Celtic Church, established before St Augustine came to England. Cornwall had been trading tin with the Phoenicians since the earliest times, and one popular local legend was that Joseph of Aramathea was really a tin merchant who travelled here with Jesus when he was a boy. Whatever the origins of the story, it is certainly very possible that the sailors who traded between Cornwall and the Middle East brought the 'Good News' of the gospel to these shores.

TREBETHERICK
St Enodoc *(above)*
The 13th C church of St Enodoc, on the east side of the Camel Estuary near Trebetherick, was once buried in sand. Local people even gained entrance through the church roof, and archaeologists have discovered houses in the area engulfed so quickly by a storm that some still contain furniture. A collection of stone bowls, found nearby, lines the entrance to the church. The bowls are not religious vessels, but medieval domestic mortars for grinding corn.

The burial of the church is evidence of the ferocious storms that once battered this coastline. Many gravestones in the churchyard are those of 'unknown sailors', whose ships were wrecked on these shores.

But it is perhaps because of a different burial that St Enodoc is noted. It was here that Sir John Betjeman, Poet Laureate to Queen Elizabeth II, was buried in 1972, near his mother, just inside the lych-gate.

TRURO
Truro Cathedral (below)
When the Prince of Wales laid the foundation stone for the building of Truro Cathedral in 1880, it was the first Anglican cathedral to be built on a new site since Salisbury in the 13th C. The occasion is remembered in the cathedral's stained-glass windows.

However, the newly consecrated bishop, Dr Edward White Benson, had to administer his Diocese from a wooden hut for the years the cathedral was being built! It was during these years that he revived the nine lessons and carols that are now a part of so many Christmas services.

The cathedral's style mimics the Early English or Gothic style prevalent in the 13th C, and is influenced by the medieval buildings of Brittany and Normandy. The prime emphasis is on the choir, while the nave is comparatively small. The architect, John Loughborough Pearson, also wanted to preserve the medieval parish church of St Mary's, so some of it was kept as St Mary's aisle, therefore achieving a 'church within a church'.

After Pearson's death in 1897, his son Frank continued the project. The cathedral's cloisters were begun in 1935, but work was stopped during World War II. However, Truro was to triumph over adversity. The last building was the addition of a chapter house in 1967. On the north transept is a painting, 'Cornubia—Land of the Sainta' by John Miller, unveiled for the cathedral's centenary celebration in 1980. The aerial view of the county is shown, with Celtic crosses placed where churches exist, and a beam of light falling on the cathedral.

Cumbria

APPLEBY-IN-WESTMORLAND
St Lawrence
An Early English style church with Perpendicular overtones. Among a number of fine fittings, it contains the tomb of Lady Anne Clifford, who restored this (1655) and numerous other churches in the area. It also has probably the oldest working organ in England (c.1542), brought here from Carlisle cathedral in the late 17th C.

BURGH-BY-SANDS
St Michael
Built largely of stone from Hadrian's Wall, on which line it stands. In the vicinity is a monument to Edward I who died in camp on Burgh Marsh in 1307.

CARLISLE
Carlisle Cathedral (right)
The old red sandstone cathedral of

Carlisle has a historic past; some of the stones in its fabric were taken from Hadrian's Wall or the old Roman city. The city was later believed to have had a monastery (although no trace of it has yet been found), and was visited by St Cuthbert in 686. An early painted mural in the north aisle shows the monk guided by a flying eagle and fed by a dolphin.

Excavations during the 1980s have shown that an ancient Christian graveyard was situated on this site. Viking objects have been discovered and it is suspected that there were two Christian settlements in old Carlisle. By 1102, King Henry I had given grants for a religious house. Soon afterwards, he founded a church and priory, later to become the cathedral.

The west end of the nave was demolished in the mid-17th C. Only two bays of the Norman nave still remain, and a new west end was built. The magnificently-decorated 15th C choir and east end, masked in the nave by the organ, can be reached through one of the aisles. The stalls are richly ornamented, and there are interesting misericords, including one of a legendary mermaid.

The roof is a wonderful piece of work, painted by Owen Jones in 1856, five years after he had decorated the Great Exhibition. The large east window, showing The Judgment of Christ and scenes from Jesus' life, was begun in the 14th C and is one of the best remaining examples of Decorated tracery.

The labours of the month are depicted on the 14th C capitals around the presbytery and choir. One shows a farm-worker warming his toes in the February cold; another, a man gathering grapes in September.

The treasury has many beautiful objects, including a unique black jet medieval cross, found during construction of the treasury in the 1980s. The library holds several rare books, as well as other documents, including the marriage certificate of Sir Walter Scott, who was married here in 1797.

A sad, sensitive and lovely feature is

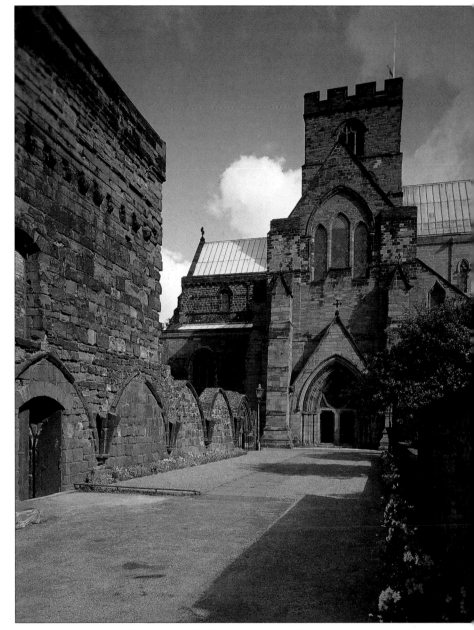

the main window in St Wilfred's chapel in the north transept, which commemorates the five daughters of Dean Tait. They died of scarlet fever within six weeks of each other in 1856. The lily is a reminder of one of the daughters, who could not remember the correct words of the 23rd Psalm and who kept repeating 'Though I walk through the lily of the valley of death, I shall fear no evil.'

CROSTHWAITE
St Kentigern

Built on an ancient site, the present church is mostly 16th C, but restored. Contains many curiosities; an 18th C pitch-pipe, a conductor's baton, and old rhymes urging bell-ringers not to swear, nor ring in spurs nor wear hats. Its greatest treasure must be its unique number of medieval consecration crosses, 12 outside and 9 inside.

GRASMERE
St Oswald *(above)*

The poet William Wordsworth is buried in St Oswald's churchyard with his wife Mary and other members of his family. He also wrote about the church, of its 'naked rafters intricately crossed, like leafless under-boughs in some thick wood'.

The church dates from the 11th, 13th and 17th C and is dedicated to St Oswald, the Northumbrian king who was killed in battle at Hexham in 642. Earlier in his life, Oswald had fled to Iona when his father was overwhelmed by King Edwin. The time spent in Iona must have been important to him because, on his return, he re-established Christianity in Northumbria with the help of the Celtic monk St Aidan. St Aidan became known as 'the apostle of Northumbria', setting up a church and monastery at Lindisfarne and founding many other churches in the area.

ISEL
St Michael

A largely Norman church, near to a medieval fortified hall. On the 15th C window, three sundials mark the monastic hours, and on one of the pre-Norman crosses is a rare three-armed symbol, a triskele, one of the earlier Christian devices.

Derbyshire

BREADSALL
All Saints

Predominantly 13th and 14th C, but internally heavily restored after a fire in 1915 started by Suffragettes. Possibly the finest steeple in the county.

CHESTERFIELD
St Mary and All Saints *(right)*

St Mary and All Saints is best known for its 14th C twisted spire, one of the most eccentric in Europe. Some say the twist is due to the drying out of the comparatively green, unseasoned wood used to make it. Certainly, the herringbone patterns of the lead plates that encase it accentuate its peculiar form.

The church is the largest parish church in the county, and has many interesting features from the medieval period to modern times. The interior of the church was redesigned by Sir Gilbert Scott in 1843, and restored again after a fire in 1963.

The oldest parts of the church are the massive arches of the Early English period, which date from around 1234.

DALE ABBEY
All Saints

Near to the site of 12th C abbey, with a hermitage close by. Minuscule church with farmhouse under one roof. 17th C furnishings—'cupboard' altar; pulpit of 1634; reading desk and box pews. Pleasant 14th C mural of the Visitation.

DERBY
The Cathedral Church of All Saints *(below right, opposite)*

Derby Cathedral testifies to the trading prosperity of this area, which was renowned for its silk, porcelain and iron work. The city gained a bishop in 1927, and at the same time an unusual bishop's throne from Constantinople.

The church was once an important medieval collegiate church, but all that remains of the medieval building is the west tower, one of the largest Perpendicular towers in England. It was built in 1520 (to replace one that was demolished overnight by a rector in dispute with the city officials) and has a fine battlement top, with pinnacles.

The rest of the church was rebuilt between 1723–25, over older burial vaults, by the London architect James Gibbs, renowned for designing St

Martin-in-the-Fields. The design is a combination of early designs for St Mary-le-Strand and a rejected design for St Martin-in-the-Fields.

In the interior, the nave and aisles are separated by wonderful Tuscan columns on tall pedestals. The nave was extended eastwards in the 1960s to form a new sanctuary. The retro-choir by Sebastian Comper is a successful addition that was completed in 1972.

There is an interesting and colourful tomb to Elizabeth, Countess of Shrewsbury, also known as Bess of Hardwick, who died in 1607, having outlived four husbands. There is also a tablet erected in 1945 to commemorate the 200th anniversary of the arrival in Derby of Bonny Prince Charlie (the Young Pretender).

Derby's most important feature is a richly-carved 18th C Flemish chancel screen. The ironwork screen bounding the sanctuary was made locally by Robert Bakewell and is embellished with a heraldic coat of arms of the

house of Hanover.

The east windows of both aisles represent All Saints and All Souls. They were designed in 1967 by the Welsh artist Ceri Richards, and made by Patrick Reyntiens.

■ EYAM
St Lawrence *(above right)*

Attracting more than 120,000 visitors each year, Eyam is famous for the events during the Great Plague of 1666 when the villagers halted the spread of the disease by breaking off all contact with the outside world. The church, which is Norman (though probably resting on Saxon foundations), has many reminders of this great act of courage and selflessness.

The plague came to Eyam by means of a bundle of cloth sent from London. Because the cloth was damp, it was aired in front of the fire, allowing the escape from the cloth of the fleas which were carrying the dreaded bubonic plague virus. Soon after, the

village was struck by the disease. The church and churchyard were closed, and the burial of victims took place in the fields and gardens around their

own homes. Elaborate precautions were taken to ensure that people leaving supplies for the villagers did not come into contact with the plague.

In the church, the terrible effects of the plague at Eyam are seen in the *Plague Register* in the south aisle, which gives the names of all the people who died during the 14 months of the plague. In all, 276 of the 350 villagers died. In the north aisle is the so-called *Plague Cupboard*, said to have been made out of the box in which the plague-infested cloth was brought to Eyam.

Major restoration was carried out in the church after the bicentenary of the Eyam Plague in 1866, and in the 20th C the church renovations include a new window, installed in 1985.

MELBOURNE
St Michael and St Mary
Once part of an abbey, this huge and ambitious Norman church is dated c.1130. It has twin west and central towers, a stone-vaulted narthex, and circular apses to the chancel and aisles. Internally, it is similar to St Bartholomew-the-Great, London, with ponderous round inscribed pillars; triforium with clerestory, and processional all the way round.

TIDESWELL
'Cathedral of the Peaks' *(below)*
Hidden away on the remote and misty moorland of Derbyshire is one of the county's grandest parish churches. It is impressive from any distance and well deserves its title of 'Cathedral of the Peaks'.

As a piece of ecclesiastical architecture its main interest lies in its completion within a 75-year timespan in the 14th C. This has given it a unity of style, being largely Decorated with some Perpendicular additions. It is dominated by its impressive west tower, the last part to be built, which in turn is surmounted by tall corner turrets finished in crocketed pinnacles. The church is strongly battlemented with angle buttresses carrying pinnacles.

Over the chancel arch is a small niched bell-cote, again with pinnacles. The windows are a mixture of two styles, the broad, tall, square-headed windows showing the move to Perpendicular. The only later work was the restoration of the church in the early 1870s.

Inside the tower, the arch is very tall and the nave roof medieval. The nave and aisles have box pews and the church is rich in pre-Reformation monuments (stone effigies and brasses). There are some large tomb chests and a stone screen behind the altar.

Devon

BRANSCOMBE
St Winifred
Isolated church of architectural importance, built 11th–16th C. Inside, the woodwork is worth close inspection, especially the Elizabethan west gallery, the altar rails enclosing the altar on four sides, and the magnificent three-decker pulpit—rare in Devon.

BUCKLAND MONACHORUM
St Andrew *(above, opposite)*
More than a third of British parish churches are partly or wholly Perpendicular in style. In St Andrew's church, Perpendicular features include the tall, upright bars in the windows and the splendid wooden nave roof with its 16 figures, each playing a different musical instrument.

A church inventory of 1805 records that St Andrew's church music was provided by violin, cello, flute and bassoon. In 1849, a church organ was introduced. There is also some

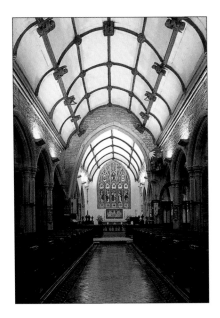

interesting Victorian stained glass by Charles Kempe, and the roughly-hewn old granite font is worth close inspection—on the rim, a small area of damage indicates it once had a lid. Many fonts had lids after the 13th C, when the then Archbishop of Canterbury ordered fonts to be closed, to prevent holy water from being stolen.

CHITTLEHAMPTON
St Urith
Dedicated to a local saint, murdered c.700 by pagan villagers. Urith is buried in the church of ancient date, and her holy well lies at the east end of village.

EXETER
Exeter Cathedral (below)
Exeter's west elevation, lit at night by floodlights, is stunning, and highlights the efforts of 14th C masons to create wonderful statues of saints and monarchs for those who came to worship.

The present cathedral was begun in 1275 by Bishop Bronescombe, who had previously been at the consecration of Salisbury Cathedral. Indeed, it was Richard Farleigh, architect of Salisbury's spire, who gave Exeter its most outstanding feature—the longest uninterrupted stretch (300 ft) of Gothic stone vaulting in the world, made possible by the Norman towers that rise from the transepts rather than the main body of the church.

The interior of Exeter is one of Britain's glories. It is well known for its detailed carvings in wood, for example the oldest set of misericords in Britain (c.1260), including one of an elephant. In the nave there is a famous series of carved corbels, one showing an acrobat performing before the Virgin Mary. The bishop's canopied throne is another splendid piece of medieval woodwork. Made of Devon oak, it rises to 57 ft.

There is also a touching memorial to Matthew Goodwin, who died at the age of 17 in 1586. He is recorded as a genius, 'very worthy and very learned,

Master of Music at Canterbury and Exeter Cathedrals'.

Exeter was hit by a bomb during the Second World War. The ecclesiastical artist Herbert Read and master mason George Down (who carved a modern corbel of himself as a rugby forward in St James's Chapel) restored much of the fine work.

OTTERY ST MARY
St Mary the Virgin (above)
This 13th C church was remodelled into a collegiate church in 1338–42 by Bishop Grandisson, and is modelled on Exeter Cathedral. The interior is full of light and colour, and in the Dorset aisle (c.1520), there is a spectacular fan-vaulted roof with pendants, with very special roof bosses. The church was partly restored in 1850 by architect William Butterfield, a leading exponent of the Gothic revival.

The medieval clock is one of the oldest surviving mechanical clocks in Britain. Based on the Ptolemaic theory that the earth is the centre of the universe, hours of the day and night are shown by the movement of a golden sun. Arabic numerals are written on an inner circle that has 30 discs for the days of the Synodic month. The phases of the moon are described by a moving star, while a black-and-white orb revolving on its own axis completes a revolution every 24 hours.

The father of the poet Samuel Taylor Coleridge was vicar here, and Coleridge was baptized in the church in 1772. Outside the church, there is a fine series of consecration crosses.

REPTON
St Wystan
Originally a Saxon foundation, the chancel and crypt (with its crude stone vault) date from this period. It has all styles of architecture from 10th to 15th C.

SAMPFORD COURTENAY
St Andrew
Mainly 16th C work; inside simple, light and spacious. This village was the hatching ground for the Prayer Book Rebellion of 1549 which began and ended here.

WIDECOMBE-IN-THE-MOOR
St Pancras
The delightful church of St Pancras (the patron saint of children) is situated in a perfect little niche, surrounded by typical Dartmoor countryside.

The cruciform church dates mostly from the late 14th C, but it has had a number of alterations. The transepts were extended into the aisles and the splendid granite tower was raised to 135 ft in the 16th C, funded by the prosperous local tin-miners.

During a service in 1638, a bolt of lightning struck the church. Local records tell how one of the tower's pinnacles toppled, and a great ball of fire, possibly a meteorite, swept through the choir, killing and injuring many people. The incident is illustrated on the rood screen, with 32 figure paintings and verses about the disaster, and on floor tablets close to the chancel steps.

Interesting features include some finely carved bosses. One in particular, of three one-eared rabbits, form a Trinitarian symbol—also a symbol connected with tin-mining.

Dorset

BRIDPORT
Chapel (Quaker)
Typical of the origins of so many Quaker meeting houses, this chapel was first a barn, adapted to its present use following a visit to the town by George Fox in 1655. Like many Quaker meeting places, the exterior is hardly recognizable as a chapel. This was often deliberate, to avoid persecution.

Internally, all is plain and simple, yet managing to appear rich. A gallery and benches forming three sides of a square are all that mark this as a building for worship.

CHRISTCHURCH
Christchurch Priory *(below)*
This is the longest parish church in England, crowned by a glorious golden weather-vane of a salmon—a reminder that fish had long been the major source of food for the local people.

The first church here was built some time after the baptism of Cynegils, King of the West Saxons, in 640. The Domesday Book called it the monastery of the Holy Trinity, and its monks contributed a great deal to the local community.

The present church is impressive. The 13th C north porch is 35 ft long, and the nave (c.1150) is beautifully simple, with marvellous geometric patterns carved into the stone. The view east, past massive pillars and towards the Great Late Perpendicular choir, really is uplifting.

Because the central tower collapsed in about 1420, only the reredos remains of the old choir. Its wonderful stone carving is based on Isaiah's prophecy, 'There shall come forth a rod out of the stem of Jesse', and it shows David, Solomon and Jesse resting beneath a nativity scene.

Christchurch is not short of fine detail: the choir screen includes two small animals, possibly from the Ark, chasing each other around a pillar; there is also a caricature of a man's head, and some wonderfully chiselled foliage and acorns.

In the Montacute Chantry, there is a carving on the capital depicting the 12 disciples and a two-faced Judas. The Ascension tablet depicts the 11 disciples looking heavenwards, gathered round a stone with the imprint of Christ's feet.

The most famous object in the church is the Miraculous Beam, near the ceiling beside the Lady Chapel. It was believed by some that an extra 'carpenter' mysteriously exchanged a beam cut too short for one that was too long; the new beam then miraculously placed itself in the correct position and was left exposed in the church for all to see.

HILTON
All Saints
An example of a Dorset county church which could well have been built for the pages of a Hardy novel. Mainly late Gothic, its features include a fine range of 15th C windows from the now destroyed Milton Abbey, and 12 panels with early 16th C figure paintings of the Apostles from the same source.

LONGBURTON
St James
Predominantly Perpendicular, the tower is Early English with a 13th C upper stage. Noted for its monuments, including ancestors of Sir Winston Churchill.

WHITCHURCH CANONICORUM
St Candida and Holy Cross
An Early English building for the most part, unique in this country for retaining relics of its patroness in a 13th C shrine. Good monuments in a spacious and light church.

WIMBORNE MINSTER
St Cuthberga
Cruciform church, formerly collegiate and the only instance of a two-towered church in the county. Full of medieval interest, but of especial note are the coloured tower ceilings and the vaulted crypt, simple and moving.

County Durham

BRANCEPETH
St Brandon
Built between the 12th and 17th C, St Brandon's church is especially noted for its woodwork, given by John Cosin, rector here from 1626 and later Bishop of Durham. This includes a magnificent chancel screen, pews, pulpit, ceilings, choir stalls and more, all of which carry fine detail. Fragments of medieval rood screen.

CHESTER-LE-STREET
St Mary and St Cuthbert
Practically engulfed by 20th C development, it is recognizable by its curious tower with octagonal storey and capped with 14th C spire. Of various dates, it possesses an anchorite's cell with squint to afford the occupant a view of the altar.

DURHAM
Durham Cathedral (opposite)
Durham is the greatest and most innovative of Britain's Romanesque cathedrals. Perched on a wooded cliff high above a horseshoe bend in the River Wear, its fortified position is absolutely awe-inspiring.

The only English cathedral to have been built as a shrine, it fulfilled St Cuthbert's wishes that the monks never left his bones alone on Holy Island. When they left their monastery in fear of Viking raids, they took his coffin with them and eventually found a resting place for it at Durham. In 995, 'The White Church' to shelter St Cuthbert's body was dedicated.

Seven years later, a new cathedral was begun by the second Norman bishop, William of Calais. In less than 40 years, the building was complete, and the only significant changes since that time have been the Galilee Chapel (where the Venerable Bede is buried); the Chapel of Nine Altars of 1240 (so called because of the need for many altars to celebrate the Mass); and the 15th C central tower.

The Norman design is quite remarkable, the whole cathedral covered by a simple rib vault—the first example of rib vaulting in England. The stone vaulting in the aisles is the oldest of its kind in Europe.

The lofty central tower is Perpendicular, but was later 're-Normanized' by Sir Gilbert Scott. The nave is richly decorated, and has great pillars incised with unusual deep channels. The great west window was added in the 14th C, as was the imposing reredos, known as the Neville screen, which now stands behind the high altar. This was probably carved by Henry Yevele, master architect of Westminster Hall and much of Westminster Abbey. There are also some beautiful misericords in the 17th C choir stalls.

Remains of the monastic buildings include the monks' door into the cloister, which contains ironwork that has been there since the church was consecrated 850 years ago. The monks' dormitory has its original roof timbers, and is now a museum. The sanctuary knocker on the north door is a bronze replica of the 12th C original (now in the treasury). Any fugitive seizing the door knocker could claim the right of sanctuary.

There are also several memorials in the cathedral. The head of Oswald, who founded the see of Lindisfarne in 635, is buried in Durham, and St Cuthbert's remains are buried under a plain stone slab behind the high altar. One 17th C memorial is dedicated to the miners who gave their lives, while another pays tribute to those who work today in the pits of County Durham.

ESCOMBE
Escombe Church
A simple, untouched Saxon church of majestic beauty. Inscribed stone from Roman fort at Binchester built into north wall, and an interesting sundial above the porch. Textbook long-and-short work as well as Roman masonry.

SEAHAM
St Mary the Virgin
Like so many County Durham churches of ancient origin, Roman masonry is incorporated. Simple, almost austere architecture. There is a nice double piscina, with a mysterious design of a priest's hand raised in blessing cut into its arch. Parish registers record Lord Byron's marriage.

Essex

BRADWELL-ON-SEA
St Peter-on-the-Wall (overleaf, top)
St Peter-on-the-Wall has a unique atmosphere, located as it is, on the shore of the Blackwater Estuary. Only a rough track leads to this simple brick building, although Christians have been worshipping here for more than 1,300 years.

It was in 653 that St Cedd came to convert the East Saxons at the request of King Sigbert. The monastery became a cathedral after Cedd was consecrated bishop in 654. It is one of the few links in this part of Britain with Celtic Christianity.

A simple stone chapel, of which the 7th C nave remains, was built using materials from the old Roman fort of Othona. In fact, the name St Peter-on-the-Wall came from the fort's west wall, and there are Roman tiles above the rectangular doorway.

The chapel was rebuilt in the 14th C. Then, in the 17th C, it fell into disuse and was converted into a barn. It continued to be used as such until 1920, when it was reconsecrated.

CHELMSFORD
St Mary, St Peter & St Cedd (below)

Although a parish church until 1914, Chelmsford Cathedral now serves the largest diocese (by population) in England. It is not an ancient church, but was rebuilt in the 15th and early 16th C, after damage caused during the Civil War. Extremists broke windows when the bells were rung to commemorate 'deliverance from Guido Fawkes' and youths burned many of the church's objects—it is amazing that the beautifully-coloured 16th C monument to Thomas Mildmay survived.

In 1800, the nave collapsed and had to be rebuilt, but the special quality about this cathedral remains. Its entrance through the two-storeyed 15th C south porch is beautiful, and its 1983 restoration tells a story of renewal. The cathedral's modern, polished limestone floor replaces the stone slabs and Victorian glazed tiles of so many Christian sites while its cool, light colour sets off work by contemporary artists.

This cathedral church has the feeling of constant use by its congregation. The cathedral contains a banner of the Virgin Mary and a colourful

patchwork-like wall-hanging by Beryl Dean, which contains 1,520 pieces. The simple grey altar is by Robert Potter, and a modern bishop's chair, unusually made of stone, is by John Skelton.

As you step through the unusual 15th C twin pointed arch, off the chancel, you face St Peter's Chapel, dedicated to all who suffer in the world. There, a magnificent bronze screen by Guisseppe Lund has the appearance of large upturned nails; the screen contrasts with a sculpture of a mother and child that sits inside. 'The bombed Child', by George Ehrlich, refers to war—a reminder of the verse in Luke's Gospel saying that Mary, mother of Jesus, 'kept all these things in her heart'.

St Cedd's Chapel is indeed for quiet and thoughtful prayer, as well as daily communal and private worship. It also has some interesting modern work.

COPFORD GREEN
St Michael and All Angels
As Pickering is to Yorkshire, so Copford is to Essex. The whole of this 12th C church interior is a blaze of coloured wall-paintings, the finest of which is the beautiful depiction of Christ in Majesty on the half-domed vault over the apse. In the south aisle (c.1300) are some of the oldest medieval bricks in the country.

GREENSTED-JUXTA-ONGAR
St Andrew (*above, right*)
This amazing little Saxon church at Greensted (the name literally means a clearing in the forest) was built in 845, from huge oak logs. These were split vertically, tongued and grooved to keep out drafts, and held in place by wooden pegs set in a more recent sill-and-brick base. It is the oldest wooden church in the world and the earliest example of a Saxon wooden-framed building; as such it is a national treasure.

There were no windows in the original pre-Conquest nave, only holes drilled through the logs for ventilation. After some 1,100 years, its oak walls have become so hard it is

practically impossible to drive a nail into the timber.

14th C stained glass in the east end depicts the head of St Edmund, martyr and first patron saint of England before the Normans substituted St George. His body was believed to have rested here in 1013 when it was being taken back to Bury St Edmunds (after a period of safe keeping in London).

HADSTOCK
St Botolph
Probably the Minster erected by Canute in 1020 to commemorate his victory over Edmund Ironside at Assendum. A remarkable Saxon cruciform church entered through a south door, which must be one of the oldest in the country.

NEWPORT
St Mary the Virgin
A large town church of 13th–16th C work. Among its furnishings is an unusual and important 13th C portable

altar in the form of a chest, the lid of which opens to form a reredos with early paintings.

STEBBING
St Mary the Virgin
Predominantly 14th C. Full of interest—good timber roof even in a county renowned for its timbered churches; fine stone chancel screen; and a rare pulley block in the chancel for drawing the Lenten veil.

Gloucestershire

ASHLEWORTH
St Andrew and St Bartholomew
Notable church with 14th C spire. In its setting near the tithe barn and court house, it admirably demonstrates the church's place within the local community.

BROMSBERROW
St Mary (*below*)
This small village church was built in
Norman times c.1170. Its 'tub' font is
one of only 60 or so in the country.
Inside the church are standards of both
the Royalist and the parliamentary
sides in the English Civil War.

CHIPPING CAMPDEN
The Parish Church (*below*)
The church of this town at the
northern end of the Cotswold Way
boasts a tower 120 ft high, and can be
seen as the town is approached from
any direction. It was built almost

entirely in the 15th C when the town
prospered through the wool industry.

In a case beneath the tower are a
unique set of altar hangings, the only
complete set remaining anywhere
from the 15th C. They are still used at
Westminster Abbey for coronations or
special services.

CIRENCESTER
St John the Baptist (*above*)
The Perpendicular parish church of
Cirencester is not only the largest in
Gloucestershire, but one of the

grandest in the country. Cirencester,
or Corinium, was one of the largest
towns in Roman Britain. The church,
one of the Cotswold 'wool' churches,
was founded by King Henry I.

The three-storey porch is one of the
most impressive in England, and
secular business could be transacted
here—it was at one time the town
hall. The nave was the last part to be
completed, in 1515–30.

The most famous possession of St
John's is the Boleyn cup, given to
Anne Boleyn by Henry VIII in 1535,

two years before she died. The cup is unique, and is on permanent display here. The church also has magnificent medieval stained glass, and is noted for its two-storey oriel window.

There are medieval murals in St Catherine's Chapel and a rare 'wine-glass' pulpit from around 1450, one of the only pre-Reformation pulpits in Gloucestershire. There are also many brasses and examples of fine fan vaulting.

▓ DEERHURST
St Mary
Originally founded in the 8th C as an Anglo-Saxon monastery, St Mary's was rebuilt in the 10th C after the Vikings

had left it in ruins. The interior appears to have immense height, with curious double triangular-headed windows opening high up from the tower into the nave. The sanctuary is set out in 17th C manner. Nearby is a chapel erected by Earl Odda in 1056.

▓ FAIRFORD
St Mary the Virgin (below)
The exterior of this completely Perpendicular church is impressive enough, with its embattled parapets and pinnacles. But it is the interior that reveals the amazing talents of the ecclesiastical craftsmen, probably including King Henry II's glazier.

The whole church is a monument to

the builder and cloth merchant, John Tame. With its complete set of 28 medieval stained-glass windows, it has the greatest display of 15th and 16th C glass in any British church. In times of danger, the glass has been removed: once in the time of Cromwell, and again during World War II.

The biblical stories in glass begin in the north aisle. The first large window portrays Eve tempted by the serpent. Moses and the burning bush, and the Queen of Sheba and Solomon follow. In the Lady Chapel, the important times of Mary's life are shown: Mary as a child, a wife, a mother and a woman who watched the death and experienced the resurrection of her son and saviour. The pinnacle of this visual feast is a set of images of the Last Judgment, in the great west window of the nave. Mary and St John the Baptist kneel at Christ's feet, while hellish images of devils and Satan are bathed in a blood-red glow.

▓ GLOUCESTER
Gloucester Cathedral (overleaf)
The old city of Gloucester was once a crossroads for travellers to Wales or to the Midlands, and the great Perpendicular cathedral would have dominated the skyline as it still does today. Yet when you get close, the small area of the college green that surrounds it suddenly reduces the size of this great building, giving the visitor a sense of intimacy.

The nave is cool and dark with relatively small windows. The great Romanesque arches, with large rotund columns, were finished in 1160, and give it a grand scale without reducing the sense of well-being. Reminders of the cathedral's monastic history include an unusual lavatorium (washing place) and recesses for monks' desks in the cloisters, where the fan vaulting is the earliest in the country to have survived.

The first Christian community was started here by Osric, Prince of Mercia, in 681 and was handed over to Benedictine monks in 1022. William the Conqueror's order to compile the Domesday Book was made from

Gloucester and the book was completed in 1086, half a century later.

Gloucester's present splendour is due to Abbot Thoky who, in 1327, buried the murdered King Edward II at the abbey. Donations from the swarms of pilgrims that came to his tomb funded the rebuilding of the abbey in the then little-known Perpendicular style. Gloucester thus became the birthplace of English Perpendicular Gothic architecture and the Perpendicular Lady Chapel is the finest example of its period in England.

Like many of the monasteries in Britain, Gloucester was dissolved in 1540 and became a cathedral. However, it is probably the best example of an abbey church that escaped destruction in this period. The colossal 3,000 sq ft east window is the largest in Britain, and commemorates those who fell in the Battle of Crecy.

A more recent addition is the interesting memorial to Dr Jenner, who pioneered vaccination in 1796, and whose work was the first step to ridding the world of smallpox.

TEWKESBURY

Tewkesbury Abbey *(below, opposite)*
It is often thought that Britain's best church buildings are all cathedrals. This is not so. In fact, some cathedrals are architecturally just like large parish churches, while magnificent places of worship such as Tewkesbury Abbey have never been a cathedral.

Tewkesbury is one of the largest abbeys largely to have survived the Reformation. After the Dissolution of the Monasteries Act 1541, the people of Tewkesbury purchased the building from the king to use as their parish church. As a result, they saved the finest monastic building in Britain after Westminster Abbey for future worship and enjoyment.

The 12th C Norman tower and the nave, with its 14 massive columns, are very fine. Once highly decorated with medieval paintings, the interior would have been dark and richly illustrated, illuminated by flickering wax candles. The great 65-ft west window (1686), recessed with a six-fold arch, is the tallest of its kind in Britain.

The medieval tombs of the De Clares, the Despencers and the Beauchamps, who bestowed so much on the abbey for its adornment, are themselves some of the best in Britain. Also buried here, in the choir, is Edward Lancaster, Prince of Wales, killed during or after the Battle of Tewkesbury in 1471.

One of Tewkesbury's most treasured possessions is the 17th C 'Milton Organ', so called because it once sat in Hampton Court Palace, where it is thought it was played by the poet.

Hampshire

■ BEAULIEU
Blessed Virgin and Child
Established in the refectory of the Cistercian abbey. It still retains the monastic reader's desk approached through the thickness of the wall by a graceful arcaded stair.

■ BREAMORE
St Mary
An architecturally important church c.1000. Originally cruciform, it is made up of and contains much textbook work. The nice timber roof is often overlooked in favour of other features, and there is a delightful array of hatchments in the tower crossing. The inscription over the south transept archway reads 'Here the Covenant becomes Manifest to Thee'.

■ ELLINGHAM
St Mary
An 18th C rustic simplicity which hides an interior of complex design and rare treasures. Medieval screen with hourglass; 16th C tympanum with painted Decalogue, texts and Royal Arms. Near the west door, a fine reredos by Grinling Gibbons surrounds an Italian painting.

Externally, the south porch carries an interesting and huge blue-and-gold painted sundial.

■ PORTSMOUTH
The Cathedral and Parish Church of St Thomas of Canterbury *(above)*
In 1180, Jean de Gisors, a ship owner, gave an acre of land to the Augustinian monks of Southwick to build a chapel for the seafaring community. By 1320 it had become a church, and served in this capacity for 700 years.

Due to the subdivision of the Winchester diocese in 1927, Portsmouth became a cathedral. Sir Charles Nicholson began to turn the old parish church into a new cathedral, but the work was left incomplete. Recent additions, including an altar and font, are the work of Michael Drury. The church is named after Thomas à Becket, who was murdered in Canterbury Cathedral in 1170.

The cathedral has a 12th–13th C sanctuary and choir, surmounted by an exquisite Jacobean tower (1691); a cupola was added (1703) to accommodate bells given by Queen Anne's Consort and a clock that

chimed hymns every four hours. The
light in the tower acted as a beacon to
sailors at sea.

King Charles II was married in the
Domus Dei Chapel, on the Grand
Parade, to Catherine of Braganza of
Portugal. The King was given Tangier
in North Africa as a wedding present,
and the church plate used in the
colony's Anglican services is on
display. There is a bronze plaque to
Captain John Mason who founded New
Hampshire in America. The grave of
an unknown sailor from Henry VIII's
flagship, the *Mary Rose*, lies in the Navy
aisle.

ROMSEY
Romsey Abbey (St Mary and St Ethelflaeda) *(left)*

Romsey Abbey, north-east of
Southampton and Hampshire's largest
parish church, is renowned for its
Norman architecture. Its blocky shape,
with a central tower and wooden bell-
cage with eight bells, is unique.

The abbey was founded in 907 by the
son of Alfred the Great, who made his
daughter, Elflaeda, Abbess. It was
later refounded as a Benedictine
nunnery by King Edgar.

The present buildings date largely
from 1120–40, and were built as
Henry I's memorial to Queen Matilda,
who died in 1118. The arcading on the
south side of the chancel is fine
Norman architecture. The triforium
above the main arches has unique
twinned sub-arches surmounted by a
single column. Carved capitals above
the pillars in the south choir aisle are
by craftsmen who worked on the crypt
at Canterbury Cathedral. Some
interesting Arabian 'stalactite'
decoration must have been brought
back from the crusades.

On the outside, the Abbess'
doorway is flanked by a Saxon rood
dated 1000 and protected by a
contemporary canopy of Christ on the
cross, with the hand of God reaching
out to him. A rectangular niche to his
side was probably once used for
burning candles. A second Saxon rood
is in the chapel of St Anne.

Also of interest are 14th C floor

tiles in the Chapel of St George, the medieval coffin lid of an abbess, and an exquisitely painted wooden reredos in the north transept. The abbey has had a long association with the Palmerston and, more recently, Mountbatten families who lived nearby on the Broadlands estate.

▨ WINCHESTER
Winchester Cathedral *(above)*

'In this year was built a Church at Winchester which King Cenwalh made and consecrated in St Peter's name,' says an Anglo-Saxon chronicle of 648. The bones of Saxon kings and bishops rest here, including those of King Canute and his wife, Queen Emma, and William Rufus, third son of William the Conqueror.

Winchester has had a bishop since 679. The pre-Conquest cathedral lay north of the present site and was the ceremonial place of worship for the

Wessex kings, but nothing remains of it, or the earlier Saxon cathedral.

By the time of the Normans, Winchester was the second most important town in England. Construction of the cathedral under Bishop Walkelyn began in 1079. The building took more than 300 years to complete and encompasses a variety of styles. The church that resulted was probably the largest Romanesque church in Europe, larger even than Durham or Peterborough Cathedrals.

The building was a bold undertaking, considering the marshy ground. The builders had to drive thousands of wooden piles into the ground before they started laying foundations. Traces of this early Norman cathedral can be seen in the north and south transepts, the crypt and the crossing with its low tower.

However, the early Norman cathedral was made Gothic. Its nave was

transformed to provide a tunnel of light, with large lofty perpendicular arches, elegant balconies and an open clerestory. The choir stalls are the oldest in England and there are excellent early-13th C wall-paintings in the Chapel of the Holy Sepulchre. The font, like Lincoln's, is of black Tournai marble, with carvings of St Nicholas, and there are seven elaborately carved chapels.

Jane Austen (1775–1817), author of *Pride and Prejudice*, is buried under a simple floor slab. Isaac Walton (1593–1683) is also buried here. He wrote *Lives* of many people, including John Donne.

The cathedral's library houses a 10th C copy of Bede's *Ecclesiastical History* and the famous 12th C Winchester Bible.

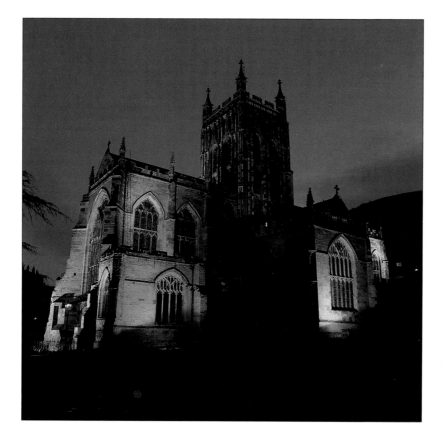

patriarchs, the Nativity and Passion of Jesus, and legends of the Saints. In addition, Richard III is thought to have presented the west window above the font, and King Henry VII was the donor of the 'Magnificat' window in the north transept. In the east and north transepts there are further colourful windows showing 11 medieval musical instruments.

Other medieval features of the Priory are some fascinating misericords, several beautiful tombs and sculptures, and the finest set of medieval wall and floor tiles of any church in the country.

In the 19th C, renovations were directed by Sir George Gilbert Scott (famed for his work on Westminster Abbey). Amongst other things, he was responsible for the superb restoration of the ceiling, new designs such as the oak pulpit, and several new windows.

▦ HEREFORD
Cathedral of Our Lady and St Ethelbert *(above, opposite)*
Hereford Cathedral has a wonderful tower and is superbly furnished, but perhaps most special is its library of more than 1,500 chained books. These include a wonderful set of 8th C gospels, more than 90 12th C manuscripts, and a unique national treasure, the *Mappa Mundi*—a map drawn on vellum c.1290 by Richard de Haldingham, a prebendary of the cathedral. Its flat world, pivoting around Jerusalem, shows the garden of Eden, the Tower of Babel and the Red Sea.

The diocese is one of England's oldest, established about 700. Even before then, there was probably an ancient Celtic bishopric, and the first church was dedicated to the king and martyr St Ethelbert. Of this there are no remains.

The cathedral as it stands today is quite majestic, soaring as it does above the river Wye. Much of it is 12th–14th C, but no other major cathedral in England has had so many 'improvements' or attempts at restoration. It reminds one of the words of King Solomon in the book of

Hereford and Worcester

▦ BESFORD
St Peter
Slightly restored in 1880, it remains for the most part a 14th C church and has the distinction of being the only timber-framed church in the county. 14th C bells, a complete rood loft, and 16th C triptych with painted figures.

▦ BREDWARDINE
St Andrew
Predominantly Norman, with a Georgian tower. Associated with Francis Kilvert, the famous diarist, who was rector here from 1877 until his death in 1879.

▦ GREAT MALVERN
Malvern Priory *(above)*
The first glimpse of Malvern Priory through the trees of the churchyard is a breath-taking experience. Its majestic structure, its variety of coloured stone and its position on the side of steep, ancient hills, all serve to create a graceful sense of harmony.

The priory was founded at the end of Saxon times by a hermit monk called Aldwyn, and was formally recognized as a Benedictine priory in 1085. The first buildings were, in fact, Norman, and relatively squat and dark. (One of the tiny, Norman windows, now bricked up, is visible on the south side of the priory, just outside the vestry.)

In the 15th C, the Norman pillars came to support a glorious matrix of architectural detail in the Perpendicular Gothic style. Great stained-glass windows flooded the building with light, and today they constitute the finest collection of 15th C glass to be seen in Britain outside York Minster.

The most striking glass is in the magnificent east window, the largest of any parish church in England. It shows the creation, the Old Testament

Ecclesiastes: 'All things are full of labour; man cannot utter it; the eye is not satisfied with seeing, nor the ear filled with hearing.'

Inside, an ancient chair in the cathedral is said to have been used at Pentecost by King Stephen when he attended mass in 1138, and fine misericords can be seen in the choir stalls. There are also excellent brasses.

The early 18th C saw the beginning of the Three Choirs Festival, an annual music event that is still held by the cathedrals of Hereford, Gloucester and Worcester. As a young man Sir Edward Elgar played the violin in the orchestras here, and later he conducted all his major works in the cathedral. Ralph Vaughan Williams also composed for the festival.

One final feature worth noting is on the eastern wall of the south transept—three tapestries designed by John Piper and made in Namibia, illustrating the Tree of Life. The first tapestry is of the Garden of Eden; the second is of Jesus on the cross; and the third is of the tree standing beside the

river of life, as described in the book of Revelation.

▓ KILPECK
St Mary and St David (above)
Kilpeck, with its castle, village and church, has been described as one of

the most important rural medieval sites in England, but it is the church of St Mary and St David that is the village's crowning glory.

Built from old red sandstone in the 12th C, it is one of the most perfect Romanesque churches in Britain. The

French influence is clear, with a Norman three-cell nave, chancel and apse.

There are also superb Norse and Celtic-style carvings. The south doorway is an extraordinary depiction of creation, with wonderful reliefs of birds, fish, beasts and people. The Garden of Eden is illustrated by the tree of life, and its forbidden fruit. Even the temptation and the Fall of Humanity is illustrated, with a lion, a dragon and a serpent suggesting the battle between good and evil.

On the outside of the church, there are over 70 carvings on the corbels. Carved figures wrestle, while dancers, musicians, lovers, bears, horses, pigs and a fertility figure are lined up one after the other; there are even a hunting dog and rabbit cuddled up together—suggesting the lion lying down with the lamb.

▓ TYBERTON
St Mary
Originally Norman, rebuilt in 1720 in brick with Classical tower. Its most noted feature is the beautiful early 18th C reredos carved with the symbols of the passion, in a spirit of mysticism unusual for the period.

▓ WORCESTER
Worcester Cathedral *(right)*
Built on the edge of the River Severn, Worcester Cathedral looks splendid with its 14th C central tower reflected in the deep blue water. Its origins go back to 680, when a priest named Bosel, from Whitby in Yorkshire, was consecrated as the first bishop, although there is evidence of even earlier Christian burials here. By 993, Oswald, Archbishop of York and Worcester, had founded a Benedictine monastery here.

Many more buildings were to follow over the next few hundred years. Some survive, such as the notable circular 12th C chapter house of 1120, with its green and white bands of stone decoration.

After Oswald, the most important figure to follow was Wulstan, the only Anglo-Saxon to keep his position as a

bishop well after the Norman Conquest. He built first the crypt, and then the Lady Chapel and remodelled the choir. The present nave was rebuilt in the 14th C, in Decorated and Perpendicular styles. It has a dramatic black-and-white patterned floor, which contrasts with the brightly coloured west window (a superb example of Victorian stained glass, depicting the story of creation).

Worcester Cathedral contains the tomb of King John, buried here in 1216, and also has a window and a memorial in the north aisle to the composer Sir Edward Elgar, whose birthplace was only three miles away.

Hertfordshire

ANSTEY
St George
A deceptive building, giving the impression of being larger than it actually is. Of many periods—transitional central tower c.1200; 13th C chancel, transepts and squints affording a view of the altar; 16th C stalls and misericords; and the rest comprises 14th and 15th C work.

AYOT ST LAWRENCE
St Lawrence
Set as a focal point in parkland view, the old parish church stands in ruins next to the new. It was designed in 1778–79 by Revet on the lines of a Greek temple with flanking pavilions and linking screens. Internally, however, the detail is Roman Classical tempered to Anglican 18th C. The east end is a coffered apse.

HITCHIN
St Mary
A sumptuous church—architecturally 12th–15th C with a rich interior full of monuments, woodwork and brasses. Spectacular two-storey south porch, undoubtedly built by a merchant.

ST ALBANS
St Alban's Cathedral *(above, right)*
Few cathedrals have exuded such an outpouring of human emotion as has St Alban's, built on the execution site of Britain's first-known Christian martyr. Neither a monk, nor a devoted missionary, Alban was a Roman soldier from Verulamium (now St Albans), who was beheaded c.300 for sheltering and changing clothes with a fugitive priest who had shared the gospel with him. According to the historian Bede, he also refused to offer a sacrifice at a pagan altar, and said, 'I worship and adore the true and living God who created all things.' Christianity was outlawed in the Roman Empire, and he was put to death.

In 793, King Offa of Mercia

rediscovered the saint's relics and founded a Benedictine monastery on the execution site. To this day, there has been Christian worship on this site, and the altar in St Albans' north transept is dedicated to the 'Persecuted Church'.

By the reign of King Edgar and St Oswald in the 960s, the reputation for miracles at St Alban's shrine was drawing many pilgrims, and Oswald's monks collected material from the ruined Roman city to expand the building. After the Norman conquest, the first abbot—an Italian named Paul de Caen—brought over from Normandy the notable architect and builder, Robert Mason. By 1115, the abbey had been completely rebuilt, becoming the largest and richest church in England.

The central tower, the oldest of England's great cathedrals, is built with Roman tiles, already 800 years old when the Normans used them. The same bricks can be seen in the triforium in both transepts. Paul de Caen also founded a scriptorium here, which later encouraged the artistic talents of Matthew Paris, William of Colchester and other men of the 13th C.

Most of the cathedral as it is today dates from the 13th–15th C. However, the nave contains early wall-paintings and a beautiful stone rood screen that separates the choir from the nave. Doors from both sides of the reredos lead into St Alban's shrine, rebuilt from 2,000 fragments in the 19th C—a time of major renovation for the cathedral generally.

St Albans was raised to cathedral status in 1877. In 1982, a new chapter house was opened by Her Majesty Queen Elizabeth II.

TRING
New Mill Chapel (Baptist)
A beautiful red-brick chapel and schoolhouse set in a spacious graveyard. Well worth a visit to savour the contemplative atmosphere of the unrestored early-1800s interior.

WARE
St Mary
Mainly 14th and 15th C periods; the most notable features are the transepts, unusual in being carried to full nave height and embellished with clerestories. Another fine feature is the octagonal font c.1380, the most elaborate in Hertfordshire.

Humberside

ALDBROUGH
St Bartholomew
One of the few churches retaining an inscribed Anglo-Saxon sundial, which reads 'Ulf who ordered this church to be built for his own and Gunware's souls.' Also of note is a late 14th C military effigy.

APPLEBY
St Bartholomew
Largely rebuilt in 1800, when fragments of masonry from Thornholme Priory were incorporated. Of considerable interest are the remains of an old church custom, traces of funeral blacking applied to the interior walls on the death of a notable parish personage— in this case, a former Lord St Oswald.

BEVERLEY
Beverley Minster (right)
Beverley's twin towers dominate the red-tiled roofs of the town. Its Perpendicular west front and unusual west door are exquisite, and were made under Nicholas Hawksmoor, a pupil of Sir Christopher Wren.

The first Anglo-Saxon church was founded by St John of Beverley, famous for curing a deaf and dumb boy. The Frid-Stool (Old English for 'peace stool'), that sits near the altar is probably the only remaining part of this church.

The second Saxon church was refounded as a collegiate church and was given the right of sanctuary for a mile in all directions by King Athelstan (c.937). Records from 1478–1539 show that 469 self-confessed criminals sought sanctuary during those years.

The present minster was built between 1220 and 1420. In 1548 it was reconstituted as a parish church and has remained so ever since. The nave is light and airy, with the clerestory directing light down onto the floor. The oldest part is the Early English east end with its altar. The transepts followed as the masons worked from east to west.

A wonderful Norman font with 18th C cover is one of the few remaining parts of the Norman church.

The Percy Tomb, dedicated to Lady Eleanor, wife of Henry, first Lord Percy of Alnwick, is possibly one of the finest examples of medieval European art. It is situated on the north side of the sanctuary. Carved between 1340–49, it is an exquisite example of Decorated Gothic, an elegant canopy with intricate details, overflowing with fruit, leaves, angels and beasts.

The Black Death in 1349 brought work to a halt here as it did in so many other churches and cathedrals across Britain. As a result the nave from the north door westwards was completed in the later Perpendicular style. The great Perpendicular west window is Victorian, and portrays the early history of Christianity in Northumbria.

The elaborate choir stalls date from 1520, with their 68 misericords. Other interesting carving is found on the west door where a set of figures represents the four evangelists and the four living creatures described in the book of Revelation.

BOTTESFORD
St Peter's Chains
An Early English church with a rare dedication. The lancet windows of the chancel are said to be the longest of any parish church in England. The north transept, formerly known as the Morley choir, was used for a considerable period as the burial place of the ancient Catholic family of that name.

GOODMANHAM
All Saints
This church is reputed to occupy the site of a pagan temple which Bede tells us was destroyed by Coifi, the chief priest, after his conversion to Christianity in 627. The most ornate font in the area is here, probably made on the eve of the Reformation and inscribed 'with owt baptysm no soull ma be saved'.

SWINE
St Mary
Formed out of the aisled chancel of a cruciform church which was part of a Cistercian nunnery. Beautiful assembly of alabaster effigal tombs, 16th C screenwork and misericord stalls to assist the clergy to stand during the long medieval church services.

Isle of Wight

CARISBROOKE
St Mary
Overshadowed by the castle, the church, with its stately Perpendicular west tower, has been described as 'the most important ecclesiastical building in the Island'. It was originally monastic, while simultaneously parochial, but the priory was suppressed in 1414 and none of the convent buildings have survived. The church suffered the loss of its chancel in c.1565.

SHORWELL
St Peter
An almost unchanged, wholly Perpendicular church with an extraordinary collection of poppy-headed pews. There is also an important wall-painting of St Christopher, depicting several episodes in the life of the saint.

WHIPPINGHAM
St Mildred
A 'royal' church, in the sense that it was much patronized by Queen Victoria and the then royal family, who gave a number of sumptuous fittings. Architecturally Germanic Gothic and partly designed by Prince Albert. There are various memorials to members of the royal family.

Kent

BROOKLAND
St Augustine
The most remarkable architectural feature of this mainly 13th C church is the detached timber belfry, octagonal in plan, with three stages stacked on one another like cones, and shingled from top to bottom. The interior is unrestored with the most exquisite 12th C lead font.

CANTERBURY
Canterbury Cathedral *(above)*
In 597, Augustine was sent to England by Pope Gregory the Great to convert the Anglo-Saxons and establish the See of Rome. He was welcomed at Thanet by Ethelbert, king of Kent, and a new monastic residence was set up at Canterbury.
Nothing remains of the first Saxon cathedral, destroyed by fire in 1067.

129

The first Norman bishop, Lanfranc, set about rebuilding the cathedral, but it is to his successor, Anselm, that we owe much of Norman remains today. The 12th C crypt is the largest of its period in England, and has excellent carving influenced by Byzantine and Middle Eastern art.

It was in the Norman church that Thomas à Becket, one-time Chancellor to Henry II, became Archbishop of Canterbury in 1162. His disagreements with the King led ultimately to his martyrdom in 1170 and his canonization in 1173. These events made Canterbury one of the most important centres for pilgrimage after Jerusalem and Rome; even King Henry II came here in 1174 to do public penance for Becket's death. In the same year, a fire left the new eastern arm of the cathedral gutted. Becket's tomb survived, and people claimed miracles at his shrine.

Much of the splendour of the present architecture at Canterbury was based on money from pilgrims. William of Sens, a Frenchman, was employed to take on the rebuilding. He was succeeded by William the Englishman, who continued building the transepts, the Trinity Chapel (for St Thomas' shrine), the extension to the crypt, and the Corona.

The architecture affords a processional route for the pilgrims, as the cathedral is on a series of levels: pilgrims literally ascend to the shrine. The choir is above the nave, the presbytery and altar above the choir, and the Trinity Chapel and Corona even higher.

The new Early Perpendicular nave was built in the 14th C, probably by Henry Yeveley. With its increased roof height, tall elegant columns and large windows for light to pour through, there is a wonderful sense of loftiness—a masterpiece of contemporary design. The central arcade and clerestory were begun in 1391, while a 15th C stone pulpitum separates the choir from the nave.

The tower, with its fan-vaulted lantern, is one of the finest in Britain; begun by Thomas Wastell in 1496, it is known as Bell Harry, and is the most perfect Perpendicular tower in England.

The cathedral has many tombs, including that of Edward Prince of Wales (The Black Prince) who died in 1376. His effigy on the south side of the Trinity Chapel shows him in full, gilded armour.

The stained-glass windows show stories of Jesus' miracles, patriarchs from the Old Testament, incidents from the life of Jonah, the Queen of Sheba, and even the story of Becket's life and death.

St Martin
Possibly the oldest parish church in England, it was here that St Augustine first worshipped.

HARBLEDOWN
St Nicholas
Originally the church of a leper hospital founded in 1084 by Lanfranc, builder of Canterbury cathedral. Norman and 13th C work in evidence.

HYTHE
St Leonard
Norman with later restoration, notably 13th and 14th C. Chancel contains finest Early English work in the county. 18th C tower. An unusual feature is the crypt and ambulatory stacked to the ceiling with vast quantities of skulls and bones, all carefully separated and sized.

MINSTER-IN-SHEPPEY
St Mary and St Sexburga
Unusual in being two churches in one; north part originally serving nunnery founded in 670, south part is parochial and Early English. Internally impressive and moving.

ROCHESTER
Cathedral Church of Christ and the Blessed Virgin Mary (below)
When the Norman bishop, Gundulf, decided to rebuild the ancient Saxon cathedral at Rochester, the church had already served the community for more than 400 years. The Bishopric of Rochester, founded by Augustine in 640, is the second oldest in England after Canterbury, on whose pilgrim route it stands.

Bishop Gundulf set up his Benedictine monastery here with 22 monks sent from Archbishop Lefranc. By the time he died, 60 were living here. The oldest part of the building is functional and lacks design. The second phase of building, by the Normans, used rich ornamentation and new building techniques. Most of the Norman work now remaining in the cathedral is from this second

phase, and was conducted by Bishop Ernulf (1115–24). Typical of Bishop Ernulf's work is the delicate ornamentation fringing the arches and the wonderful arcades in the nave.

The cathedral's west front has a magnificent Romanesque facade, resembling that of Chartres. It was built during the third phase of Norman building, about 1160, but was altered with the insertion of a Perpendicular window. The doors show Christ in Majesty, flanked by Solomon and the Queen of Sheba, and a further 14th C Gothic door leads to the Chapter Room inside.

In the crypt, there are some interesting medieval paintings. One of the best fragments of 13th C wall-painting, illustrating the 'The Wheel of Fortune', can be found in the choir.

The most visited memorial in the cathedral is to Charles Dickens, who lived just outside the city in Gad's Hill. He knew the cathedral well; in fact, it was the setting of his last, unfinished novel. But perhaps most touching is a small ledger on the floor of the Lady Chapel and dedicated to a local doctor. It illustrates the parable of the Good Samaritan (dressed in 18th C dress), and includes the words *abi fac simile*—'Go and do likewise'. No greater sentiment could surely be offered by such a centre of historic worship.

▓ WROTHAM
St George
Sited actually on the old London Road, the tower has a vaulted passage beneath to allow public right of way to pass unhindered. Mainly 13th and 15th C; brasses; vaulted porch with room over.

Lancashire

▓ BLACKBURN
Cathedral and Parish Church of St Mary the Virgin (*above*)
The Cathedral Church of St Mary is positioned opposite Station Square, in a sloping churchyard endowed with trees. You enter through a cast iron gate.

Blackburn Cathedral is a good example of a parish church turned cathedral. The transformation was in 1926, although the church has pre-Conquest and medieval roots.

The present cathedral is mainly the work of John Palmer, a pioneer of the Gothic Revival, and was built between 1820–26. It was consecrated in 1826, but unfortunately in 1831 it was set alight and had to be reconstructed. It was W. Forsyth who converted the church for cathedral use after 1933, using a simplified Gothic style. He retained the west tower and nave, including some magnificent early 19th C roof bosses. The east end with transepts was then added. In 1961 Lawrence King added the corona above the high altar. For such a new cathedral it is surprising that the stalls in the north transept aisles have 15th C misericords; this is because they came from Whalley Abbey.

There is an interesting organ case and a variety of stained-glass, from 18th C Flemish glass to some Burne-Jones windows in the transepts.

▓ HALSALL
St Cuthbert
Architecturally an important church in the county. Mainly 14th C, with a 15th C spire rising from a tower with

an octagonal upper stage. There are spired turrets to each side of the chancel arch, one of which gave access to the rood loft.

▓ HEYSHAM
St Patrick's Chapel
Near to the later parish church of St Peter, it is here that St Patrick is said to have set up a monastery. Fragmentary ruins stand impressively on the cliff-top overlooking the sea. The doorway is notable, and there are a number of deep, shaped graves hollowed out of the solid rock, with a hole at the head of each for the now lost headstones.

▓ SALMESBURY
St Leonard
Both externally and internally, many periods are reflected here: a 16th C clerestoried nave; c.1900 aisles and north tower; Norman font; Jacobean altar rails; 17th and 18th C lowered box pews, and cut-down three-decker pulpit. There is evidence of old church customs: a funeral helm, and a sword and shield placed in the church after the death of the owner.

Leicestershire

▓ BREEDON-ON-THE-HILL
St Mary and St Hardulph
Sited within an Iron Age camp, the church was originally a Saxon monastery. What remains is mainly Norman and 13th C, but there are also a series of very fine 8th C carved stones.

▓ GADDESBY
St Luke
A medievalist's delight (mainly from 1290 to 1340), its exterior, in particular the south aisle, is a riot of the 14th C stone-carver's art. Inside, the church is graceful and light, and noted for a life-size statue of Colonel Cheney on his horse at Waterloo.

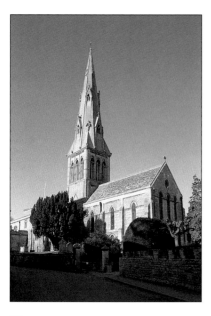

KETTON
St Mary the Virgin *(above)*
The beautiful church of St Mary the Virgin has an elegance of design that imitates a small cathedral, so much so that some compare this tiny little church with the nearby cathedral in Lincoln.

Its most notable architectural feature is the tall 14th C spire that rests on an Early English bell tower. Inside, the renovated chancel roof illustrates how a medieval panelled roof would probably have been decorated.

LEICESTER
The Cathedral and Parish Church of St Martin *(below, left)*
St Martin's parish church became a cathedral in 1927, and its bishop's throne was made the same year by Sir Charles Nicholson. Much of the church is Victorian on a medieval plan, but the site may well go back to the 12th C according to a piece of billet moulding *in situ* in the south wall at the east end of the north aisle.

The tower (1861–62) and spire (1867) are loosely modelled on Ketton (Rutland), and were designed by Raphael Brandon, whose work replaced the Norman tower. The splendid spire reaching 220 ft is unusually high for the Leicester region.

The nave has a 19th C hammer-beam roof with angels holding heraldic shields. The cathedral's most unusual feature is the double south aisle.

There is an interesting stained-glass window in an expressionist style, with Pre-Raphaelite influences, by Christopher Whall (1920), and some fine memorials in the Herrick chapel.

The 18th C furniture in the medieval Lady Chapel is well worth looking at, as are the grotesque corbels.

LYDDINGTON
St Andrew
Predominantly Perpendicular with good wall-paintings; a sanctuary arranged in the 17th C manner, with the altar enclosed by railings on all four sides; brasses; and an unusual medieval feature—acoustic jars in the chancel to help improve the quality of chanting, singing and preaching.

MELTON MOWBRAY
St Mary *(below)*
This cruciform church is spectacularly long—more than 150ft—and it has an impressive 100-ft central tower. In

style, it is Early English, Decorated and Perpendicular, and it dates mainly from 1280–1320. Parts of the original Norman church can still be seen, but it was during the Middle Ages that the church became so important.

Most striking is the clerestory wall, which has 48 windows containing more than 15,000 pieces of glass. There is a superb crossing tower, and unusual transepts that have both east and west aisles. The nave is very spacious, with impressive quatrefoil piers, and there is richly carved woodwork in the chancel.

There is also a window commemorating the three bishops, Latimer, Ridley and Cranmer, who were martyred in Oxford for their Protestant beliefs. Latimer came from Leicestershire, and it is possible that he preached his last sermon in St Mary's before his arrest in 1553.

The porch has had a varied history—it was even used as the garage for the local fire engine at one time.

RYHALL
St John the Evangelist
St Tibba lived and died here c.690. Against the west wall of the north aisle are the remains of a medieval hermitage associated with her, against which the first church was erected c.1200.

STAUNTON HAROLD
Holy Trinity
Historically important church erected by Sir Robert Shirley in 1653, as a gesture of defiance against the Commonwealth when, an inscription over the door proclaims, 'all things sacred were throughout the nation either demolished or profaned'. For his actions, Sir Robert was imprisoned in the Tower, where he died in 1656. Today, the church, externally Gothic but with a complete Jacobean interior, is cared for by the National Trust.

Lincolnshire

BARLINGS
St Edward, King and Martyr
Originally Norman, the church was built near the ruins of a Premonstratensian monastery, whose abbot was hanged for his part in the Lincolnshire Rising of 1536.

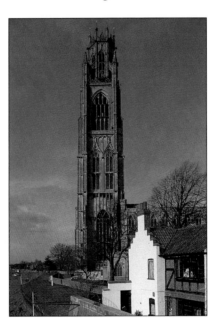

BOSTON
St Botolph (above)
It was from Boston, in 1607, that a group of Puritans (later called the Pilgrim Fathers) tried to sail to America via Holland. The captain of their boat was not on their side, however, and they were disembarked at Fishtoft. But in 1630, 10 years after the sailing of the *Mayflower*, another group of Boston citizens landed in New England. There they set up a colony named 'Boston', now one of America's most famous cities.

In the 13th and 14th centuries, Boston became the centre of the English wool industry, itself believed to be the finest in Europe at that time. Records show that by 1300, Boston was Britain's leading port, frequently

paying more in customs duties than London. The present church dates from 1309, when the port was rich, on the site of a chapel established by an Anglo-Saxon missionary monk named Botolph in the 7th C.

The tower is the most striking feature of the church, and is locally and affectionately called 'The Stump'. It has no spire and can be seen from miles around, rising above the roof tops.

It is said that the church has 365 steps leading to the top of the tower, one for every day of the year; 12 pillars supporting the roof, one for each month; 7 doors for the days of the week; and 52 windows for the weeks of the year. As such, it has been called a veritable 'calendar in stone'. St Botolph's also claims to be the largest parish church in England.

LINCOLN
Lincoln Cathedral (overleaf)
One of the most graceful of all medieval buildings, Lincoln Cathedral has been described as the finest building in Europe.

The Norman cathedral was started by Bishop Remigius (the first Norman bishop of England) in 1072, and took twenty years to build. Various fires led to its restoration and elaborate adornment by Bishop Alexander the Magnificent (1123–48). Today the only remains of this period are the two west towers and the lower parts of the west front, with its magnificent display of weathered friezes illustrating the Old and New Testaments.

On 15 April 1185, an earthquake shattered the Norman cathedral, and it was Hugh of Avalon, a Carthusian monk who became bishop, who started the plans to rebuild it. He was one of the greatest saints of medieval England and was so loved that when he died in 1200, King John and his nobles carried his body to the cathedral door to be received by no fewer than three archbishops and thirteen bishops—an event illustrated shortly afterwards in the cathedral's famous rose window, 'The Dean's Eye'.

St Hugh's tomb is housed in the Angel choir, (c.1256–80), so called because of the angels around the arches. The detail, richness of carving, use of Purbeck marble and square termination make it one of the greatest achievements of Gothic architecture in this country. It also contains the little mischievous figure called the 'Lincoln Imp'.

'The Dean's Eye' is at the north end of the transept, and is believed to have been longer in its setting than any other glass in the country.

Reconstruction began in 1192, with the choir and eastern transepts having work done between 1192–1210. This was followed by the rebuilding of the great transept, the chapter house, the nave (Lincoln has a simple beautiful nave with soaring columns of Purbeck marble), the extension to the west front, the Galilee entrance and the lower part of the central tower. Other interesting features include a superb choir screen and choir stalls with their misericords.

A walk around the exterior, looking for the details of angels, grotesques and heads, is an exciting experience. Lincoln's profile of three great towers perfectly complements the hill it stands on. The two west towers are 206 ft high, while the central one reaches 271 ft, and has a 5$\frac{1}{2}$ ton bell called Great Tom of Lincoln. The towers all had spires at one time—the two western ones until 1807. The central tower replaced an earlier tower topped by a lead-encased timber spire that had apparently given it the unbelievable height of 525 ft, the highest in the country. This was destroyed in a storm in 1584.

The classical library (1674) is Sir Christopher Wren's only design for part of a cathedral outside London. It houses one of the four original copies of the Magna Carta.

LITTLE BYTHAM
St Medard
An ancient, pleasing church with Saxon work. An interesting early tympanum over the south door possibly contained the skull and arm bone of St Medard, the patron saint.

MARKBY
St Peter
Externally, with its thatched roof, it reminds us of how the great majority of England's humble parish churches might have looked. Inside, 17th C with box pews and two-decker pulpit.

PINCHBECK
St Mary
A restored church of the Decorated and Perpendicular periods. Of interest is the early 19th C graveside shelter for the protection of the vicar in inclement weather.

RAITHBY
Chapel (Methodist)
Typical of early non-conformist places of worship, Raithby Chapel was adapted from a stable in the corner of a stable yard to the hall. It bears the inscription 'Wesley's Chapel Built by Robert Carr Brackenbury 1779, Dedicated July 5 1779 by John Wesley'. Internally quite simple. From the vestibule, a divided stair (men right, women left) leads to a landing and gallery.

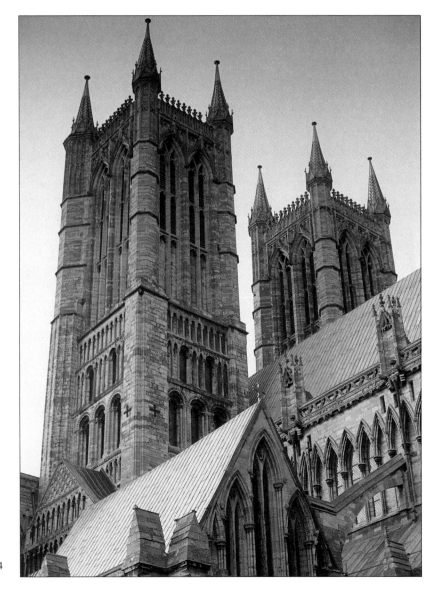

London
City and Greater

All Souls, Langham Place (below)

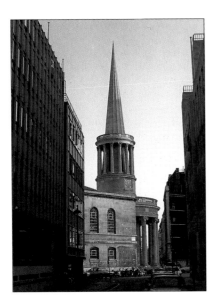

All Souls is situated at the top of Regent Street, against the somewhat unusual backdrop of the old BBC Broadcasting House. A curious feature is the semi-detached porch and steeple, built out from the nave so as to appear at the centre of Regent Street. The rounded porch supports a unique conical steeple.

This church was built in 1822–24 during the reign of George IV. It is the only church left in London designed by the famous John Nash, the person responsible for the architecture of Regent Street. His bust on the porch looks down the street that he created.

The interior of All Souls has been beautifully restored. Underneath is a church hall constructed in the early 1970s for more than £655,000—paid before completion, with contributions from around the world. The church was reconsecrated on All Souls Day (2 November) 1976.

A parish church with one of the largest congregations in London, All Souls is also well known throughout the English-speaking world for its frequent use in broadcast worship, and for the international ministry of many of its ministers. Attendance of 1,000 or more is not unusual.

Brompton Oratory (right)

Brompton Oratory is, officially, the church of the London Oratory. Unique in the Roman Catholic Church, it emphasizes the aesthetic and artistic in its devotions. A beautiful Italian Renaissance building, it is furnished with a statuary and paintings of the highest quality, and its Oratory Choir sings the finest traditional Christian music at vespers and at solemn Mass.

The Oratory was designed by 29-year-old architect Herbert Gribble, a recently converted Roman Catholic. It was consecrated in 1884, and features a very wide nave with seven side chapels, and a great dome with a surround of circular windows. These shed rays of light down before the sanctuary and the ornate high altar.

Perhaps the most noteworthy feature of the church is St Wilfrid's Chapel at the right of the sanctuary. Outstanding among its many splendours is the Altar of St Wilfred, a fine example of Flemish Baroque from

the 18th C, and the Altar of the English Martyrs. Above the latter is a triptych by American painter Rex Whistler, showing St Thomas More on the left, St John Fisher on the right, and a scene of the executions at Tyburn in the centre.

Chapel Royal, St James Palace (below)

St James Palace on Pall Mall was built by Henry VIII in 1531, on the site of a former lepers' hospital. While the official home of the sovereign is now Buckingham Palace, the royal court is still known as the Court of St James.

The Chapel Royal dates partly to the 16th C, when the palace was built. Its beautiful ceiling is said to have been

designed by Holbein in 1540. There is also a tradition of fine music, which is provided today by the private choir of the sovereign, and is composed of 6 men and 10 boys. Famous organists have included Orlando Gibbons and Purcell. At Epiphany (6 January) the service is conducted by the Bishop of London, and an offering of gold, frankincense and myrrh is made on behalf of the sovereign.

This has been the site of several royal marriages, including those of William III and Mary II (1677), Queen Anne (1683), George IV (1795), Queen Victoria (1840), and George V (1893). Visitors may attend services in the Chapel Royal if there is no service in the Queen's Chapel nearby.

St Bride, Fleet Street (below)

This celebrated church is sometimes called the 'Cathedral of Fleet Street', and has close ties with the world of journalism. Just off Fleet Street, it occupies the site of Roman buildings and of a very early Christian church, perhaps the first in London. Seven church-building foundations of different sizes and ages have been identified, and numerous objects have been found, dating from Roman times to the 19th C.

St Bride's as it is today was designed by Christopher Wren in 1670–75,

except for the tower and spire, which were added in 1701–3. It was gutted by incendiaries in December 1940 and restored in 1957.

The most prominent physical feature is the church's 226-ft high steeple of Portland stone, made up of four stages of diminishing octagons with open arches and pilasters. This steeple was struck by lightning three times in the early 18th C, and in 1764 George III consulted with Dr Benjamin Franklin regarding the best type of lightning rod. Later that century, a pastry cook who lived nearby, named William Rich, invented the wedding cake modelled after St Bride's steeple. The twelve bells of St Bride's were also well known for their distinctive peal.

Interior features include the oak reredos (a memorial to the Pilgrim Fathers) and a separate memorial to Virginia Dare, the first English child to be born in America and whose parents were of this parish.

Famous figures of Christian history associated with St Bride's include Wynken de Worde, who brought Caxton's press from Westminster to St Bride's in 1500; John Taylor, who became vicar in 1543 and was later burnt at Smithfield under Bloody Mary; Samuel Pepys, who was christened here; and John Milton, Izaac Walton and Samuel Johnson, all of whom lived nearby.

In the crypt, there is a fascinating museum exhibiting remains of Roman walls, a tessellated pavement, part of a Saxon font, medieval carvings and various samples of medieval glass left from the Great Fire.

St Giles, Cripplegate (right)

St Giles Church was originally founded in 1090 by Alfune, an associate of the famous prior Rahere who founded St Bartholomew's, Smithfield. The site of the church, on swampy ground near the Walbrook where it flowed under the walls of London, caused construction problems in early days. Even today, the water forms a pond below a retaining wall which runs around the perimeter of the building.

Being at the north of the City and outside its wall, the church survived

the Great Fire. The earliest part of the present structure dates to a rebuilding in 1545. The tower was raised 15 ft in 1682, and various alterations were made in the 19th C. It was burned out in 1940 and for nearly 20 years stood in ruins, before being restored by Godfrey Allen in 1960.

Several of London's great Christian figures are associated with St Giles, including John Foxe the martyrologist; Launcelot Andrewes, court preacher and a translator of the King James Version of the Bible; and renowned poet John Milton. During the Great Plague of 1665, the parish of St Giles suffered heavily because of the swampy location, with some 8,000 deaths. On one day, 18 August, there were 151 funerals. The following year, the churchyard became a campground for refugees from the Great Fire. Today, however, the location of this church—away from the street traffic, and surrounded by water and gardens—gives it a pleasant distinctiveness.

St Margaret's, Westminster (above, opposite)

This is the mother church of the City of Westminster and the parish church of the Lower House of Parliament. On special occasions, services are held for the Commons—led by the Speaker, whose pew is directly in front of the lectern. In addition, the bells are rung when the sovereign passes or is nearby.

The original church was probably founded alongside Westminster Abbey by King Edward 'the Confessor' in the 11th C, but a second building replaced it during the reign of Edward III (1327–77), and that in turn was replaced during the time of Henry VII and Henry VIII.

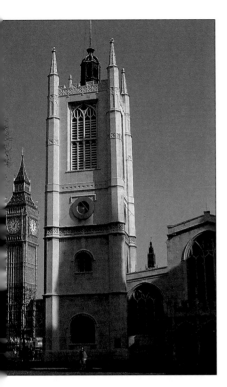

A number of famous Puritan divines preached here, including Dr John Reynolds (whose proposal at the Hampton Court Conference led to the King James Version of the Bible); John Owen, the chaplain of Oliver Cromwell; and Richard Baxter, author of *Saint's Everlasting Rest*.

The large and impressive stained-glass window at the east end is a particular treasure of St Margaret's. Originally intended for Westminster Abbey, it was made by the magistrates in Dort, Holland, as a present to Henry VII on the occasion of the marriage of his son Arthur to Catherine of Aragon.

St Margaret's has been associated with numerous famous persons, from William Caxton, a member of this church who set up his printing press in 1477 in Almonry and who is buried in the churchyard, to Winston Churchill, who was married here in 1908. Sir Walter Raleigh's decapitated body was buried in front of the altar after his execution in Palace Yard; he is commemorated by a brass memorial near the east door and in a memorial window, which also depicts Elizabeth I. Another window commemorates John Milton. Samuel Pepys, who was married here in 1655, records several visits to services at St Margaret's, at one time hearing common prayer for the first time (5 August 1660). George Whitefield preached at St Margaret's one Sunday evening in February 1739, apparently taking the pulpit without official sanction. The sexton thereupon locked him in, 'to the great confusion of the bewildered congregation'!

St Martin-in-the-Fields (below)
This famous church occupies a prominent site at the north-east corner of Trafalgar Square and across the street from the National Gallery. It is probably the one parish church in

London recognized by most tourists. St Martin's has an active ministry of social welfare. It is also internationally known for the classical music broadcasts of the Academy of St Martin-in-the-Fields, under the direction of Sir Neville Marriner.

The church itself probably started as a chapel near the village of Charing, to serve the monks of St Peter's at Westminster on their visits to the monastery gardens (on the site of the present Covent Garden). St Martin's is a royal church, and the names of royal children may be found in the register. It has even had one royal church-warden, George I.

St Mary-le-Bow (below)
This historic church in Cheapside sits on the ancient 'chepe', or main market street, of Old London. To be born within the sound of its bells identifies the true Cockney. Its 12 mighty bells can be heard as far away as Highgate Hill, and it was they that chimed the message 'Turn again, Dick Whittington, thrice Lord Mayor of London!'

The original Bow Church was probably built during the reign of William the Conqueror (1066–87). It was rebuilt by Wren after the Great Fire in 1670–83, and restored after the War by Laurence King.

First called St Mary Newchurch, the 'Bow' in the name was added to refer to the stone bows or arches which the Normans used for a foundation.

Bow Church has had more than its share of violence over its 900-year life. During Norman times, a hurricane-force wind lifted the roof off and deposited it in the street, driving the rafters deep into the ground and killing several people. A hundred years later (in 1196), a murderer took refuge in the tower and was subsequently smoked out. The tower itself collapsed in 1271, and the whole church was a victim both of the Great Fire and the blitz.

The steeple is one of Wren's masterpieces and the most elaborate in the City, taking seven years to build. Another celebrated feature is the Norman crypt, rediscovered by Wren and rebuilt after World War II. Here one can see the stone 'bows' upon which the church rests. From medieval times to the present day, a church judicial body called the Court of Arches has met in this crypt, to decide cases of ecclesiastical law and to confirm the election of bishops.

St Paul's Cathedral (left)

St Paul's Cathedral is one of the most magnificent buildings in Old London, and one of the world's great churches.

It was some time before the Great Fire of 1666 that the renowned architect, Sir Christopher Wren, was consulted on the restoration of St Paul's, and he originally planned to extend the Renaissance influence even further than his predecessor, Inigo Jones. But the Great Fire reduced the old cathedral to ruins, and Wren began fresh plans for a new, totally classical design in the shape of a Latin cross, with a great dome in the centre. Despite division amongst the commissioners, the king gave his approval—and considerable freedom to the architect. A model of the first building plan can be seen in the crypt of the present cathedral.

Before construction could begin, however, the site had to be cleared. Demolition of the old ruins, which included several massive 200-ft columns, posed a particular problem. Pick-axes were slow and sometimes ineffective; gunpowder worked better, but proved somewhat hazardous to the surroundings; and the final solution had to be a kind of battering ram.

Wren himself took charge of the surveying. He laid out a circle for the new dome, marking the exact centre with an old tombstone inscribed with the word *Resurgam*: 'I shall rise again'!

Completion of the new cathedral took more than 40 years, by which time its cost—most of it funded by a tax on sea-borne coal entering London—amounted to almost £750,000. After Queen Anne died in 1714, Wren himself had less influence over the final details. Nevertheless, he had the satisfaction of seeing the great church completed largely to his design. In later life, he came every Saturday to view his handiwork, and after his death in 1723 he was given a simple grave in the crypt. The inscription read *Si monumentum requiris, circumspice*—'If you seek his monument, look around you.'

The visitor entering St Paul's for the first time is likely to be drawn to the centre under the great dome. Everywhere—above to the painting by Sir John Thornhill of the life of St Paul, eastward to the magnificent quire with its exquisite wood carvings by Grinling Gibbons, beyond that to the high altar canopied by a splendid baldachino, westward to the spacious nave, and northward and southward to the aisles with their richly decorated bays—St Paul's fully deserves its position as the cathedral of England's capital city.

St Peter-ad-Vincula (St Peter in Chains) (overleaf, above)

The chapel on this site next to the Tower of London was built during the reign of Henry I (1100–35). A major fire in 1512 destroyed the first building, and the oldest parts of the present chapel therefore date from the 16th C.

The Tower was a royal residence as well as a prison for persons accused of

up in anger, he was promptly murdered! His daughter, Mary, donated her inheritance to found a nunnery on the spot—later funded by profits from the ferry.

Between the 9th–16th C, other monastic institutions followed until the Reformation, when this became the parish church. During the reign of Mary Tudor, the retro-choir was also used as a consistorial court, presided over by Bishops Gardiner and Bonner.

As might be suspected from its location near the old Globe Theatre, the church has associations with Chaucer and Shakespeare as well as many other literary figures. Shakespeare is commemorated by a memorial window as well as an alabaster monument. John Harvard, founder of Harvard University, was baptized here and a beautiful chapel is dedicated to him. The famous divine, Launcelot Andrewes, one of the translators of the King James Bible, has a fine tomb in the south aisle.

Over the centuries, the church has undergone considerable alteration and repair. The stone vault collapsed in 1469, while the famous Lady Chapel became a bakery in the 17th C; both have twice been rebuilt. Despite this, Southwark is still one of London's great medieval treasures. It became a cathedral in 1905.

offences against the crown, so St Peter-ad-Vincula came to be used both by royalty, and by the warders and soldiers on duty and their families. It also became the burial place of a number of the more important prisoners who paid the extreme penalty: the site of the execution block is only a few yards from the church door.

The history of executions at the Tower is closely linked to the history of England itself and, in particular, of the English Reformation. Most of those who died on the block were famous—among them, Anne Boleyn, Catherine Howard, Sir Thomas More and Lady Jane Grey—and some were of noble or royal blood. Some were truly guilty, others merely the unfortunate victims of circumstance. In several cases, the facts are still a mystery. As the famous essayist Thomas Carlyle wrote, 'In this little Golgotha are interred mighty secrets now never to be solved; for half the crimes of our English monarchs were wrought out on the little plot outside the church-door of St Peter-ad-Vincula.'

A number of fine monuments have survived from the 16th and 17th centuries. Despite various changes and inevitable modernization, this royal chapel has, in a small way, much in common with Westminster Abbey as a church of great historic interest.

Southwark Cathedral (below)

According to legend, the site of this cathedral was once the home of a ferry-man who feigned his own death in order to see what would happen afterwards. In fact his servants held a party, and when the ferry-man sprang

Temple Church (above, opposite)

During the Crusades, many churches were built by the Knights Templar and Knights Hospitaller, often 'in the round', to imitate the Church of the Holy Sepulchre in Jerusalem.

Temple Church (c.1161) is the most historically prominent of all the Round Churches in Europe, of which there are four in England. It unites the round arches of Norman architecture with the Gothic pointed arches of the Early English style in one building, and has the only Norman doorway in London.

Originally the church consisted of a round nave (the one seen today) on the west and a rectangular chancel on the east. An inscription above the entrance door describes the dedication

140

Despite several expansions and reconstructions, John Wesley's Chapel on City Road is essentially the same building in character and appearance that Wesley himself knew.

It was on 21 April 1777 that John Wesley pushed his way through a huge crowd to lay the cornerstone of the new chapel. The building work took about 18 months, and the first public worship meeting was held on All Saints Day, 1778. Most of the money for the chapel came from small gifts, but there were a few large ones as well. The pillars used to support the gallery were masts from warships donated by King George III.

In 1879 the chapel was damaged by fire but was restored in the original style. Then, in 1891, 100 years after Wesley's death, a major renovation was undertaken, with contributions from Methodists in many countries. King George's masts were replaced with marble pillars; stained glass windows and the present oak pews were installed; and the foundations were strengthened with concrete.

During World War II, Wesley's Chapel and his nearby house were miraculously left unharmed. Thirty years later, however, the chapel again needed major renovation. Nearly one million pounds was raised from Methodists in 24 countries.

by Heraclius, the patriarch of the Church of the Holy Sepulchre. The chancel was later enlarged in Early English style and was consecrated in 1240 in the presence of King Henry III.

After several stages of renovation and restoration, Temple Church is now very much like the original and has various striking reminders of the days of the Knights Templar. There are details of several 13th C figures on the floor, and there is an early double piscina (a drain where the chalice was cleansed). The Crusader brotherhood also appears to have been extremely strict: the door in the north-west corner opens into a tiny penitential cell where disobedient members were confined in chains, with no room to lie down. One brother, Walter le Bacheler, knight and Grand Preceptor of Ireland, actually starved to death here.

Today, Temple Church serves as a private chapel for the lawyers of the Temple, and is not under the

jurisdiction of the Bishop of London. It also has a tradition of outstandingly fine music.

Wesley's Chapel (below)

On All Saints Day, 1978, the restored building was reopened in the presence of Queen Elizabeth and the Duke of Edinburgh. Today, Wesley's Chapel, with the founder's grave at the back and an impressive statue of him in the forecourt, is open daily to visitors (apply at Wesley's House). It is a shrine, not only to Methodism, but to the entire Nonconformist heritage in London.

Westminster Abbey (above)
Westminster Abbey is one of the world's most famous churches, certainly the best known in the English-speaking world. The site was chosen by the pious King Edward 'the Confessor' (1042–66), who decided to build a monastery abbey which would serve as his final resting place. It was the first Norman building in England (and the largest in either England or Normandy), and although nothing now remains of this church above ground, scholars estimate that its foundations

occupied roughly the same area as the present abbey.

On Christmas Day, 1066, the same year that Edward the Confessor was buried in the abbey, William the Conqueror was crowned here as William I of England. Since then, the tradition of holding the coronation here has continued to the present day. In addition, 32 sovereigns or their consorts have also been interred here, though only 17 have monuments.

Many of history's finest architects have lavished their skills on Westminster Abbey. From the 13th to the 16th centuries, it was altered structurally to the Gothic Perpendicular style. Magnificent sculptures and glass, and priceless works of art were added. Sadly, much of this was lost during the Reformation, but the building itself was spared.

Two interesting developments during Reformation times were the founding of the famous Westminster

School and the ending of the right of sanctuary for debtors. Founded by Henry VIII, Westminster School now takes its place beside Eton and Winchester as one of England's most renowned public schools. The right of sanctuary for debtors, however, goes back much further, having originally been granted by Edward the Confessor. Within the abbey's precincts a fugitive was safe from his adversaries providing he behaved himself properly, wore no weapons and stayed within bounds. This right was finally abolished by Parliament in 1623.

A further development was the commemoration of great commoners in particular groups—statesmen around Chatham, poets around Chaucer, musicians around Purcell, scholars around Casaubon, scientists around Newton, and so on. Of special Christian interest are the grave of David Livingstone in the centre of the nave, the monument of the seventh

Earl of Shaftesbury near the west door, a table to William Tyndale, and medallions to John Wesley, Charles Wesley and Isaac Watts in the south choir aisle.

The two imposing west towers of Westminster Abbey were built in 1738–39 by John James, successor to Nicholas Hawksmoor, who in turn was a successor to Christopher Wren. Wren had been appointed Architect to the Abbey in 1698, and planned to have a central tower with a spire. Neither he nor Hawksmoor was able to complete this plan, but they did recase the exterior of the abbey and fill the north and west windows with glass by Joshua Price.

In the 19th C, Sir Gilbert Scott was appointed architect, becoming the first one to use scientific means to preserve the abbey. Throughout history, the value of this great London monument has been amply recognized. It stands now not only as London's number one tourist attraction, but as a living reminder that England's history is inseparable from the Christian faith.

Westminster Cathedral (right)
This imposing Byzantine-style structure is the Mother Church of the diocese of Westminster. It is also the Metropolitan Church of all England and Wales, and was built at the end of the Victorian era (1895–1903) specifically for the purpose—its archbishop being the ranking Roman Catholic prelate in the country.

The church measures 360 ft deep and 156 ft wide, with the cross atop its bell tower reaching a height of 284 ft. It is constructed of brick but ingeniously retains the impression of Byzantine ornateness. A great arch stretches over the main doorway, under which is a mosaic representing Christ and an open book, on which is written (in Latin): 'I am the gate: if any one enters by Me he shall be saved.' Mary and Joseph stand on either side, and kneeling are St Peter and St Edward the Confessor. Above the arch is the inscription (also in Latin) 'Lord Jesus, King and Redeemer, save us by Thy blood.'

The visitor entering Westminster Cathedral steps into a vestibule (narthex) from which an unobstructed view can be gained of the awesome 342-ft nave and beyond, to the sanctuary with its high altar and towering baldachino. Along the aisles and in the transepts are 12 side chapels where mass is offered. Above are three towering domes, and from the main arch hangs a great 30-ft rood. The eight dark-green columns that support the galleries are from the same quarry

that supplied the marble for Santa Sophia in Istanbul.

The chapels themselves abound with works of religious art. The Chapel of the Holy Souls is said to display in completed form what the entire cathedral will be like some day. Of particular interest is the Chapel of St George and the English Martyrs, where Thomas More and John Fisher are represented in the altar-piece.

Manchester, Greater

ASHTON-UNDER-LYNE
St Michael
In common with numerous churches in the area, St Michael's has suffered under Victorian zeal. But despite this, the church retains an important collection of stained glass c.1500: in particular, 18 scenes from the Life of St Helena, and the figures of kings.

MANCHESTER
The Cathedral Church of St Mary, St Denys and St George (below)
The cathedral's present site in Victoria Street on the River Irwell may well have been occupied by a church since the 8th C, and today's may be the third ecclesiastical building on this site. Built principally in the 15th C, it was founded by Thomas de la Warre as a collegiate church.

The nave is very impressive and very wide. It has some magnificent medieval woodcarving, particularly on the pulpitum screen dividing the nave from the choir. The screen is made of solid oak with three double doors and painted panels. The choir stalls show exquisite 16th C craftsmanship, with canopies and cleverly detailed

misericords of medieval scenes and legends. These designs have recently been repeated in the tapestry kneelers.

To the left of the pulpitum is the angel stone. This is a fragment of the carved 8th C Saxon church, depicting an angel, which was discovered when the north porch foundations were being dug in the late 19th C. Its inscription, translated, quotes from a psalm: 'Into thy hands, O Lord, I commend my spirit.'

The church became a cathedral in 1847 and has since undergone a series of restorations, especially following an air-raid in 1940 which blew out all the windows. After Coventry, Manchester was the cathedral most damaged in the Second World War. One of the worst casualties was the Lady Chapel, but the 15th C screen separating the retro-choir escaped damage.

Although there is a regimental chapel, and a fine window as a memorial to the architect who restored the cathedral after the war, the new tapestries concentrate on peacetime activities and life, depicting the Nativity and the importance of women and children in the life of the church. On the outside wall of the now restored chapel is a gilded bronze of the Virgin and Child, by Sir Charles Wheeler. The Virgin is dressed as a Lancashire mill girl.

St Anne
A fine, gracious town church, providing an oasis of tranquillity in an otherwise commercial city. Erected in the style of Wren between 1709 and 1712, in a mellow red sandstone. Internally, Classical, galleried and arcaded with a flat coved ceiling and good carved frieze in the east apse. Much contemporary woodwork.

WARBURTON
St Werburgh
This church is more typical of adjoining Cheshire, insomuch as it is of timber. Some walls were replaced with stone in 1645, while the brick tower dates back to 1711. Inside, construction timbers divide off the aisles. Most of the fittings are Jacobean. The box pews are 19th C.

Merseyside

LIVERPOOL
Liverpool Anglican Cathedral
(above, opposite)
The sheer size of this cathedral is stunning, made even greater by its position on a hill. Designed in 1901 by Gilbert Scott, it is the largest cathedral in Britain and the largest Anglican church in the world. Sir John Betjeman said of it, 'This is one of the great buildings of the world . . . Suddenly, one sees that the greatest art of architecture, that lifts one up and turns one into a King, yet compels reverence, is the art of enclosing space.' It is Scott's own interpretation of Gothic.

The whole building was designed with total symmetry to form a double cross, with the nave and choir of equal length, giving it a grandeur and vastness well beyond expectation. In 1904, in a service with a 1,000-strong choir and a congregation of 8,000, King Edward VII laid the foundation stone. The red sandstone cathedral slowly took shape from east to west, and by 1910 the Lady Chapel was consecrated and was used for services.

Building was interrupted by the war, but by 1924 the high altar, the chancel and the eastern transepts were consecrated. The 300-ft tower was completed in 1978, one of the tallest structures of its kind on earth, holding the highest and heaviest peal of bells anywhere in the world.

The baptistry has some of the most beautiful wood carving in the cathedral. The font, sitting on marble patterned with waves and fish, and the stained glass by Carl Edwards, are interesting modern pieces. Everything, from the light fittings to the carving of Liver Birds—the symbol of Liverpool—reveals Scott's interest in detail.

Shortage of funds and a lack of skilled labour made the progress very slow. 74 years after her great-grandfather had laid the foundation stone, Queen Elizabeth II attended the great Thanksgiving Service when the cathedral was completed in 1978, thirteen years after the architect's death. Scott is buried just beyond the entrance steps to the cathedral—he was a Roman Catholic.

Cathedral of Christ the King
(below)

On entering Liverpool's Roman Catholic cathedral there is an overall impression of being bathed in blue light—as if to suggest some heavenly place. The most spiritually symbolic colour of religious artists has been used here in the stained glass of the outer perimeter of the cathedral.

In the centre, the cathedral's famous 290-ft lantern dome sits above the sanctuary, creating a focal point at the altar to which every other part of the building is related. A magnificent variety of coloured glass and light, it also serves as a beacon rising into the night sky, illuminated from within—a symbol of hope across Liverpool's skyline. It is the most outstanding feature of the cathedral and was designed by John Piper and made by Patrick Reyntiens (who also collaborated in the large stained-glass window in Coventry).

Designed by Sir Frederick Gibberd, the building is 'a cathedral in our own

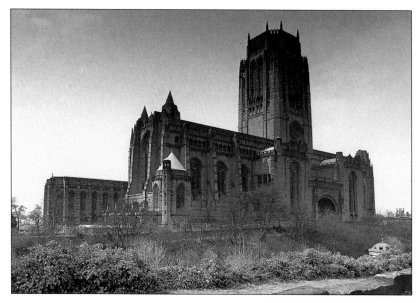

time', in the words of Archbishop Downey. Steel and reinforced concrete created a space where 2,000 people could sit and take part in a service within easy sight of the altar. In turn, the altar is a simple rectangular block of white marble quarried near Skopje in the former Yugoslavia. It sits beneath the lantern and has a wonderful boldness that contrasts with the fragile crucifix showing Christ with his arms flung open, by Elizabeth Frink.

The whole cathedral has a sense of unity. Glass, metal, wood all play with the mysterious light, contributing to the impression that this is a special space and place to be.

In the past, illustrative pictures in glass windows taught the illiterate the stories of the Bible. Today, the abstract design has taken over. Even the stations of the cross (representations of the stages of Christ's way to Calvary to be crucified) are simple numbered wooden crosses attached to the weight-bearing supports.

Norfolk

ATTLEBOROUGH
St Mary

A magnificent church, sadly engulfed by the 20th C chancel and 14th C nave. The chancel was collegiate at one time, the nave being erected for parochial use later. Unrivalled anywhere in East Anglia is the rood screen with intact loft, which stretches right across from north to south, and is topped by frescoes c.1500. It is all the more remarkable for its colour and liveliness after all these centuries.

BEESTON REGIS
All Saints
Here in this cliff-top church, in a county famed for the quality of its painted panels, those on the beautiful 15th C rood screen surpass all.

BRISLEY
St Bartholomew
Predominantly Perpendicular architecture with a striking west tower. Inside, three-decker pulpit; 15th C screen; and good font cover. An interesting feature is the crypt situated beneath the altar, supposed to have been used to lodge prisoners on their way to Norwich gaol.

BURNHAM THORPE
All Saints
Lord Nelson's father was rector here, and the interior is resplendent with many memorials to Nelson himself. It also contains relics of the Admiral.

EAST DEREHAM
St Nicholas
Historically and architecturally interesting church with work of many periods and styles. Norman south doorway; early 16th C detached tower; decorated nave, transepts and chancel with fine sedilia, piscina and aumbry niche for the storage of the communion vessels. In the churchyard is the well of St Withburga, daughter of King Annas, who founded a convent here.

GREAT YARMOUTH
St Nicholas
This is the largest parish church in England, and it does not disappoint the ardent church-crawler. Begun in the 12th C, each successive generation extended the building. Unfortunately, much was destroyed in 1942. Many of the old fittings are therefore from other places or worship, but they are well arranged to create an impressive church.

HALES
St Margaret
A textbook church, typical of the county, with round tower, apse, fine Norman doorways and a charming thatched roof. Inside, there are wall-paintings and a screen. Sadly, its isolation has meant redundancy, and it is now vested in the Redundant Church Fund.

HEACHAM
St Mary
Particularly noted for its monuments, especially one to Pocahontas, Red Indian wife of John Rolfe, who was squire of the manor in the reign of James I.

NORWICH
Norwich Cathedral *(below)*
The first church at Norwich was a wooden building founded by St Felix in 630. Herbert de Losinga laid the foundation stone for the present

Norman church in 1096 (a unique early Christian effigy in the ambulatory may well be of him). The very long nave which leads into a wonderful ambulatory around the famous and beautifully proportioned apse at the east end is typically Norman. Even the 13th and 14th C cloisters, the most extensive and probably the finest in Britain, are Norman in origin.

Norwich's great spire, the second highest in England after Salisbury, was a replacement for one that collapsed during a storm in 1362, but it was struck again in 1463. The Norman tower, the highest in Britain, remains.

The roof has some of the best examples of roof bosses. Many resemble designs from illuminated manuscripts and are often of historical events. One depicts Henry II doing penance at St Thomas of Canterbury's tomb. Further carving of some of Britain's finest 15th C misericords can be found in the choir.

But it is a couple of weather-beaten stones from the old cathedral that are Norwich's rarest treasure. They form part of the oldest bishop's throne in the country, dating back earlier than the 8th C. Unique in England, the throne sits behind the high altar, as in early basilican cathedrals.

The city of Norwich is famous for one of Britain's female saints, Julian of Norwich, a remarkable woman of the Middle Ages who became an anchoress for a short period and who wrote down a series of visions that she experienced in May 1373. One of her better-known sayings, expressing the essential Christian hope in the love of God triumphing over evil, is 'All shall be well and all shall be well, and all manner of things shall be well.'

Another woman associated with and buried in the cathedral is Edith Cavell. A nurse and daughter of a local rector, and matron in a Brussels Red Cross hospital during World War I, she was arrested by the Germans in August 1915 for helping 200 allied soldiers escape to neutral Holland. She was then executed.

Octagonal Chapel (Unitarian)
Undoubtedly the finest of all non-conformist places of worship. An elegant mid-18th C brick building of architectural complexity designed by Thomas Ivory, a provincial carpenter. Detail is restrained and all the more effective for it. Instead it relies on form to achieve a sense of richness. Illumination is via a dome supported on massive Corinthian columns carried from floor level through the gallery front, which are then linked to each other by a series of arches—quite stunning.

■ SPARHAM
St Mary
A noble exterior, mainly Perpendicular, with an exceptionally tall tower. Scratched onto a door jamb is a mass clock, similar to a sundial, but which served to tell the times of the church services. This was obviously done before the building was completed. Inside are panels of the old screen, brasses, bench-ends and a good roof.

■ TIVETSHALL
St Margaret
Contains a rare treasure which is possibly the finest of its type in existence—the Royal Arms of Elizabeth I in the tympanum above the chancel arch.

■ TRUNCH
St Botolph
A medievalist's delight, full of interest and history. Of particular note are a screen of 1502; medieval glass; a fine 15th C roof with angels; return stalls with holes for ink pots, and with much graffiti (there is evidence that a school was once held here); and the greatest glory, a superb wooden font-cover c.1500 over a font of 1390.

■ UPPER SHERINGHAM
All Saints
All Saints is famous for its 15th C rood screen (with loft), its painted beam with a pulley for raising the ornate font cover, and its excellent bench-ends with quaint scenes. These include a mermaid, a nurse with the Christ child, and a cat with a kitten.

■ WALPOLE
St Peter
Even in its reduced circumstances, perhaps the finest church in the county. Unusual is the processional way under the east end. Vast Perpendicular windows; fine porches, especially the two-storey south porch, and many other interesting features.

■ WESTOW LONGUEVILLE
All Saints
James Woodforde, who wrote *Diary of a Country Parson*, was rector here 1776–1803. His portrait and memorial are in the church. Other notable features include the sedilia, a piscina for pouring away consecrated wine after communion, and the south aisle window with figures of the Apostles.

■ WYMONDHAM
St Mary and St Thomas of Canterbury
An important and noble church with twin towers east and west. Originally part of a Benedictine abbey, it was also always parochial. Predominantly Norman, with splendid arcades and triforium, while above is a clerestory and magnificent roof of 15th C date. Nice two-storey in which can be seen the famous Corporas Case, a rare example of a 13th C Opus Anglicanum.

Northamptonshire

■ ASHBY ST LEGER
St Leodegorius
A rare dedication of a saint who gave his name to the village and, ultimately, a horse race. Associated with the Catesby family, once of a nearby hall, where the gunpowder conspirators met. There is a brass of William Catesby, beheaded after the battle of Bosworth, in the church. Numerous features include beautiful rood screen, benches and musicians' pew.

147

BRIXWORTH
All Saints (below)

All Saints was built c.680 and has not only Saxon, but Italian and Syrian influences in its architecture. Old Roman tiles, probably from a locally demolished villa, are to be found around the arches, and there are other Mediterranean and Eastern touches.

Reddish bricks in the tower probably indicate that the church was sacked by the Danes, and used as a watch-tower and refuge, and yet it was rare before the Norman Conquest for a tower to rise above the central section of a cruciform plan.

The simplicity of the interior is superb, and a set of small windows from the tower overlooking the nave are of special importance. A sacred relic, a neck bone of the great preacher, St Boniface, is kept in the church. During the Reformation, it was hidden in a bricked-up part of the Lady Chapel.

CHARWELTON
Holy Trinity

A relic of changing fortunes, now isolated when the nearby road was diverted following the War of Roses. Architectural features include the fine priest's room over south porch.

EARLS BARTON
All Saints (right)

In 1086, the Domesday Book revealed that 'Buartone' even then had a church dedicated to All Saints. Sitting on high ground beside an earlier fortified mound and ditch, it was probably built during the reign of Edgar the Peaceful in the 10th C.

The unique 10th C tower (made of stone, plaster and rubble) is often described as the finest Saxon tower in Britain and, surprisingly, it has its original wooden west door. The whole tower is not unlike a fortress, and was probably used as such. Tradition in the village suggests that when raiders approached, people ran up a rope ladder through a doorway which can still be seen on the tower's first storey.

The rest of the church was built later and is made of rubble. It is entered through a fine Norman arch, decorated with carved birds, fabulous creatures and an angel.

FINEDON
St Mary

A stately, Decorated period edifice chiefly remembered for the excellent private theological library over the south porch.

FOTHERINGHAY
Fotheringhay Church (below)

Only part of Fotheringhay church

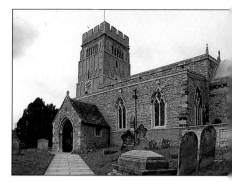

remains today. Most of its buildings were dismantled, as was the nearby castle and its great hall, after Mary Queen of Scots was beheaded on 8th February 1587.

Despite such a depressing history, the great tower and the tall nave with its flying buttresses stand majestic above the River Nene. The original, much larger collegiate buildings which stood only 20 ft from the present building were built in 1411, by Edward, Duke of York.

STANFORD-ON-AVON
St Nicholas

Light and airy, this church is most famous for its 17th C organ-case, thrown out by Cromwell from a building in Whitehall. However, there is a splendid east window with 14th–16th C stained glass. Archbishop Laud was once rector here.

SULGRAVE
St James

Traditional English church, not too large, not too small. It has an important historical association with the USA: the Washington family were lords of the manor here from 1540 until 1659. There is a brass memorial to Lawrence Washington of Sulgrave Manor 1584. A small panel of stained glass depicts the earliest Washington arms.

Northumberland

ALNMOUTH
St John the Baptist and the Friary Chapel *(below)*

Three churches have been built in Alnmouth. The first was Saxon and stood on an isthmus called Church Hill at the mouth of the River Aln. It was here, at the synod of Twyford in 684, that St Cuthbert was elected Bishop of Northumbria. Almost 500 years later, the first Norman Earl of Northumberland built his church on the same site, and dedicated it to St Waleric.

Coastal erosion and the shifting of the river mouth ate away at this site. The nave was the first casualty, falling

into the river, and it was soon followed by the chancel and north transept. The remaining structure was blown down in a storm in 1806. The site of the church was therefore moved onto higher ground on the north side of the river, and the parish church of St John the Baptist was built.

The new church was consecrated by the Bishop of Durham in 1876, and has an attractive sanctuary ceiling that has been painted in medieval style. A modern Friary chapel is also situated nearby. Built in 1902 and extended in 1920, it is a retreat and guest house.

ANCROFT
St Anne

A Norman foundation with, at the west end, a 14th C 'Vicar's Pele', or fortified tower; a relic of the county's troubled past when it was often ravaged by Scottish raiders.

HEXHAM
St Andrew

The first church was built here by Wilfrid c.675, and of this the crypt alone remains. Some of the crypt's passages are closed, and a display of church treasures has been incorporated which mars the atmosphere. In 876 this church was laid waste by the Danes and not refounded until 1113, and then as an Augustinian priory. Among the many

splendid and varied medieval features, of particular note are the unique monks' night stairs remaining from the priory, and a Saxon 'Frith' stool.

LINDISFARNE (Holy Island)
Lindisfarne Priory and Church
(above)

The great monk and historian Bede tells us that Lindisfarne (the name probably meant 'Water Island') had a monastery here from 635, 'built in the Irish manner of sawn oak' and founded by St Aidan. Cuthbert also came here, in 664. Because miracles were associated with his missionary work, Lindisfarne drew more and more people to its shores and there followed a great golden age for the community. The famous illuminated *Lindisfarne Gospels* were written here, completed by Bishop Edfrith (698–721). They are the earliest fully illuminated English books, and are now held in the British Library.

The Danish Viking invasion, however, sent the monks of Lindisfarne on a long journey in 875. With them they carried their most precious possession—the body of St Cuthbert—but it was more than a century before the saint's remains reached their final resting place at Durham in 998.

The Norman name 'Insula Sacra' or Holy Island has been in existence since the 11th C. The island's surviving monastic buildings date from c.1190 and comprise cloister and outer court. There are later 13th–14th C additions.

The present church of St Mary the Virgin is late 13th C Early English work with an 18th C bell-cote. It has an interesting altar carpet, based on a

149

page from the *Lindisfarne Gospels*, made by women from the surrounding area.

Holy Island is reached from the A1, south of Berwick upon Tweed. From the village of Beal, there is a tarred road across the tidal causeway which is covered twice a day by the sea. During the six hours around high tide it is not possible to visit or leave the island. Times of safe passage are posted at the start of the causeway and on the island itself. Yearly tide tables are obtainable from the Post Office, Holy Island (Tel: (0289) 89271).

Nottinghamshire

▓ HAWTON
All Saints
Externally, All Saints is mainly 15th C, surmounted by a fine tower. The east window is curvilinear and exhibits superb 14th C stonework. Internally, it is simple, with old pews. The Easter Sepulchre is the finest in the county, and there are well-executed sedilia, which bear a striking resemblance to craftsmanship seen at Southwell.

▓ NEWARK
St Mary Magdalene
A town church in the grand manner with transepts, aisles, nave and choir under the shadow of a splendid spire. Inside there is a great deal of 15th C woodwork, including poppy-heads, a screen and a number of modern additions—a 1937 Comper reredos and sculptural contributions from R. Kiddey.

▓ SOUTHWELL
Southwell Minster *(above, right)*
Southwell is the smallest town in England to boast a cathedral. With a church here as long ago as 956, the minster itself was begun in 1108 under the direction of Thomas, Archbishop of York.

Much of the early Norman work has survived, including the nave, transepts, facade and three towers, a superb example of Romanesque style.

The nave is imposing with its great cylindrical columns, large triforium arches, simple clerestory and wonderful set of round windows. The Early English choir was added in 1234.

However, it is the chapter house (c.1290) that is the real gem of Southwell. Approached through a magnificent doorway, it has some of the best late 13th–14th C stone carving in Britain. Nowhere has a greater collection of naturalistic carving than Southwell, except perhaps the little Herefordshire church of Kilpeck.

Oaks, buttercups, apple, maple, vine, hop and ivy foliage are just a few of the subjects that decorate capitals, bosses, arches and spandrels. Even the green man of primeval folklore sits here, near grotesque beasts and human heads. One of the oldest Anglo-Saxon sculptures in Britain can be seen above the door to the belfry: St Michael with lion, lamb and dragon.

Outside, the unusual west front is a wonderful example of its period, and has its 'Rhenish' spires added in the 19th C.

A brass eagle lectern and candlesticks were recovered after 300 years in a nearby pond at Newstead Abbey. They had been put there by monks to protect them at the dissolution of the monastery.

Oxfordshire

ABINGDON
Ock Street Chapel (Baptist)
A particularly good example of a severe Classical-style chapel, nicely situated within its own graveyard.

BURFORD
St John the Baptist (below)

Burford town is set on a hill at the south-eastern corner of the Cotswold hills. Its church sits close to the lovely River Windrush, and the tall spire can be seen from miles away on the A40 road.

Like many Cotswold towns, Burford grew rich in medieval times on the wool trade, and the church saw frequent extension from the first part of the building (c.1500). The 'bale' tombs in the churchyard symbolize this link with wool.

The many renovations have led to a rather unusual internal layout, and the porch is three storeys high, with external buttresses to support it.

In the south-east corner of the church, by the burial place of the ancient Bartholomew family, there is a mural inscription in a 16th C hand.

The passage is quoted in the Bible translation of William Tyndale, whose work pre-dated the Authorized King James Version and formed the basis of that work.

COTE near BAMPTON
Cote Baptist Church
Built in 1664, it retains a charming, untouched interior with gallery, flagstone floor, box pews, communion table, and possibly the earliest surviving baptistry within a chapel.

KELMSCOTT
St George
Historical association with William Morris, artist, writer and social reformer, whose tomb is in the churchyard.

OXFORD
Christ Church Cathedral (below)
Oxford's cathedral is the only one in the country to serve also as a college chapel. To visit it you have to enter the courtyards of the magnificent Christ Church college, built by Cardinal Wolsey in the 1520s.

Before that, the church was part of an Augustinian monastery, St Frideswide's Priory, named after the 8th C Anglo-Saxon princess who is Oxford's patron saint. The splendid 19th C east window, designed by Burne-Jones, tells the story of St Frideswide warding off the advances of the brutal Prince Algar.

The choir is vaulted in Perpendicular style—an excellent example. At the top of the pillars are

wonderfully decorated capitals, very similar in style to those in Canterbury cathedral and probably carved by the same masons. Adjacent to the church are an ancient cloister and chapter house.

Iffley Parish Church of St Mary

The superb, late-Norman west front of St Mary's, Iffley, is a fine example of architectural decoration. A Romanesque showpiece, the bold beak-head and zig-zag carvings are of Scandinavian origin. One of Britain's most famous late 12th C churches, St Mary's has a central tower, no transepts, a Norman nave and chancel, and is probably based on a two-cell Saxon church.

The wealth of ornamentation is fabulous, both inside and out. The doorway is highly decorated, probably because church doorways were the first place of baptism and marriage services. In this instance, the signs of the zodiac run around the arch.

The aisled interior is dark and has two elaborate Norman arches, an Early English vaulted west end, and medieval glass. The boss set in the chevrons of the choir depicts a seraph.

A blocked-up arch was probably a cell for the anchoress, Annora, who lived at Iffley for nine years until 1241. Religious devotion was such that hermits would be walled up in a small cell with only a small opening to view the altar, and to receive gifts of food and clothing, in Annora's case from King Henry III.

Magdalen College Chapel (left)

Magdalen College enjoys a beautiful position beside the River Cherwell. It is well worth a visit, if only as an example of the Oxford colleges, and is laid out on the intimate courtyard plan which makes the colleges such oases of peace.

Each college has its own chapel, most of which are arranged with the pews facing each other across the building—the 'collegiate' style. Many of the colleges have a long-standing tradition of choral singing, and it is worth trying to be present at the time of the evening service.

On May Day, the Magdalen College choristers climb the tower at daybreak and sing madrigals, while the streets below are packed with students, many of whom have been partying through the previous night.

St Aldate's (above, opposite)

As you come into St Aldate's church, its shape immediately appears unusual—no traditional cross-shape, but instead an open design, geared to the needs of the congregation, the people. In medieval times, the area nearby included a bustling market-place, the old Jewish quarter, and the city's commercial centre. And of course, all around has been the life of the university.

St Aldate's dates back to Norman times, with the south aisle added in 1336 by John of Ducklington, fishmonger and five-times mayor of Oxford. The tracery of the original

east window (the outline of which can still be seen partway down the south aisle) was in magnificent Decorated style, like the three original windows in the south wall. Later, in 1445, the north aisle was added in the Perpendicular style of the time by Philip Polton, Archdeacon of Gloucester.

The church as it now stands, however, is largely the result of the work done in the last century. There are numerous tributes to industrialists of that time, in particular to Lord Nuffield, founder of Morris Cars. On one screen you can even see the motor industry called upon to praise God, the ultimate creator! On another, a spider and a snail are among the creatures that tell how creation praises God. The words are from an ancient Hebrew song popular in Christian worship from earliest times.

Even more up to date are the amusing carvings outside and round to the back of the church, on the 1961 extension. However, St Aldate's is probably best known not as a church full of artefacts, fascinating though they are, but as a vibrant community committed to evangelistic mission and outreach. As such, it continually strives to ensure that the unchanging message of Jesus Christ is relevant to new generations.

St Mary the Virgin *(right)*
This fine church in the High Street has had close connections with Oxford University since the 13th C, and is now the University church as well as a parish church.

The tower is the oldest part, built in 1280 and supporting a richly decorated 14th C spire. The tower can be climbed, to give fine views of the city and the colleges. The chancel is 15th C and the nave 16th C.

St Mary's has seen many key events of English church history. When Queen Mary attempted to restore England to the Roman obedience after the Reformation, Cranmer, Ridley and Latimer were all tried here before being condemned to be burned. In the days of the Commonwealth, Archbishop Laud was condemned for installing the statue of Virgin and child above the 'Virgin Porch', by which one enters the church from the street. (The bullet holes in the statue were put there by Cromwell's soldiers.) Then, in the 19th C, John Henry Newman was vicar here, and John Keble's 'assize sermon' marked the beginning of the Oxford Movement to revive Catholic spirituality.

RYCOTE
St Michael and All Angels
Now in the care of the State. Queen Elizabeth I and Charles I worshipped here in this remote parkland chapel to the nearby house. It has a sumptuous interior, full of diverse fittings.

Shropshire

BATTLEFIELD
St Mary Magdalene
Founded in 1406 as a chantry chapel to commemorate the dead of the battle of Shrewsbury in 1403. It is predominantly 15th C, with later reticulated tracery to some windows. Unfortunately, by the 19th C the nave had lost its roof and become ruinous, but was restored in 1861–62.

OMNIBURY
St Michael
A rural simplicity, echoing the crafts of our ancestors, is captured in this Norman church of tower, nave and chancel. Plenty of rough-hewn oak in the west gallery, pews, and the old guileless roof. A Decalogue, or panel of Ten Commandments, dates from 1902.

STOKESAY
St John
The consequence of siting a church next to a castle can be seen here. During the Civil War, this church was much damaged, and subsequently had to be rebuilt and refurnished, the nave in 1654 and the tower in 1664.

TONG
St Mary and St Bartholomew
(overleaf)
According to Robert Eyton, in his *Antiquities of Shropshire*, 'If there be a place in Shropshire calculated alike to impress the moralist, to instruct the antiquary, and interest the historian, that place is Tong.'

St Mary and St Bartholomew was built between 1411 and 1430 by Lady Isabella de Pembruge, so that Masses could be said for her three husbands. Many alabaster tombs dominate the interior, particularly in the church's famed Golden Chapel, named after its gilded fan vault. The 15th C alabaster tomb chests and effigies of Sir Richard and Lady Margaret Vernon are quite exquisite, and show them in period costume and armour.

153

Interestingly, St Mary and St Bartholomew survived the Reformation almost intact because a relative of the family was one of the inspecting commissioners.

Somerset

St Margaret
Unequivocally Georgian, this church is complete and unaltered, making it the most splendid example of its type in the county. Interestingly, it has an apsidal sanctuary, and the west tower though small, is topped with a cupola.

▨ **BRYMPTON D'EVERCY**
St Andrew
Part of a group with a manor house, outbuildings and charnel house. Predominantly 14th–15th C with an ornate bell-cote instead of a tower or spire. Inside is a fine stone screen of early 15th C date.

▨ **CULBONE**
St Culbone
Of Norman origin, the building is arguably the smallest parish church in England, but still manages to contain a 17th C screen, old benches, and a family pew. Externally it carries a quaint diminutive spire.

▨ **GLASTONBURY**
Glastonbury Abbey (below)
Before the universities of Oxford and Cambridge were founded, Glastonbury Abbey was one of the main places of learning in southern England. It was a foundation of such wealth that it was second only to Westminster Abbey, and in fact Henry VIII left it till last before sacking and breaking it up at the time of the dissolution of the monasteries. At that time there were 100 monks there and the revenue of the abbey was around £3,500 a year.

The present ruins of the abbey date from 1184 to 1250; a severe fire engulfed the earlier buildings, and destroyed all books and records of the early history of the abbey, as well as its relics. The towers on the west end are particularly striking, as is the abbot's kitchen, a 14th C addition. Overlooking the abbey on Glastonbury Tor sits the tower of St Michael's Chapel (c.13th and 15th C).

Although the abbey was founded c.700, legends take us back further, to the time of Joseph of Arimathea. The Bible records that he took Jesus' body down from the cross and put it in the tomb. According to legend, he was a tin and lead trader who brought Jesus here as a child. The legend says that soon after Jesus' resurrection, Joseph arrived once again from the Holy Land, sent by St Philip to evangelize Britain, and brought with him the Holy Grail—the cup Jesus used at the Last Supper.

LULLINGTON
All Saints
A Norman church, with original tripartite plan. Rich in period detail, and a notable north door with Christ in Majesty. Inside, a massive font is inscribed 'In this holy font sins perish and are washed away'.

TRULL
All Saints
Perpendicular, inside is a treasure house of late medieval art: rood-screen, pulpit with painted panels depicting the Doctors, a fine array of carved bench-ends and an unusually extensive series of late 15th C glass.

WATCHETT
Chapel (Baptist)
Dated 1824, a chapel of unusual architectural quality, owing its outward appearance to Spanish influence. Gentle, ogee-curved gable end. Architectural lettering across the front is particularly good.

WELLS
Wells Cathedral (right)
The Gothic frontage of Wells Cathedral is a masterpiece, and is like an elaborate altar screen, with 300 statues of kings, prophets, apostles, saints and angels, half of which stand lifesize or larger.

A Saxon church was founded in Wells by St Aldhelm in 705. Today a font of that period is still in use for baptisms, and there is evidence of Saxon and even Roman burials nearby.

The present cathedral was begun c.1180, and is the earliest Gothic cathedral in Europe. The pointed arch was used here for the first time. Today the earliest part is the east end of the nave, while the choir, transepts, north porch and exquisite west front were all completed by 1240.

The arch structure is the result of the weight of the great central tower (1315–22). The tower, one of the finest in Britain, was so heavy that cracks started appearing only thirteen years after it had been finished, and it began leaning westwards. A series of ingenious inverted arches designed to

transfer the load from west to east were inserted around 1338.

The capitals in the nave are some of the best in England, full of foliage or showing people working in the vineyards that were in this area during the 1200s. Further into the cathedral the transept carvings are exquisite. One illustrates a man with toothache, another a lizard eating berries.

A magnificent well-worn staircase leads to the octagonal chapter house, added between 1286 and 1306. It has a fan-vaulted ceiling branching out from a central column.

The stone choir screen was built in the 14th C and, in the nearby choir stalls, craftsmen created an amazing collection of misericords.

There are some fine medieval tombs and chantries, made in 1200 when the remains of some Saxon bishops were brought from the old cathedral.

Note the early Renaissance pulpit and the superb east window (c.1340) with predominantly gold and green glass. It is known as the Golden Window and shows Christ's family relationship with King David; the 'tree of Jesse' is one of the best Jesse windows in Britain. The Lady Chapel is a triumph of medieval architecture and craftsmanship and the presbytery has a wonderful vaulted

retro-choir with a set of early stained-glass windows.

There is also an interesting clock face (first mentioned in 1392), which is the oldest in Britain.

The cathedral library holds about 6,000 books. Mostly from the 16th and 18th centuries, they cover not only theology but also travel, medicine, botany, mathematics, science and law.

Outside the cathedral is a wonderful 14th C street called the Vicars Close. It was built for the vicars of the canons ('vicar' means 'deputy'; the vicars were chosen for their singing ability— a central part of cathedral life). They are still occupied by people who work at the cathedral. Many residents are members of the Vicars Choral, who still sing daily in the cathedral.

WITHAM
St Mary, St John Baptist and All Saints
A small, late 12th C 'French' church, apsidal and stone-vaulted. Possibly erected by Sir Hugh, later Bishop of Lincoln, who came from Burgundy as prior of the first English Carthusian monastery (founded here by Henry II).

Staffordshire

BRADLEY
All Saints
This 13th–15th C church is of great antiquarian interest, with its well-lit nave containing well-proportioned arcades of c.1260. It has a carved Norman tub font, and a medieval rood-stair leading to a modern rood screen. Contains some good stained glass and 16th C effigies.

ECCLESHALL
Holy Trinity
Here can be seen the tombs of four bishops of Lichfield, of which the 17th C memorial to Bishop Overton is finest of all. Two other features of interest are the mass clock, similar to a sundial but which indicates the times of the church services; and a relic of an old church custom, arrow whets on the south side. These were made by those practising archery in the churchyard after service—a fineable offence if not undertaken.

LICHFIELD
The Church of St Mary and St Chad *(below)*
Two Irish pilgrims on their way to the Holy Land in 1400 are quoted as saying that Lichfield Cathedral was 'of the most gracious and wondrous beauty'. Certainly, its unique three spires in striking red sandstone—locally called the 'Ladies of the Vale'—and its decorative west front give it a very distinctive silhouette.

The first Norman church was probably built by Bishop Roger de Clinton, in 1085, and an apse for St Chad's shrine became a favourite destination for pilgrims.

By the end of the 12th C, however, the present Gothic cathedral was being built on the same site. Work began with the Early English choir, and by 1285 the nave was completed in the Geometric style. It is very fine, with a wonderful view right down to the Lady Chapel (c.1300). The Lady Chapel is renowned for its 14th C traceried windows, with 1530s glass that came from a Cistercian church near Liège before the French Revolution. It is the finest continental glass in any English cathedral.

Terrible damage occurred to the cathedral during the Civil War. In 1643 Royalist troops barricaded themselves inside to withstand a siege. Parliamentary forces subsequently rampaged through it. No glass was left in the windows, a steeple crashed onto the roof and tombs were desecrated and plundered. By the time the Restoration came, under Charles II, many thought that the cathedral was beyond repair.

However, as at Coventry, the congregation at Lichfield would not

let war destroy their place of worship. With a new Bishop, John Hacket, the cathedral was transformed in eight years, and Lichfield became the greatest 17th C example of a whole diocese coming together to rebuild its mother church.

The cathedral has many interesting features. The vestibule to the chapter house was where the Maundy Thursday foot-washing took place, and inside the chapter house itself is one of the cathedral's three medieval wall paintings. The Lichfield Gospels (c.730), also on show here, are some of the most beautiful manuscripts in the history of British Christian art. They contains the Gospels of Matthew, Mark and the early part of Luke, written in Latin in the Lindisfarne style.

Suffolk

▨ ALDEBURGH
St Peter and St Paul
Immortalized in the Revd. George Crabbe's book, *The Borough* , this church achieved its present symmetrical plan with broad aisles in the late 16th C. A likeness of the author, by Thurlow of nearby Saxmundham, can be seen in the north aisle.

▨ AMPTON
St Peter
Here, the most notable features are the chantry chapel of 1479, and the church's greatest treasure, a 'sealed book' of Common Prayer—neither the British Museum nor the Bodleian library possess a copy.

▨ BLYTHBURGH
Holy Trinity
A huge 15th C edifice, though much reduced in beauty by the 17th C iconoclast, William Dowsing. Founded on the wealth of the town when it was a port of some repute. Magnificent contemporary woodwork including tie-beam roof, carved bench-ends and carved chancel stalls, some of which are obviously fronted by the removed rood loft.

▨ BRAMFIELD
St Andrew
A tiny village church with thatched roof and very early detached circular tower. Internally, the beautiful vaulted screen is the best of its type in the county. Also here, the most important piece of Renaissance art in England—Nicholas Stone's exquisite effigy, dated 1634.

▨ BURY ST EDMUNDS
St Edmundsbury Cathedral (below)
Bury St Edmunds was once one of England's richest monasteries and major centres of Christianity, and its history stretches back to 636. Still standing is the abbey's free-standing Norman gatehouse. It is one of the finest Norman structures in Britain

and demonstrates what a wonderful place the abbey must have been. It was also in this abbey, however, that King John's barons secretly swore at the altar they would obtain ratification of the Magna Carta from the King.

The main body of the church stands within the abbey precinct. A medieval building, it was enlarged in the 19th C and was a parish church until 1913, when the diocese of Edmundsbury and Ipswich was created. Its fine west front has some excellent medieval moulding and panelling.

Inside, note the remarkable font, more than 20 ft high, which was placed as a memorial to those of the parish that gave their lives in World War I. (Its 'medieval' decoration, however, was added as late as 1960.) The nave with its slender pillars was begun in 1502, designed largely by John Wastell, who also built the Bell Harry Tower of Canterbury Cathedral, part of the chapel at King's College Cambridge, and many parish churches.

The roof is a Victorian restoration, undertaken by the architect Sir George Gilbert Scott, who led the Gothic revival of the 19th C. The organ, one of the greatest in the country, contains some 6,650 pipes. The cloisters are used in the summer for exhibitions of missionary work, art and literature.

CAVENDISH
St Mary
The epitome of an English village and English church, with a clerestory exterior decorated in flint flushwork panels similar to Long Melford. 14th C tower with the curious feature of a ringing-chamber furnished as a living-room, complete with fireplace and original window shutters. Two fine medieval lecterns, one 15th C brass and the other 16th C wood.

COMBS
St Mary
Architecturally of the Decorated and Perpendicular periods, St Mary's contains south aisle windows of magnificent 15th C stained glass. These depict the Old Testament kings and prophets; the genealogy of Christ; the Works of Mercy; the Tree of Jesse; and most impressive of all, scenes from the life of St Margaret of Antioch.

The whole reminds us that the medieval church was not a drab shell, but rather a riot of vivid colour and pattern, designed to inspire the lives of a population who were mostly uneducated and needed the Bible stories to be visually represented.

DENINGTON
St Mary
A wonderful church, chiefly remarkable for its aisle and parclose screens, complete with lofts and parapets. Much 15th C work predominates over other 17th–18th C fittings. A great rarity is the cover for the pyx (vessel in which Communion bread is preserved and which is suspended in front of the altar).

ICKLINGHAM
All Saints
This church saw a great deal of destruction by Reformers and Puritans, but there still remains considerable work by medieval craftsmen. There is a superb parish chest in which the church's documents would have been kept. Of historical interest are the original kneelers cut from thick tufts of reeds from which the word 'hassock' is derived. All Saints is now in the care of the Redundant Church Fund.

IPSWICH
Friar Street Chapel (Unitarian)
Originally built as a Presbyterian chapel c.1700 for a cost of £257 by a carpenter named Joseph Clarke. It was visited by Daniel Defoe in 1722, who said it was 'as large and as fine a building of that kind as most on this side of England'.

The furnishings inside include a beautiful wine-glass pulpit thought to be by Grinling Gibbons, and a gallery clock with a painted face which shows both roman and arabic numerals. The clock is believed to predate the building. Some of the box pews have hinged flaps for book rests.

KEDINGTON
St Peter and St Paul
Predominantly Perpendicular, but with earlier work including the chancel, this is one of the finest of the Puritan churches. A striking 16th C hammer-beam roof overlooks much excellent 17th and 18th C woodwork, which sets the atmosphere of the inside. Of great interest is the vault in which there are over 50 lead coffins, some of them moulded to the exact shape of the body.

LAVENHAM
SS Peter and Paul *(below, opposite)*
None of the 'wool' towns of East Anglia have such a splendid example of a 'wool' church as does the medieval town of Lavenham. The church of SS Peter and Paul sits raised on an area of grass, at the end of a road of superb half-timbered houses. Refurbishment of the church was paid for by John de Vere, Earl of Oxford, and by donations from the clothiers of Lavenham.

As a unit, the church works well as a classic of the Late Perpendicular period. Building techniques developed in the 14th C meant that roofs could rest on well-spaced slender pillars, leaving room for wide windows and creating an interior full of light.

There are also unique examples of woodwork. The Spryng parclose has an excellent example of Renaissance 'wainscot' carving, while the chancel screen c.1350 is decorated with wonderfully carved flowers and foliage, and animal and human heads.

SHELLAND
King Charles the Martyr
Ecclesiastically unusual, this parish is 'donative', meaning that it was the personal possession of the patron. This may account for the unusual dedication. With box pews and a three-decker pulpit of fine proportions, this small church has one of the most attractive 18th C interiors in the county.

TAMWORTH
St Editha
The church is generally of noble and ample proportions. Mostly 14th C, although there is Norman and 15th C work in evidence as well as 17th–18th C fittings. The most notable feature is the unique double staircase in the west tower.

WALPOLE
Chapel (Congregational)
Considered to have been converted from two cottages, this thatched, non-conformist place of worship is the second oldest Congregational chapel in England and is still in use.

Architecturally, it gave rise to the Congregational Meeting Houses of New England, USA. The interior remains totally unaltered and, in its peaceful graveyard setting with stately headstones, it is a delight to visit.

Surrey

COMPTON
St Nicholas
Set within a magnificent, old and unspoilt graveyard, this church is of 11th C origin. Here, the only two-storeyed sanctuary remaining in England can be found. The lower stage is groined, and the upper still retains its contemporary wooden balustrade. Much 17th C woodwork is in evidence.

GUILDFORD
The Cathedral of the Holy Spirit
(below, right)
Guildford was the first southern English cathedral since the Reformation to be built on a new site. When the decision was made that the diocese of Winchester had become too highly populated, it was decided to create two new diocese, Portsmouth and Guildford.

The eventual design by Sir Edward Maufe was for a modern, simplified Gothic building with a red brick exterior, using clay from the hill on which it stands. The foundation stone was laid in 1936 but, due to the outbreak of war, the work was stopped and the structure boarded up. However, soon after the war, the cathedral became a symbol of hope and an expression of faith; work began again, and the cathedral was eventually consecrated in 1961.

Guildford Cathedral is unique in that it is dedicated to the Holy Spirit. The interior is light, with tall, graceful south and north aisles and, at the east end, a relatively small rose window of a dove and gifts of the Holy Spirit—wisdom, steadfastness, knowledge, contemplation, Godliness, counsel and understanding.

Another feature that represents Christian giving during times of great trouble is the Jarrow stone situated on the left of the Regimental Chapel. A piece of the old monastic remains, it was sent by the people of Jarrow in recognition of financial assistance given to them by the people of Guildford during the Great Depression.

LINGFIELD
Saints Peter and Paul
The church was rebuilt during the 15th C when a college was founded by the lord of the manor. Internally the arrangement leans toward a Kentish style. An interesting lectern holds a chained Bible, secured to prevent theft during the medieval era. There are monuments, stalls and a screen.

LOWER KINGSWOOD
The Wisdom of God
A Victorian eccentricity, unique in England, is this replica of a Balkan church with narthex and apse. A great deal of it was brought from Balkan ruins. Byzantine in every respect.

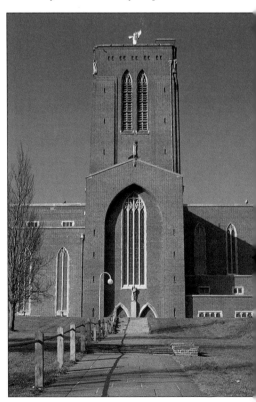

STOKE D'ABERNON
St Mary

Famous for its important series of brasses, that of Sir John D'Abernon (1277) being the earliest surviving in England. Architecturally, the church is pre-Conquest in origin, and the south wall dates from this period. There is 12th and 13th C work in evidence, and remains of 13th C paintings in the chancel. The most notable fixture of later periods is the early 17th C pulpit with a tester for producing better acoustics.

Sussex
East and West

ALFRISTON
St Andrew

A transitional cruciform church built of flint (c.1360), it stands away from the village, with a central tower and shingle spire. The inside has been refurnished, but unaltered are the piscina and sedilia of unusual design, and there is an ancient Easter Sepulchre, the focal point of medieval Easter services.

BATTLE
Battle Abbey (below)

The weathered ruin of the Benedictine abbey at Battle stands on a ridge overlooking the site of the Battle of Hastings (1066).

The abbey was founded by William the Conqueror to celebrate his victory at Hastings over King Harold of Wessex, and to atone for the loss of life suffered in the battle. The high altar of the first church was built over the spot where King Harold was thought to have fallen.

The buildings were consecrated after William's death, and he left substantial endowment for the survival of the Benedictine community. The abbots of Battle were responsible for organizing defences against French raids in the 14th C and a great monastic fortified gatehouse was rebuilt as a stronghold in 1338. After six centuries it still dominates the town.

Of the first abbey church, the undercroft (guest house) with its twin towers and 13th C Dorter (dormitory with novices' rooms) are very beautiful. Sadly, other buildings were demolished after the dissolution of the monasteries, and the abbey ruins and battlefield are now in the care of English Heritage.

The church of St Mary the Virgin nearby has a magnificent Romanesque nave, a Norman font with a medieval cover, rare 14th C wall-paintings and the gilded alabaster tomb of Sir Anthony Brame, to whom Henry VIII originally granted the abbey.

BOSHAM
Holy Trinity

A small but important church, which has the distinction of being one of the few featured on the Bayeux Tapestry. Its foundations are historic, originally

a Roman site. There was an Irish monastery here before the mission of St Wilfrid. The chancel is part Saxon and part Early English. In 1064, King Harold said prayers here before setting out on his fateful journey to Normandy.

CHICHESTER
Chichester Cathedral (above, right)
Chichester is the only one of England's medieval cathedrals visible from the sea. Its high spire can be seen from miles around rising upwards through tree-lined streets and lush green fields.

The spire is an excellent Victorian copy by Gilbert Scott of the original spire (c.1400), which had collapsed after a severe storm on 17 February 1861.

The cathedral's most unique architectural structure, however, is its free-standing bell tower—the only one in England. Its broad nave, transepts and much of the choir are basically Norman, but they underwent Gothic remodelling c.1200.

Chichester has had two great fires, one of which destroyed the east end and led to the building of the retro-choir. This has superb early Gothic work by Walter of Coventry. It is square-ended, with rounded arches and early foliate capitals.

Some of the fine examples of medieval stone carving can be seen in the superb 12th C south choir aisle, showing Christ at the raising of Lazarus, greeted by Mary and Martha. The 14th C stone Arundel tomb is also unusual, and was probably for Richard Fitzalan, who died in 1375, and his countess.

20th C features include a beautiful altar tapestry (1966) symbolizing the Trinity, designed by John Piper and woven in France; a magnificent stained-glass window (1978) illustrating Psalm 150, by Marc Chagall; and a Graham Sutherland painting of Mary Magdalen and the risen Christ, in the Mary Magdalen Chapel.

PARHAM
St Peter
Mostly Perpendicular, but remodelled in the 19th C, the church stands in a park next to an Elizabethan house. Nevertheless, good box pews, and a notable 18th C pulpit and screen. Of particular interest is the 14th C font, one of only 35 lead ones in the country; this has Lombardic lettering.

ROTHERFIELD
St Denys
Despite two restorations, the interior of this hilltop church remains totally unspoilt and includes many fine features, including a wall-painting of Doom on the chancel arch and of the Annunciation over the entrance to the north chapel. The elaborate canopied pulpit of c.1630 came from the Archbishop of York's private chapel.

RYE
St Mary the Virgin (below)
St Mary's literally crowns the town of Rye, high up as it is and visible from miles around. Built early in the 12th C, it is sometimes called 'the Cathedral of East Sussex', although it is in reality a small parish church.

The French raided the church in 1377, and it was rebuilt by the monks of Fecamp in Normandy, who then governed Rye for two centuries. In the raids, the French also took the church's six bells back to France, but these were later recovered by a raiding party from Rye and Winchelsea. Between 1562 and 1572, many Huguenots fleeing from persecution in France settled here.

The present church retains its original

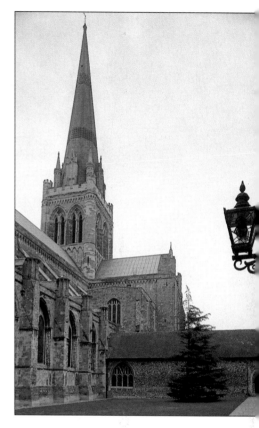

basic cruciform shape, and its best-known feature is its clock. Known as 'tquarter boys' (striking only the quarter and half hours), its original chime played part or all of a psalm or hymn. It is one of the oldest church turret clocks in the country, and still has its original works. The pendulum swings in the body of the church.

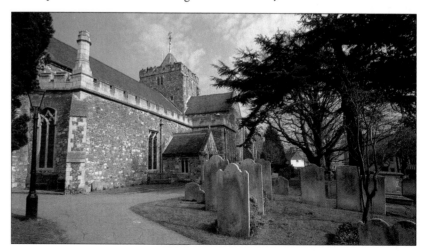

SOMPTING
St Mary

The Saxon church of St Mary's, Sompting, is set at the foot of the South Downs. Surrounded by open fields, it has an uninterrupted view over Worthing.

Its original pyramidal shingled roof is made of oblong strips of cleft oak; the original Saxon timbers are still in place beneath them. This shape is unique among Saxon churches in Britain, although it was copied in the 19th C at Flixton in Suffolk. An example of the 'Rhenish Helm' style found in the Germany, it is the nearest the Saxons came to building a spire.

St Mary's has some Roman tiles, and some small Saxon windows. The main body of the church was rebuilt in the 12th C by the Templars, an order of crusading monks whose wealth and power grew throughout the Middle Ages. The administration of the church then passed to the Knights of St John, who opened it up to local congregations.

Tyne and Wear

JARROW
St Paul's Priory (above)

Half a mile south of the Tyne Tunnel, surrounded by the Jarrow docks, is the exceptional monastic parish church of St Paul's. It was founded by Benedict Biscop and Benedictine monks from Monkwearmouth in the 7th C, and its dedication stone of 685 to St Paul is one of the oldest in the country. The stone is set into the arch of the central tower.

The Venerable Bede (673–735), the Anglo-Saxon chronicler, historian and monk, was buried here until his remains were moved to Durham Cathedral in 1020. The church itself became a dependent priory of Durham, and then—after the dissolution of the monasteries—the parish church of Jarrow.

Inside, the nave is dominated by a modern wooden sculpture of the ascending Christ. A beautifully crafted stained-glass window by John Piper shows the heavens, the Earth and the Pentecostal flame, around the Jarrow cross. The initials of Benedict Biscop are inscribed on the cross.

Saxon masonry is on display, including frieze material and baluster columns recovered from the adjacent monastic site. There is also a glass floor-section in the nave, showing the original 7th C foundations, and some Anglo-Saxon window glass. A chair, probably 800–1,100 years old, is traditionally believed to have been from Bede's cell. There is a museum about Bede's life nearby.

MONKWEARMOUTH
St Peter and St Cuthbert

Typically Saxon in proportion, with a tall tower bearing a carved figure on the exterior above the west door. This was originally the chancel arch and thus internal! This is all that remains of the first church here, built to serve a Saxon monastery by Benedict Biscop in 674. Inside the church is a fine collection of Saxon carved stone, and recent restoration has unearthed a pane of original stained glass, now identified as the oldest in England, brought over from France by Biscop c.675.

NEWCASTLE UPON TYNE
The Cathedral Church of St Nicholas (below)

The first church on the site of the present cathedral was set up not long after 1080, and is believed to have been founded by St Osmond, Bishop of Salisbury.

Most of the cathedral's finest features, however, were the result of much later building. There is a unique 15th C stone lantern tower, 203-ft high, and paid for by two families, the Jameses and the Rodes. St Margaret's Chapel has a 15th C pre-Reformation roundel of the Madonna and child, while a double brass of the early 15th C covers the altar tomb; it is probably Flemish. A brass pre-Reformation lectern, which came from East Anglia, dates from 1500.

In 1813, considerable effort was expended on buttressing, underpinning and reconstruction of the crown. In 1882, a Bishopric of Newcastle was created and on the south wall of the ambulatory there is a memorial to Ernest Roland Wilberforce, first Bishop of Newcastle and grandson of William Wilberforce, the slavery abolitionist. There is also a memorial to the Newcastle-born Admiral Collingwood, second in command to Admiral Nelson at the Battle of Trafalgar in 1805.

ROKER
St Andrew
A surprising church built in 1906–7, a time little likely to produce a masterpiece of ecclesiastical architecture. Here we have just such a one. A massive and original design by Prior, with Arts and Crafts furnishings to harmonize; Burne-Jones, William Morris, Eric Gill and Gimson were among those who contributed.

Warwickshire

HAMPTON LUCY
St Peter ad Vincula
Standing beside Charlcotte Park on the River Avon, this is essentially a Victorian church, with work mainly by Gilbert Scott and Hutchinson. Rickman also constructed the window tracery in moulded cast-iron and built the nearby cast-iron bridge over the Avon. The nave is lofty in proportion, and has a sensitive plaster vault, giving the impression of a cathedral in miniature.

KENILWORTH
St Nicholas, Abbey Fields (above)
To the north of Old Kenilworth are the Abbey Fields, in which stand the remains of an Augustinian Priory. Founded in 1122 by Geoffrey de Clinton, Chamberlain to Henry I, the priory's surviving ruins are now partly incorporated in the parish church of St Nicholas.

The church has one of the finest Norman doorways in Warwickshire. In the graveyard, parts of the priory walls have been re-used to create a terraced bank, which contains a haphazard collection of old window tracery, pillar fragments and decorative stones.

LOXLEY
St Nicholas
All that an English church should be.

Nestling in a valley setting, it was consecrated in 1286 and the chancel is substantially 13th C. The 18th C saw much restoration, leaving a charming interior of box pews, clear glass, and interestingly, a pulpit high-up on a wall which is approached through the vestry.

STRATFORD-UPON-AVON
Holy Trinity (below)
Yews, cedars and lime trees brought from the Garden of Gethsemane surround this collegiate church which overlooks the calm waters of the Avon. It has splendid Early English and Perpendicular architecture, but is most famous for its associations with William Shakespeare.

On 26 April 1564, William Shakespeare was christened here. 52 years later, after his death on 23 April 1616, he was also buried in the church grounds and his tomb reads, 'Good friend for Jesus sake forbeare To digg the dvst enclosed heare; Blest be ye man y spares thes stones, And cvrst be he yt moves my bones.' This 'curse' probably refers to the old practice of recycling grave spaces, and removing bones and storing them in the 'charnel-house', or 'bone house', which until 1799 stood against the north wall of the chancel.

Shakespeare, who became a 'lay rector' of the church in 1605, would have known of this practice. The thought of his bones being moved after his death obviously did not please him.

There is also a bust of Shakespeare, erected only seven years after his death when his wife Anne was still alive—probably, therefore, a good likeness.

The earliest part of the church is dated c.1210, and the south aisles were built between 1280 and 1330. The spectacular chancel and clerestory were put up c.1480.

Another interesting tomb is that of George Carew, The Earl of Totness, and his wife Joyce. A contemporary of Shakespeare, he commanded the *Mary Rose* when the Spanish fleet was destroyed at Cadiz in 1596. He became an Ambassador to France and was Lord Justice of Ireland. Carved by Edward Marshall, later master mason to King Charles II, the tomb has been described as 'the grandest Corinthian monument in England'.

WARWICK
St Mary

Perhaps the finest of all the county's town churches. The two most notable features are the Gothic-style tower—richly decorated and raised on arches to accommodate the ancient public right of way beneath—and the 15th C Beauchamp chapel with its important and richly coloured interior and monuments.

Its own tiny chantry chapel has pendant vaulting. Also of note are the south nave windows with curiously designed tracery.

West Midlands

BIRMINGHAM
Birmingham Cathedral (opposite)

The Anglican church of St Philip was begun in 1709 in the reign of Queen Anne, and consecrated in 1715. The tower, however, remained unfinished. George III gave £600 to complete it in 1725, when Robert Walpole asked

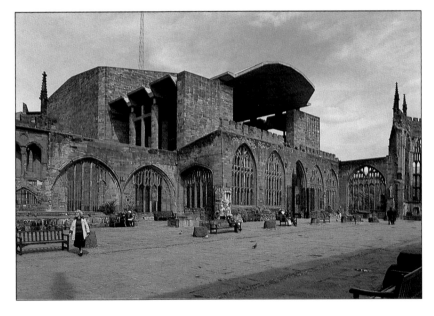

him on Sir Richard Gough's behalf to do so. The contribution made by Sir Richard Gough himself is represented by the boar's head weathervane which bears his crest.

The building was designed by Thomas Archer (1668–1743), an architect who designed in English Baroque style. He was also responsible for St John's, Westminster (1714) and St Paul's, Deptford (1712). Archer drew much of his inspiration from Christopher Wren but, unlike Wren, who only went as far as Paris to see continental architecture, Archer travelled more extensively, visiting Italy and other places on the continent for a number of years.

Birmingham Cathedral is a truly elegant building of English Baroque composition, a single-celled building in an east-west orientation with extensions of chancel and tower. The great tower with its concave sides is unique, and the parapet surmounted by urns is a wonderful detail.

Inside, the vast windows, strong fluted piers and Corinthian capitals (which are painted to simulate marble) give the church a bright and spacious dimension. A gallery of panelled oak runs down the sides of the church.

Four large Pre-Raphaelite stained-glass windows are by Sir Edward Coley and Burne-Jones (who was born in

Birmingham and baptized in this church), a designer of stained glass and tapestries for William Morris.

The new diocese was founded in 1905, and St Philip's was designated a cathedral. A statue of Bishop Gore, the first bishop, stands in front of the tower at the west end. During the Second World War, extensive damage was done by incendiary bombs, resulting in the loss of the roof. It was renovated when peace came.

COVENTRY
Coventry Cathedral (above)

'It will be rebuilt in the name of God' were the words of faith uttered by Provost Howard after the old Cathedral of Coventry was burnt to the ground in 1940. The task of reconstruction lasted nearly 22 years, until the new cathedral was opened by Her Majesty the Queen, in 1962.

Coventry Cathedral, designed by Sir Basil Spence, is one of the most original modern buildings in Britain: modern and medieval sit comfortably side by side, linked by a great porch. There has been a Christian community here since the 7th C, when St Osburga founded a convent for nuns. In 1043, this developed into a Benedictine monastery, funded by Earl Leofric and his wife Lady Godiva.

Today, the cathedral approach is

overlooked by Jacob Epstein's enormous bronze sculpture of St Michael subduing the Devil. The great entrance has an exhilarating patchwork of clear glass, each panel 8 ft high and nearly 3 ft wide, and in good weather the ruins of the old cathedral are reflected in it. Angels, patriarchs, prophets, saints, apostles and martyrs are all represented here, engraved by the artist John Hutton.

From the glass entrance one can see right through to the high altar. In the nave, five pairs of windows illustrate the journey from birth to death, and a large stained-glass window that extends from floor to ceiling, by John Piper, represents the light of the Holy Spirit. At its foot sits the roughly-hewn font, chiselled from the Barakat Valley near Bethlehem, and a gift of the Jordanian Government.

The nave is dominated by 'Christ in Glory', the largest woven tapestry in the world (75 ft by 34 ft), funded by an anonymous Coventry citizen. Set above and behind the altar, it replaces the traditional east window and represents a vision of St John from the book of Revelation. Christ sits in a mandala with the symbols of the four evangelists around him. It was designed by Graham Sutherland, and woven in France by Pinton Freres, using over 1,000 different shades of wool.

There are a number of beautiful chapels in the cathedral. The Chapel of Unity, designed like a crusader's tent, has stained glass windows by Margaret Trehearne, and a marble mosaic floor by Einar Forseth. The circular Chapel of Industry, or Christ the Servant, takes the place of the Guild Chapels of the old cathedral. Jesus's words, 'I am among you as one who serves', are inscribed around the circumference of a stone slab made by the local Technical College. The Christ in Gethsemane Chapel, adorned by a magnificent angel holding a chalice, is by Stephen Sykes.

The walls of the cathedral also hold eight stone tablets, with Christian texts and symbols, by the artist Ralph Beyer.

Wiltshire

▨ AVEBURY
St James
Adjoining a famous prehistoric stone circle, the church dates from Saxon times (there are remains in the nave). Aisles are 12th–13th C; work present on the tower is 15th C. Fixtures and fittings include a Norman font and a good 15th C rood loft.

▨ BISHOPS CANNING
St Mary the Virgin
A Norman foundation extensively rebuilt in the 13th C leaving a finely proportioned and interesting church.

The present spire, clerestory and upper sacristy are 15th C.

Of note are the nave roof of 1670, the early windows at the west end of the north aisle, and the fine arcading for recessed altars in the transept; also the rebuilt Chapel of Our Lady of the Bower with its monuments and Jacobean Holy Table. In the church, too, is a unique 'carrel', or meditation chair.

BRADFORD-ON-AVON
St Laurence (below)

In the mid-19th C, Canon Jones, a vicar and keen archaeologist, found two carved angels while repairs were being undertaken in a three storey cottage.

The result was the rediscovery of one of Britain's most complete Saxon churches. Passages from William of Malmesbury, dated c.1125, mention 'a little church which Aldhelm built in the name of the most blessed Laurence', and this is believed to be that church. In old deeds it is referred to as a 'Skull House', which probably means it was used as a charnel house (burial place).

The first impression on seeing St Laurence's is one of great loftiness; the height of the walls is greater than the length of the nave. For some time, the nave had been used as a school, with domestic windows and a door added to its west end. The chancel had been converted into a cottage, where the carved angels were spotted. Canon Jones' enthusiasm for the church

resulted in it being bought back from its private owners and reconsecrated.

DAUNTSEY
St James
11th C north and south doorways lead into a mainly 14th and 15th C building. The church is important for its contents which include screens of the 14th and 17th C; good painted glass of the 16th C; monuments; and a wood tympanum with a Doom painting, which served to point out graphically the manner of afterlife expected for those that might feel tempted to succumb to sin in the present.

HORNINGSHAM
Chapel (Congregational)
Founded in 1566, this is the oldest surviving chapel in England to have continuous use as a religious building. There have been many alterations, notably the removal of the box pews, but enough remains of considerable

antiquity to be of major interest.

The chapel is sunk beside the road under a thatch roof, resembling a cottage (except for its oversized windows). Internally, however, it has all the hallmarks of a traditional medieval chapel, including an ancient wooden gallery, of which the panelling to the front is of particularly fine quality. Some candle holders remain on the edge of the gallery and gallery pews.

The pulpit is mounted high on a pedestal and is complete with sounding board. Also original are the hat-pegs which line the rear wall of the men's gallery. Such an arrangement gave rise to the saying 'her eyes stood out like chapel hat-pegs'!

MALMESBURY
Malmesbury Abbey (below)
The town of Malmesbury was possibly the first town to receive the status of 'borough', when King Alfred conferred his charter around the year

880. Nevertheless, for 200 years before that, it had been a great centre of Christian teaching and worship.

According to tradition, Maildulph, a Celtic hermit, came to this part of Wiltshire in the early 7th C. Noblemen started sending their sons to him to be educated and one such was Aldhelm, a relative of King Ina of Wessex.

Aldhelm accepted the Christian faith and followed the traditions of St Benedict of Nursia. He founded a Benedictine monastery, was the first Abbot of Malmesbury, and later became the first Bishop of Sherborne. But he instructed that his body should be brought back here for burial. Aldhelm was indeed a great scholar—some of his Latin verses and riddles survive to this day—and an important cleric. But above all, he had a great longing that ordinary people should know the love and salvation of Jesus.

In the heyday of its life, the medieval monastery flourished, and in the south-west corner of the church, stained-glass windows depict the variety of activity at that time. Not all the monks are shown to have been scholars or teachers, some are shown in the gardens and vineyards belonging to the abbey.

The Reformation, of course, brought an end to life here as it was. Today, all that remains is the fabric of the Norman building—the great round pillars; the arches of the triforium with their chevron carving; and the lower Romanesque arches with the slight point at the top of the arch, surrounded by very fine mouldings ending in strange beakheads.

Some visitors to the town see the ruined open arch of the abbey and think the building is only a memorial of the old Christian monastery. But after 1,300 years the abbey, now the parish church of Malmesbury, continues the traditions of teaching, evangelism and music begun by Aldhelm. People from all walks of life gather here for worship, and work together with members of other churches to live out their faith and serve the community.

▨ SALISBURY
Salisbury Cathedral *(below)*

Salisbury Cathedral has one of the most perfect settings of any ecclesiastical building in Britain. It is renowned throughout the world, partly because of the famous painting, 'Salisbury Cathedral from the Bishop's Grounds', by John Constable.

As a building, Salisbury has near-perfect and delicate proportions, with Early English windows and buttresses, and heavy, rounded Norman arches passing into pointed arches in the nave, windows and doorways. It was built between 1220–58, and is the only ancient English cathedral to be built almost entirely in one style; no other cathedral interior except St Paul's was built to the design of one man. The cloisters and chapel were added later, but even the famous mid-14th C spire—the tallest in the country and rising to a height of 404 ft—complements the building perfectly.

The cathedral's 15th C library houses some 187 ancient manuscripts, an 8th C Latin manuscript of the Old Testament, some scientific, mathematical and medical books, and one of the only four copies of the Magna Carta—on view in the chapter house.

167

There are also interesting tombs and effigies, and a series of notable 13th C sculptures above niches in the chapter house. The 14th C clock in the north transept is believed to be the oldest in Britain.

Also quite beautiful, however, is the modern stained-glass. A window by Gabriel Loire in the Trinity Chapel is dedicated to Prisoners of Conscience, and is a reminder that the cathedral is still a place to offer prayer.

▓ STOCKTON
St John the Baptist
An archetypal English church but with Eastern flavour brought about by the curious arrangement of a solid stone wall, pierced by a central doorway and two squints, closing off the chancel. 15th C in date, a rood loft once existed on the nave side supported on corbels. As to the rest, predominantly 14th C.

Worcestershire
See Hereford and Worcester

Yorkshire

▓ ALMONDBURY
All Hallows
Essentially a late 15th C church with some 13th C work. The very fine nave ceiling has decorative bosses and a carved gilded prayer inscription dated 1522 running round it like a frieze. A tall ornate font cover, required by medieval Church law to protect the 'holy water' from theft, is one of the best in the county.

▓ BEDALE
St Gregory
A truly outstanding building with wall-paintings, vaulted crypt and an early 14th C tower built for parochial defence against Border raiders. Complete with evidence of a portcullis to protect the internal staircase.

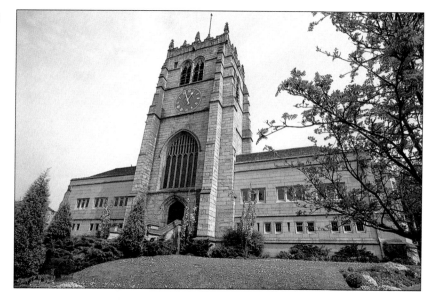

▓ BRADFORD
St Peter's Cathedral *(above)*
The parish church of Bradford was raised to cathedral status in 1919. It is built of millstone grit (a type of carboniferous sandstone), with a solid Perpendicular west tower (1493–1508), battlements and eight pinnacles. Modern wings were erected on either side of the building in the 1950s, making use of local stone.

The interior is predominantly 14th C; nothing survives of the earlier 11th C church. The south aisle, south clerestory and south porch were reconstructed in the 1830s and later remodelled. Transepts were added in 1899, and the east end—including the Lantern Tower, north and south choir aisles, choir, Lady Chapel and sanctuary—is recent (1958–63).

Note the interesting piers and oak roof decorated with heraldic shields and angel corbels. The song room is the work of Sir Edward Maufe, the architect of Guildford Cathedral. There is also a monument to Joseph Priestley, Presbyterian minister, writer, chemist and one of the discoverers of oxygen. The late Gothic font cover is marvellous, and the chancel has glass by William Morris (1862) and the artists Brown, Rossetti, and Burne-Jones.

▓ BRAMHOPE
Bramhope Chapel
With a simple, graceful interior, this chapel stands in grounds which once belonged to the now demolished hall. It was one of the first Puritan chapels in the country, built in 1645 by the lord of the manor, an early supporter of the 'Commonwealth' cause.

▓ COWTHORPE
St Michael
Attractive, late 15th C church. Inside is a rare treasure, a contemporary portable oak Easter Sepulchre which would be processed around the parish and then placed in the church, where a vigil would be kept by it from Good Friday until Easter Sunday. It would then be decorated and the curtain opened to reveal the tomb empty, signifying 'Christ is Risen'.

▓ COXWOLD
St Michael
Noted for its distinctive octagonal west tower. Contains magnificient memorials to the local gentry. Also a unique 17th C looped T-shaped communion rail, built to fit into the existing chancel space left after the erection of some of the major monuments.

EASBY
St Agatha
This long, low building with its bell-cote stands near the gatehouse of a ruined priory of slightly later date. Enlarged in the 15th C when the south aisle and a large vaulted porch (with a priests' living chamber overhead) were added.

HAWORTH
St Michael and All Angels (below)
The 17th C parish church of Haworth sits in a valley on the desolate but beautiful Yorkshire Moors. The location is lovely, but its place in English literary history is exceptional.

This small village churchyard contains the gravestones and memorials to over 40,000 local people, but in the church it is a sealed family vault belonging to the Brontës that attracts most visitors.

Anne, Charlotte and Emily Brontë were born in Thornton on the outskirts of Bradford and moved here with their brother, Branwell, and their father, Patrick, who took up the position of rector at Haworth from 1820–61.

Charlotte is best known for her novel *Jane Eyre* (1847). She outlived the rest of her family, marrying the church curate in 1854. Tragically, she died in childbirth. Emily is known for her poems and the novel *Wuthering Heights* (1847), while Anne wrote *Agnes Grey* (1847).

HEALAUGH
St John
Mainly Norman with a sumptuous south doorway showing 'Christ in Majesty' and the 'Orders of Heaven and Earth', including entwining beasts of hell on the capitals. Very fine set of corbels which supposedly represent evil spirits outside the church.

HEPTONSTALL
Octagonal Chapel (Methodist)
The epitome of northern Methodist architecture. Rugged, solid, perched on a hillside with spectacular views, this is one of the country's oldest continuously-used chapels. Built in 1764 to the favoured octagonal plan, John Wesley made many visits here to preach to huge congregations.

HUBBERHOLME
St Michael
An old church with 16th C rood loft, one of only two in Yorkshire. Here the priest would conduct parts of certain services under the great 'rood' or crucifix hung above.

KIRKBURTON
All Hallows
Much 13th C work with 15th–17th C woodwork. A squint for viewing the altar is believed to have opened out from an anchorite's cell.

KIRKDALE
St Gregory
A church with Saxon origins and the most superb Saxon sundial in England. The lengthy inscription reads 'Orm Gamal's Son bought St Gregory's Minster when it was all broken and fallen and let it be made anew from the ground to Christ and St Gregory in Edward's days, the king and Tosti's days, the Earl.' Inside, stone benches run around the walls, reflecting the days when the body of the church had no pews and people stood for services—leading to the expression 'the weakest go to the wall'.

KNARESBOROUGH
Chapel of Our Lady of the Crag
Unique single-cell shrine dug out of the wayside cliff by licence dated 1409. Guarding the entrance is a later figure of a knight drawing his sword.

LASTINGHAM
St Mary
Stands on the site of a monastery established by St Cedd in 654, refounded in 1078 by Abbot Stephen of Whitby before moving the community to York to set up St Mary's Abbey. Fine Norman chancel with apse.

The most remarkable feature of this church is a complete, unspoilt 11th C crypt built over the grave of St Cedd as a shrine for pilgrims. The crypt is unique as a complete church itself, with apsidal chancel and nave with side aisles.

PICKERING
St Peter and St Paul
A large 13th–15th C building with Norman origins. Its outstanding feature is the vast array of mid-15th C wall-paintings covering all the upper nave walls. These were important visual aids in medieval churches, and illustrated for people who knew no Latin the biblical scenes and lives of the saints.

RIPON
Ripon Cathedral *(below)*
The short, squat appearance of Ripon Cathedral is deceptive, and is due to the collapse of the spire in 1660—it was never replaced. The nave interior, by contrast, appears wide and spacious. In the past, this would have been used for gatherings, debates, meetings and to conduct business, with worship taking place only behind the 9-ft thick choir screen and sanctuary.

Today, Holy Communion is celebrated each morning in one of the chapels and private prayer is encouraged, particularly in the Pilgrims' Chapel.

This is the fourth church built on the site. Set up as a collegiate church during the 12th and 13th C, Ripon only became a cathedral in 1836. A rare Saxon crypt lies beneath the central tower, unquestionably the oldest and most complete crypt in Britain, and tradition suggests that it is the same size and shape of Jesus' tomb. It is the only remains of the 7th C Anglo-Saxon church founded by St Wilfred, according to the monk and historian Bede.

The 13th C western front has some wonderful Early English work, but the central tower fell in 1450, and was repaired in Perpendicular style. An interesting result of this change is the lopsided arch over the nave altar. The 15th C canopied choir stalls are among Ripon's most interesting features, and are mostly the work of William Bromflet and two assistants; look also for the mechanical hand used by the organist to conduct the choir after 1695. The nave is 16th C, and the east window is Decorated Gothic, shown in its stone tracery.

The misericords are exceptionally carved. The father of Lewis Carroll (Charles Dodgson), author of *Alice in Wonderland*, was canon at Ripon from 1852–68, and many think these little carvings hidden in the dark depths of the choir influenced the book.

The cathedral also has much ancient silver in display cabinets in the treasury by the north aisle, and a fine Norman chapter house.

ROTHERHAM
Bridge Chapel of Our Lady
Standing on a medieval bridge, it is one of only five such chapels left in England. Built in 1485, it was used by travelling pilgrims.

SHEFFIELD
The Cathedral of St Peter and St Paul *(below, opposite)*
Sheffield is the largest city in Yorkshire. Its cathedral lies in the heart of the old city, occupying the site of a church founded in the reign of Henry I. The north chapel of St Katherine contains a 15th C black oak sedile (seat for the officiating clergy)—the only connection with the original church. It is canopied with simple panelling and is one of only three portable sedilia in the country.

By the 18th C the church building had become neglected, which led to the nave, aisles, clerestory (without triforium) and transepts undergoing an almost complete remodelling in 1805. This century has seen its enlargement into a light and spacious cathedral.

The crossing tower has a crocketed 15th C spire. In addition there are

some fine stalls and magnificent tombs including Tudor memorials to the 4th and 6th Earls of Shrewsbury and a modern gilded cathedra by Sir Charles Nicholson, with a figure of Christ.

The church was elevated to cathedral status in 1914, a historic parish church with a strange mixture of Perpendicular and 20th C styles.

SPROTBOROUGH
St Mary

An Early English building with a fine 13th C piscina for pouring away unused communion wine. Also sedilia, or clergy seats, and a credence shelf where the bread and wine were placed before being taken to the altar for consecration.

TONG
St James

A complete Classical-style church built in 1727 by the lord of the manor, although archaeological evidence shows Norman foundations. Very good Georgian furnishings including three-decker pulpit and sounding board. Also, a squire's pew with fireplace to keep the family warm through the immense 18th C sermons.

WAKEFIELD
The Cathedral Church of All Saints (above, right)

Wakefield Cathedral, once a medieval parish church, was mentioned in the Doomsday Book. However, a Christian community lived here from much earlier times. A relic of the early Saxon church, a cross dated 960, now sits in York Museum, and there is a replica in the south transept. The earliest parts of the church to be seen today are two pillars on the north side of the nave.

The present cathedral has a Perpendicular exterior and owes much to restoration by Sir Gilbert Scott. It has Yorkshire's highest spire (247 ft), which in turn is crocketed and surrounded by pinnacles.

The nearby Bridge Chapel (c.1350) was also restored by Scott. It is one of only four remaining in England and is typical of the Middle Ages where chapels were built near bridges, both as shrines for wayfarers and as toll-raising points for the necessary upkeep of the river crossings.

The cathedral has had many phases of building, not least a series of additions in the 15th C. As a result of becoming a bishop's see in 1888 there has been an eastward enlargement this century.

WENSLEY
Holy Trinity

A church with a remarkably diverse selection of fixtures and fittings, but its crowning glory must be the large free-standing 15th C wooden reliquary taken from Easby Abbey. Containing some part of a saint, it would be taken around the parish for people to make offerings in exchange for a blessing.

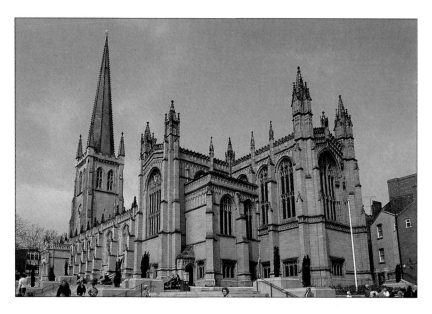

Gothic, the earliest part being the transepts (1230–60) and the wonderful polygonal chapter house with no central pier. The vestibule that leads to this is also extraordinary: its walls are practically replaced by glass—a later Gothic ideal. The west wall of the nave was finished in 1338 and the roof dates from the 1350s.

York is architecturally most famous for its stained-glass windows—there is glass from every century from the 12th to the 20th. Its greatest collection is of 13th and 14th C stained glass, including the famous Five Sisters window (seen from the south entrance). Each of the five sections is 50 ft high and only 5 ft wide. The east window, completed in 1408, is one of the largest expanses of medieval glass in the world, with over 2000 sq ft of glass. It depicts God the Father, saints, angels, stories from the Old Testament and the book of Revelation, amongst other subjects. Other windows have unexpected subject matters in their borders; for example, the bottom of the fifth window from the west on the north side of the nave portrays a monkey's funeral, a cock reading a lesson, and a fox stealing a hen.

The choir, completed in the early 1400s, is Perpendicular. There is a splendid, late 15th-C stone choir screen, with canopied niches and original statues of kings of England. (The statue of Henry VI, however, was added in 1810.)

Externally, the massive towers (c.1470) and the great central tower (the largest lantern tower in Britain at 200 ft high) are wonderfully impressive. Today's church has survived several catastrophic fires, including one in 1984.

St Martin-cum-Gregory, Micklegate

Stretching back into antiquity, with re-used Roman masonry and a Roman tombstone incorporated in its structure of many periods. Its 18th C fittings include a large pew box and cupboard for keeping the bread 'dole', before distribution to the unfortunate of the parish after the service.

▨ YORK
The Cathedral and Metropolitan Church of St Peter York (York Minster) *(above)*

On Easter Eve 627, Edwin of Northumbria (whose wife Ethelburga was a Christian princess from Kent) was baptized at York in a wooden oratory especially built for the occasion. Not long after, Pope Gregory decreed York a missionary centre, and a stone church that replaced the wooden one was built by St Wilfred in 670.

The church grew and became famous throughout Europe as a centre of learning while Alcuin (c.735–804) was head of the York Cathedral School. In 1070, Thomas of Bayeux, the first Norman archbishop, began constructing a cathedral which was larger than Canterbury Cathedral at the time.

The present minster is based on the Norman cathedral of 1070, but little survives of the original. Beginning in 1220, it took 250 years to build, and is a mixture of Early English, Decorated and Perpendicular architecture.

There is much that is entirely

Wales

ABERFRAW (Llangwyfan)
St Gwyfan
A small single-cell church of 12th C
date, sited on a tiny island, easily
reached at low tide. Interestingly, the
north wall contains 16th C arcading
which suggests a later aisle was added
and presumably demolished since.

BANGOR
The Cathedral Church of St
Deinol *(below)*
Bangor is one of the earliest cathedrals
in Britain. It was established c.525 by
St Deinol, who constructed a small
wooden church around which a Celtic
monastery developed. On being given
land by the local ruler, he drove posts
into the ground to enclose the church,
weaving branches between the posts.
The Welsh word for this type of
wattled fence was 'bangor'. Deinol
was consecrated bishop in 546, and his
church became a cathedral. He was
buried at Bardsey Island.

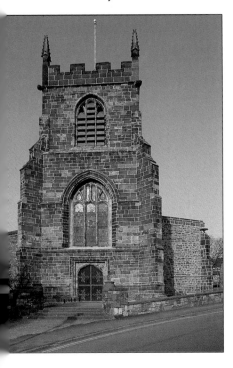

The church has been destroyed by
fire and then rebuilt many times, in
both wood and stone. The buildings
today date mainly from the medieval
period, although they were
considerably restored under Sir
Gilbert Scott in the 19th C. There is
an elegant ceiling designed by him in
the sanctuary.

The windows in the south aisle
depict Celtic saints, most of them
associated with the evangelization of
North Wales in the 6th and 7th C, and
there is also much celebration of the
achievements of Welsh princes, poets,
scholars and clergy. The cathedral
library contains 'Bishop Anian's
Pontifical', the personal service book
of Anian, Bishop of Bangor (1267–
1306), who baptized Edward II.

BODELWYDDAN
St Margaret
Often erroneously referred to as 'the
marble church', it is in fact
constructed of local white limestone.
However, the interior of this
fantastical church, with its 202-ft west
spire, contains much marble. Built by
John Gibson between 1856 and 1860,
it is lavish and ornate, and the interior
is expensive and richly carved.

BRECON
Brecon Cathedral *(above)*
Above the old historic town of Brecon
rests the imposing priory church of St
John, raised to cathedral status for the
newly formed diocese of Swansea and
Brecon in 1923.

Built mainly in the 13th–14th C, the
cathedral is linked to Brecon's busy
activities in many ways. Side chapels
are dedicated to local trades—
weaving, tailoring and shoe making—
while memorial chapels and plaques
commemorate many local soldiers
who have given their lives in strange
and unfamiliar lands.

The first recorded church was set up
here by Bernard of Neufmarche, when
he established a Lordship after defeating
the Welsh in 1093. This was a
Benedictine priory, a cell of Battle
Abbey in Sussex. The oldest object in
the building is the font, decorated with
fantastic birds, grotesques and beasts,
and which belonged to the Norman
church. The Latin inscription is
believed to refer to the baptism of Jesus. 173

The cathedral is full of interesting features, from light fittings designed with the symbol of the dove to The Bevington Chamber Organ mentioned in Kilvert's diary.

CARDIFF
Llandaff Cathedral (right)

Llandaff Cathedral was originally built in a hollow on an old Christian site, to protect it from the view of marauding Vikings sailing up the Bristol Channel. The previous religious community had been one of the first in Britain, founded by St Teilo in the 6th C.

The present buildings date from the 12th C onwards, with extensions added as recently as 1956, when the Welsh Regiment Memorial Chapel was completed.

The nave is dominated by Epstein's 'Christ in Majesty' rising powerfully upwards, a masterpiece of 20th C sculpture. The artist wrote to the Dean after its completion saying, 'I do not believe that I will ever make another act of faith similar to it.'

The cathedral is full of ancient and modern artefacts. On your left as you enter through the west door there is a large triptych by the Pre-Raphaelite, Dante Gabriel Rossetti. Originally forming the reredos behind the High Altar, it shows on the left David as shepherd, on the right David as King,

while the central panel shows a Nativity scene, with Christ from David's line.

There are a series of six panels by Burne-Jones representing the six days of creation. Above a surviving Norman arch behind 'Christ in Majesty' is a modern stained glass window, 'Our Lord at Emmaus', by the artist John Piper. It shows the events described by the Gospel of Luke after Jesus had met Cleopas and another disciple along the road from Jerusalem.

St John (left)

St John's Church is unusual in that it sits in the middle of a pedestrian precinct in the heart of the city. Businesses surround it, and cries of fruit-sellers from the local market can be heard nearby.

Records tell us that a church existed here as early as the 12th C, but that it was swept away by a flood. In 1453, a new church was built. Its most striking feature was the fine Perpendicular tower commissioned by Anne, the wife of Richard III. There is an exquisite, detailed, openwork parapet on the top of the tower and a magnificent golden weathercock. Cockerels were adopted by the Christian church in the 9th C, to be placed on spires as a reminder of Peter's denial of Christ—a warning to parishioners not to do the same.

CLYRO
St Michael and All Angels (below)

During the nineteenth century, the little church at Clyro had a curate who has since become famous—the Rev. Francis Kilvert. During his time in this part of the beautiful Wye valley, Kilvert wrote diaries which were published much later. His finely written observations on the lives of the local people, of the church, the seasons and the natural world have given these diaries a wide following.

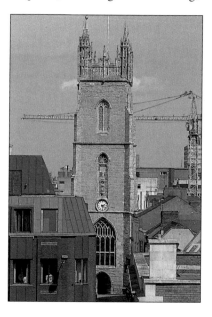

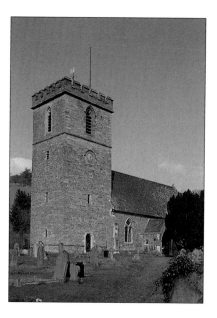

CWMYOY
St Martin (above)
This lovely ancient church, on the pilgrim route to St David's, nestles in Cwmyoy (meaning 'Valley of the Yoke', a reference to the valley's shape).

It is said that St Martin's tower leans more than Pisa—it was built on a Quaternary landslide, which is still in the process of settling. In fact, no part of the church is at right angles to any other and the chancel leans in the opposite direction to the tower.

LLANBEDR
Salem Chapel (Baptist)
In keeping with the original strictures and needs of Baptist chapels, this beautiful and ancient building is set, as so many Welsh Baptist places of worship, near to a stream for the purpose of baptism by total immersion. A simple, calm interior dominated by the pulpit.

LLANDINAM
St Llonio (right)
This mid-Wales village beside the A470 road is only a few miles from Offa's Dyke. It is also half a mile from Cefn Carnedd, an old British camp where, according to Tacitus the historian, ancient Britain's last ruler Caractacus made his final stand against the Romans.

Llandinam means 'enclosure of the fortified hill', and the 14th C church tower was once used as a fortress. This may have been needed because from here the old route from Shrewsbury to south-west Wales passed through a narrow part of the Severn Valley.

As early as 520, a Breton missionary, St Llonio, set out from here with St Cadfan on missionary journeys. Later, this became a mother church, from which monks went out to preach the gospel.

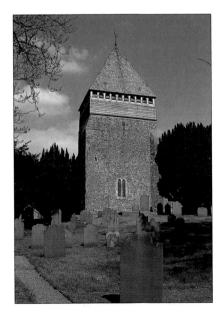

LLANDOVERY
(Llanfair-y-Bryn)
St Mary
Erected on the site of a Roman fort, this church has unusual proportions, which make it appear like a great tithe barn to which a 13th C tower has been attached. External gargoyles and parapet added c.1500.

LLANELIEU
St Ellyw
Predominantly 13th C, this church retains inside a sturdy rood screen, loft and 14th C tympanum, on which some painting survives. From an earlier church are two pillar stones of 7th and 9th C date.

LLANFACHES
St Dyfrig
Although of medieval origin, St Dyfrig was completely restored by Groves in the Art and Crafts style of 1908, retaining only coloured glass and a carved screen.

LLANGADWALADR
St Cadwaladr
An important historical church of 7th C date under ancient royal patronage of Cadfar (d. c.625) and the royal chieftain Cadwaladr, his grandson. The nave is 12th C; chancel 14th C; window 15th C; and chapel 17th C.

LLANTWIT MAJOR
St Illtyd (overleaf, top left)
When John Wesley preached at St Illtyd's, Llantwit Major, in 1777, he described it as 'abundantly the most beautiful, as well as the most spacious, parish church in Wales'.

St Illtyd's is certainly spacious, and has a wonderful set of early wall-paintings. At the rear of the church stands a unique collection of engraved stones and crosses, a reminder of the historic importance Llantwit Major has had for Christian communities.

One of Glamorgan's early monasteries was situated here, and it is claimed that the first university in Britain was started here. St David, the patron saint of Wales, was educated at the monastery, and some scholars

175

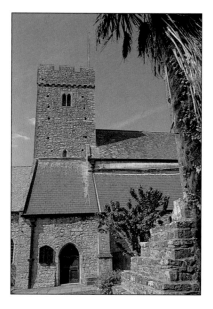

Gloucester, son of Henry I. It was one of the richest Welsh monastic houses: the Cistercian monks owned a ship, mills, fisheries and coalmines, and had a reputation for great learning. Among their manuscripts was a copy of the Doomsday Book, now held in the British Museum.

The present Margam Abbey parish church occupies most of the nave of the original abbey church. Like all Cistercian churches, it is dedicated to St Mary.

Remains of the original Norman building still exist. The west front still retains its Norman door and three Norman windows (c.1175–80) although some 19th C restoration took place, including the Italianate 'pepperpots'. Inside, massive Late Norman rectangular piers divide the nave from the two aisles.

There are some fine 16th C alabaster tombs and effigies of the local Mansel and Talbot families.

The west windows are by William Morris and there is also stained glass by Frank Roper.

MOLD
St Mary
One of the most notable medieval churches in the country. 16th and 18th C work predominates: a fine timber roof, and good early glass. Of the modern work, there is an unusual art deco War Memorial Chapel.

NEVERN
St Brynach (below)
St Brynach's parish has one of Britain's finest megalithic tombs, Pentre Ifan. Brynach, who founded a number of churches, including Nevern, was a friend of St David. He also went on pilgrimage to Rome and lived for a while in Brittany. Roman stones include the 5th C Ogham stone. There is also a 10th–11th C Great Cross.

St Brynach's has a cruciform plan, and the chancel is offset to the north. A mixture of Norman and Perpendicular, the massive battlement tower extends to the full width of the church. The grounds are crowded with mature yew trees; one special yew to the right of the entrance gate sheds its resin onto the ground, and is known as the 'bleeding yew'. Near the church is a pilgrims' cross, a wayside shrine for the pilgrims travelling from Holywell to St David's.

believe that Christian learning and worship was begun even earlier by Euragin, daughter of Caradog (Caractacus), who brought back Christianity from Rome. Euragin's father was imprisoned there, and some say Euragin met St Paul.

MARGAM
St Mary's (below)
St Mary's parish church is one of only three Cistercian churches still in use in Britain today.

The original Cistercian abbey was founded here in 1174 on the site of a Celtic church by Robert Earl of

NEWPORT
St Woolos Cathedral
(opposite, top left)
The cathedral church of St Woolos overlooks the town. It was founded about 800 by Gwynllyw (anglicized to Woolos). A convert to Christianity, he was told in a dream to search for a white ox with a black spot on its forehead, and build a church when he

found it, as an act of penitence.

The Norman church was built by Robert FitzHamon. A Norman archway, nave and lean-to south aisle were constructed. The nearby town of Caerleon is the site of the largest Roman amphitheatre in Britain, and within the old cathedral at Newport a Norman dogtooth archway, between the nave and the Lady Chapel, is supported by leafy Corinthian columns dug up from the Roman fortress of Isca in Caerleon.

The tower, south porch and north aisle are 15th C. There is also a leper window, although it is not regarded as being in its correct position, as it is too high in the wall to allow infectious people outside the building to see the priest at the altar. The tower has 13 bells, the largest peal in Wales.

A succession of restorations took place in the 19th and 20th C and in 1949 the church achieved cathedral status, although it was still short of space. This was rectified by the addition in the early 1960s of a new east end, containing a modern mural and wheel-type window designed by John Piper.

▨ OGMORE
Ewenny Priory *(above, right)*
Ewenny Priory is one of the best and most unusual Welsh examples of an early Norman church. Lying low by the river, two miles south of Bridgend, it was founded first as a church, c.1120. In 1141, however, it was converted into a monastery for a community of Benedictine monks from Gloucester.

The great walls look almost like the remains of a castle, and inside them lies the church, with a tower that also resembles a castle keep. The whole gives the impression of impenetrable strength, and as a fortified monastery, it is probably the best example in Britain.

▨ OLD RADNOR
St Stephen
Perpendicular church restored sensitively during the Victorian era. Imposing tower and beacon turret. Inside, features of note include medieval choir stalls; carved screen; the oldest organ case in Britain (c.1500); interesting Easter sepulchre in north chapel; hatchments; 18th C

painting of Aaron and Moses; and a font fashioned from a huge block of igneous rock, which is probably of pre-Christian religious significance.

▨ OXWICH
St Illtyd
An isolated cliff-top church of diminutive proportions, whose chief glory is the painted chancel ceiling executed at the expense of Dame Lilian Baylis of Old Vic fame. The chancel was restored in the 19th C and extended in the present century. The rose window above the altar has glass by John Piper.

▨ SKENFRITH
St Bridget
Attached to a lofty square tower capped with a splendid timber two-stage pyramid belfry, more at home in the county of Hertfordshire. Inside, the church's most remarkable treasure is a magnificent 15th C cope.

▨ ST ASAPH
St Asaph Cathedral *(below)*
It seems that the first church near or on the site of St Asaph was established by an exiled Scottish bishop, Cynderyn (or Kentigern), in 560. Cynderyn was succeeded by Asaph, when the former returned home to Scotland, and a 12th C *Life of St Asaph* notes that there was indeed a wooden monastery here.

One of the best known figures in the cathedral's history, however, was Bishop William Morgan (1545–1604). It was he who translated the Bible into

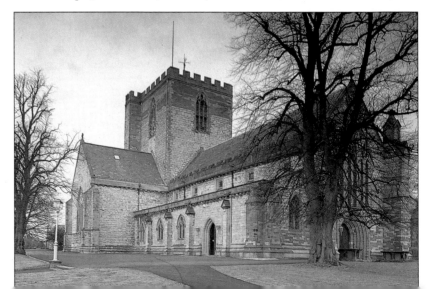

Welsh for, as he himself wrote, 'Religion, if it is not taught in the mother tongue, will lie hidden and unknown.' Bishop Morgan has been seen as a pioneer by many British missionaries who translated the Bible across the world. An original William Morgan 1588 Welsh Bible was used at the Investiture of the Prince of Wales in 1969.

On the disestablishment of the Church of Wales in 1920, the then Bishop of St Asaph, Alfred George Edwards, fittingly became the first Archbishop of Wales. A memorial to all Welsh Bible translators stands outside the church.

ST DAVID'S
St David's Cathedral (above)

According to the 11th C *Life of David*, written in Latin by Rhigyfarch, David was born into a wealthy family—the grandson of a local king. He was well educated, went on missionary journeys and is credited with having established a Christian church both here and at Glastonbury. He also visited Jerusalem and, with a group of friends and disciples, founded a monastery near the sea. According to Rhigyfarch, the monks worked the land without the help of animals: 'they place the yoke on their shoulders'. David's fame after his death spread widely, and he was much written about by Welsh poets. Today he is the patron saint of Wales.

David was canonized in 1120, and the monastery he had founded here 600 years earlier began to attract a large number of pilgrims, including William the Conqueror and, it is believed, King John. The journey to St David's is still one of the major pilgrimage routes in Britain.

The original monastery, however, was almost completely burnt down in 645. The same fate befell later buildings, and there was even an earthquake, so it is hardly surprising that no building older than the 12th C has survived. A few objects, such as the decorative Abraham stone that stands in the south transept, are older, but the buildings themselves are the design of the cathedral's third Norman bishop, Peter De Leia. A number of alterations were made by later bishops, including some rebuilding, and extensions of the tower.

St David's Cathedral has a cool stone nave, and a superb wooden roof with beautiful medieval pendants. In the south transept there is a small portable altar stone, said to have been brought back from Jerusalem by David. Today, St David's Cathedral is also the parish church, and as such continues the daily round of ordered worship begun so many centuries ago.

SWANSEA
The Tabernacle (below)

This spectacular chapel is regularly called 'The Cathedral of Welsh Nonconformity', and is the largest Nonconformist chapel in Wales. Designed by John Humphrey, it was opened in 1873. It is a mixture of styles, owing much to different episcopal traditions, but it is also huge, and has a superb gallery that looks down to the pulpit.

The Tabernacle became famous when the Prince of Wales attended a *Cwmanfa Ganu* (Songs of Praise), the same day—6 July 1969—that he had proclaimed Swansea a city.

While he was master of music at the chapel, W. Penfro Rowlands (d.1893) composed 'Blaenwern', a piece of music that is known and performed internationally.

TENBY
St Mary

Probably the most complete Perpendicular church in the county, although originally a 13th C church. It still retains the tower and octagonal spire of this period. The west door has a nice ogee arch and is the same date as the south porch, c.1500.

Scotland

ABBEY ST BATHANS
St Baothan *(above)*
Although now a small parish church, St Baothan's has an important past. People have lived at the site for thousands of years: a 4,000-year-old bronze dagger was discovered nearby, along with axe-heads, millstones and sherds of earthenware.

A Celtic church was probably situated here, followed by a 13th C priory. However, the English army later destroyed all the religious buildings in the Borders and Lothians.

After 1560, the church was restored. Pews and furniture were added, a bell tower and entrance porch were installed, and by 1726 the first glass had been put in. The east gable and north wall are the only remaining parts of the priory, and are now incorporated in the parish church. The church's most valuable item is a stone effigy of a prioress; only two others exist like it, and both are in England.

ABERDEEN
King's College Chapel
This beautiful chapel is the only remaining building of the university founded by Bishop Elphinstone in 1495. It has a flamboyant Gothic style and is famous for its wonderful, delicate, Renaissance crown spire. The spire's restoration, after a storm in 1633, was funded by the king; his initials are etched onto the lead flèche.

The great glory of King's College Chapel, however, is its rare and fine ensemble of medieval fittings, including the finest woodcarving in Scotland. The 16th C, tall oak screen is superbly worked—it was this that separated the nave from the choir. The square Cromwell tower in the northeast corner of the quadrangle originally served as student lodgings and was built in 1658.

St Macher's Cathedral
The twin spires of St Macher's have long been one of Aberdeen's most famous landmarks, but the cathedral has had a complicated history and there are many questions that cannot be answered. It has lost its crossing, transepts and choir, and now consists only of a nave and west front. Nevertheless, it is a remarkable and fascinating building.

It is believed that the original Celtic settlement was established by St Macher about 580, complying with instructions from St Columba. The see came to Aberdeen in 1130, possibly to a church that already existed, and a new cathedral was built of which nothing now remains.

In 1370, rebuilding of the nave began in red sandstone. Some of this can be seen at the east end in the wonderful naturalistic carving. The nave was finished by Bishop Leighton in 1422–40. The stone changes to granite and has a slightly stern, military appearance; the two west towers rather resemble the fortified houses of Scotland, while the stout round piers and arches, and small clerestory windows, have a Norman feel. It has an unusual seven-light window, and the whole is devoid of decoration.

The nave roof is very special, displaying 48 heraldic shields, and is dated c.1520.

ABERFOYLE
Aberfoyle Church
The ruin of the old church is of particular note, and the churchyard which features in Scott's *Rob Roy* contains cast-iron mort safes. These are designed to foil the activities of body-snatchers seeking specimens to sell to the medical profession for research.

ARBUTHNOTT
St Ternan
A magnificent cruciform church consecrated in 1242. Of this building, what survives can be seen in the

chancel. Rebuilt and restored, and notable for the aisle which forms the lower stage to a tower erected by Sir Robert Arbuthnott c.1471. The tower housed a portable altar which he had obtained under licence from Pope Innocent VIII. There is a priest's chamber above.

ATHELSTANEFORD
Athelstaneford Church (below)
The village of Athelstane was built on a ridge, and named after the defeat of the Northumbrian king, Athelstane, by the Pictish king, Angus MacFergus, in the 9th C.

According to legend, MacFergus' Scottish army had been outnumbered and surrounded by Saxons. Praying for help, he saw a cloud form in the sky in the shape of the cross of St Andrew. MacFergus vowed that if his army were victorious, he would make St Andrew Scotland's patron saint and adopt the saltire as the Scottish flag. The enemy was defeated and the king kept his word.

The church was built in 1868 on the site of an earlier building. It has transepts, a semi-octagonal chancel to the east, a bell-cote on the west gable, and some very interesting stained glass by the Victorian artist Charles Kempe.

There is a good lectern doocot (dovecot) c.1580, next to the church.

BRECHIN
St David
Formerly a cathedral of early date on the site of Culdee Abbey. Predominantly 13th C with 12th C work in evidence. Partly ruinous, the choir serves as the parish church. Notable cross-head c.900; also, one of only two round towers in Scotland (10th–11th C).

CRATHIE
Crathie Church
The second church here, opened in June 1895, it replaces a plain 19th C 'kirk'. Situated near Balmoral, this is a 'royal' church, insomuch as it is used by the royal family when in residence. Queen Victoria favoured it, and it contains many memorials to the royal family. John Brown is also buried in the churchyard, near the ruins of the medieval church.

GREAT CUMBRAE
The Cathedral of the Isles (below)

On the island of Great Cumbrae, in the Firth of Clyde, there is a considerable church known as the 'Cathedral of the Isles'. This church became widely known in the 1970s as the home of the Community of Celebration, a group of charismatic Christians originating in Houston, Texas. Their emphasis on community life, on the freedom of the Holy Spirit and on creative use of the arts in worship has been influential among churches round Britain.

DALKEITH
St Nicholas
12th C origins, the church of St Nicholas was raised to the status of a collegiate church during the 15th C and rebuilt. Inside: medieval fittings, a restored apse, and the unique Morton monument with an effigy of the First Earl of Morton in parliamentary dress rather than armour, the only effigy so clothed in Britain.

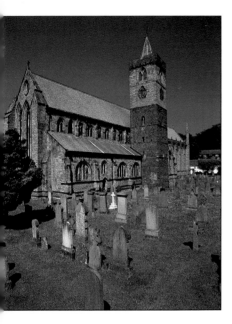

DUNBLANE
Dunblane Cathedral *(above)*
This is one of Scotland's beautiful small cathedrals. The building has been heavily restored over the centuries, so that its ancient origins are not everywhere apparent. But the bell-tower is 12th C and further building work began in 1237. Unusually for Scotland, the interesting carved choir-stalls survived the Reformation and are well worth a look.

DUNFERMLINE
Dunfermline Abbey *(below)*
Dunfermline Abbey was founded soon after 1070 and became one of the richest and most influential abbeys in the whole of Scotland. The remains of the 14th C monastic buildings—a refectory, dormitory, latrines, guest house and gate house—all give a marvellous picture of what the great monastic centre was once like.

The first abbot, Geoffrey, came from Canterbury, and during the 11th C the Abbey of Dunfermline succeeded Iona as the place of Royal sepulchre in Scotland. The magnificent 12th C nave contains 11 massive pillars, some wonderfully carved.

Outside, the grand processional west entrance displays five orders of arches, while the north entrance, for lay folk, has four.

It is in this church that the tomb of Robert the Bruce lies. He was buried here in 1329, except for his heart which he asked to be buried in the Holy Land. He was re-interred in 1889 and covered by a spectacular rectangular memorial brass in medieval form, manufactured in Sheffield and embedded in a slab of Egyptian porphyry, a gift of Lord Elgin. The battlemented 100-ft high square tower has the words 'King Robert the Bruce', cut out in stone around its four sides. In a frieze around the interior of the 19th C church at clerestory level are the memorial crests of other Scottish monarchs buried here. Charles I (second son of James VI and I) was also christened here.

The modern church attached to the nave has a very fine, beautifully carved pulpit (1890) and a splendid lectern (1931). The window of Love in the memorial chapel is also well worth studying.

EDINBURGH
Greyfriars *(below)*

Opened on Christmas Day, 1620, Greyfriars was the first church to be built in Edinburgh after the Reformation, and the first to introduce organ music, hymns and stained glass windows into the Church of Scotland. The church's name came from the grey habits worn by the monks at the Franciscan Friary that was once near the Grassmarket. Little remains of the original late Gothic church, the only furniture left being the pulpit.

Unlike many of the Border churches, Greyfriars was not affected by warfare. However, the Town Council kept their gun powder in the west end, and in 1718 it blew up; a further fire in 1845 gutted the building.

Many famous people are buried in the churchyard, built on land given by Mary Queen of Scots in 1562. The churchyard also includes the Adam Mausoleum, which houses a collection of monuments unrivalled in their architectural importance anywhere in Scotland.

The church holds Gaelic services on Sunday afternoons.

Holyrood Abbey *(below)*

Holyrood Abbey was founded by David I in 1128 and dedicated to the Holy Rood. According to legend, David's life had been endangered by a huge stag in full charge while the king was hunting near Arthur's Seat. Miraculously, a fragment of the Holy Rood (Christ's cross) was placed in his hand and the stag fled. (A similar story has been told about other saints in different parts of Europe.) It was in recognition of this that David founded the Augustine abbey of the Holy Rood.

During the 15th C, the medieval abbey benefited and prospered from the patronage of the Stewart Kings. In the 16th C, however, both the palace and the abbey suffered severe damage after the Reformation. The ruined nave of the monastery church escaped destruction for a while, when it was used as Canongate parish church, but in 1688 this church was also sacked. And when the roof finally collapsed in

1768, the damage was complete.

Today, only the processional doorway to the church's cloister survives. The remains of the abbey adjacent to Holyrood House (the Chapel Royal) consists solely of the nave, the fine west front and the north west tower.

St Giles Cathedral *(right)*

St Giles is the finest of Edinburgh's churches, and is entwined with Scottish history like no other church. St Giles, born in Athens in 640, emigrated to France; it is this connection with Scotland's oldest ally that granted him the honour of becoming patron saint of Edinburgh. His arm bone was given as a relic to the church in 1454.

There has probably been a church on the site of St Giles since 854. The four massive pillars date from about 1120, but the rest of the Norman church was largely destroyed by the English in 1385.

The present cathedral was started two years later, and finished in the 15th C. The building is surmounted by the finest of four remaining examples of crown steeples in Scotland. At one time it was used as a watch tower.

The Scottish reformer John Knox became its first Protestant minister in 1559. He was buried in 1572 in the graveyard, which now lies beneath the

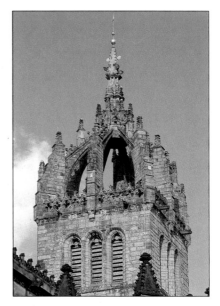

cobblestones of Parliament Square.

Considerable restoration took place in the 19th C, and there are several notable memorials.

EUROPEI (Lewis)
St Moluag

Of ancient origin, this church is now mainly 12th C. The church is in the care of the Scottish Episcopal Church, who restored and re-roofed it this century. David Livingstone presented his prayer book to this church; it can be seen today in St Peter's Episcopal church, Stornoway.

GLASGOW
Glasgow Cathedral (St Mungo)
(opposite, centre)

The site of Glasgow cathedral has been sacred for over 1,500 years, for it was here that St Ninian was buried in 397. St Kentigern (popularly known as St Mungo, and Glasgow's patron saint) also built his wooden church here in the 7th C. His tomb is now in the lower church (a unique feature of the cathedral and an extension of the east end). In 1451, there was a Papal decree that a pilgrimage to Glasgow cathedral equalled, in merit, one made to Rome, and pilgrims came from far and wide.

The present church is the fourth on

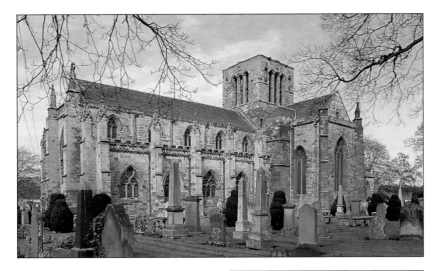

the site and is mainly 13th–14th C. It was finished in the 15th C with a chapter house (where the medieval university held its classes) and the Blacader aisle. The 15th C pulpitum has figures that may represent the seven deadly sins. There are some fine foliate capitals in the choir, and the eastern ambulatory has four chapels opening out of it, each with a double lancet window. Before the Reformation, each would have had an altar.

The cathedral has a tremendous view through to the east windows and a fine collection of modern stained-glass. The east and west windows (1951) are by Francis Spear, and show the four evangelists (Matthew, Mark, Luke and John) and creation. This latter window shows Adam and Eve, and plants, fish, birds and animals, beneath great golden rays emanating from a circle above.

The cathedral also has one of only two examples of medieval wall painting in Scotland. One painted stone is plastered and painted on two sides with a palmette symbol common in illuminated manuscripts. It is believed to be part of the east end of the earlier cathedral dedicated in 1197.

▦ HADDINGTON
St Mary *(top)*
At 197 ft in length, St Mary's is the largest parish church in Scotland. Known locally as 'The Lamp of

Lothian', it is cruciform in structure and has a splendid central tower that was once surmounted by a crown steeple. The earliest mention of a church is in 1139, at which time there were also monastic buildings; these all suffered at the hands of Edward III's army in 1355.

A new church was built, only to suffer under 'the siege of Haddington' 1547–49. John Knox, born across the river, insisted the Town Council carry out repairs in 1561, and the Victorians carried out even more changes. Even in the 1970s, restoration continued, as local people looking for a centre of renewal converted nearby buildings into youth and community buildings.

The west front of the nave is very impressive. In the choir is the tomb of Jane Baillie Welsh, the wife of writer and historian Thomas Carlyle. The Scallop Shell records early pilgrimages made between St Mary's and St James of Compostella in north-west Spain.

▦ INVERNESS
St Andrew's Episcopal Cathedral
(below)
Inverness is in a special position as gateway to the Highlands, and is a centre for many of the region's activities. It was also the capital of the Pictish kingdom as long ago as 565, when St Columba visited King Brude.

The massive, rose-coloured, twin-towered Episcopal Gothic cathedral was built in 1869–74 to the design of

Alexander Ross, and was the first cathedral to be built in Britain after the Reformation. Its many features include 11 bells, with the great tenor bell weighing a ton. The peal can be used as a carillon to play melodies. There is superb stained glass by John Hardman of Birmingham (1867–1910) and excellent woodwork in the choir rood screens and stalls. There are also polished pillars in the nave with a series of stone masks of men's faces.

But perhaps most remarkable are five gold engraved icons presented to Bishop Eden, the founder of the cathedral, by the Tzar of Russia in 1861 (his monument is in the north aisle). There is also an interesting painting of the Madonna and child, by the artist Sano di Pietro.

IONA
Iona Cathedral (below)

The sight of the cathedral on this small Hebridean island is unforgettable. White sandy beaches and low green hills provide a unique atmosphere, while the cathedral's 70-ft tower and pitched roofs dominate the entire landscape. In many ways, Iona is the cradle of Christianity in Britain, a place of pilgrimage and a centre for spiritual retreat and renewal.

It was on Iona that Columba arrived from Ireland in 563, when he was already 42. He soon founded a small monastery, and for another 36 years carried on the work of introducing Christianity to the Scottish mainland. He converted the northern Picts, and later sent out the missionary Aidan to Northumbria and Lindisfarne.

The cathedral still has some of the best examples of early Christian tombstones and crosses (many now housed in the church of St Ronan near the cathedral). With 48 kings of Scotland, Ireland and Norway buried here (including Macbeth), it is the oldest Christian burial ground in Scotland. It is also believed that part or whole of the *Book of Kells* was undertaken by the scribes and illuminators of the Iona community.

Nothing remains of the original monastery. Norsemen raided Iona time and time again, and it is believed that the relics of St Columba and the Book of Kells' eventually went back to Ireland. A 13th C Benedictine monastery here was also destroyed in 1561.

The present cathedral is dated 15th–16th C. The nave has no aisles, but it does have an ancient oratory in its north west corner, which apparently once held the shrine of St Columba. The Iona community (now an ecumenical community) was founded here in 1938, and those who live and work here continue a long tradition and ensure the rebirth of reflection and worship.

KIRKWALL (Orkney Islands)
St Magnus Cathedral (above)

St Magnus Cathedral would be an impressive building anywhere in the United Kingdom, but situated here on the main island of Orkney it is unique. It does not belong to any particular denomination, but is the property of the townspeople through a royal charter granted by James III in 1486.

Kirkwall has been capital of the Orkneys for many centuries, and is truly a cathedral city. The town has many Scandinavian-style buildings, and the Orkney See was part of the Norwegian diocese from 1154 until 1472.

The cathedral was founded in 1137 by Rognvald Jarl III as a penance for his uncle, who murdered St Magnus in 1115. It is cruciform in shape and built of flagstone, and red and yellow sandstone, in a massive Romanesque style. Similar to Durham and Dunfermline, the interior is massive and severe, but has a strong sense of unity. There is an interesting series of tombstones of Kirkwall's eminent men from the 16th C onwards. There is also a plaque that commemorates the 833 men lost in the Royal Oak in 1939.

Nearby, the 12th C bishop's palace—with its massive tower and Earl's Palace (added later, c.1600)—has been described as the 'most mature and accomplished piece of Renaissance architecture in Scotland'.

LEUCHARS
St Andrew

The 11th C apse and chancel show the finest Norman work in Scotland. Later a monastic church, St Andrew's has a 13th C tower and belfry and was restored 1914. Inside, there are crusaders' tombs and finely carved grotesques.

MONREITH
St Medana

Two chapels of the same dedication stand opposite each other over a promontory. They commemorate the maritime feat of the patron maiden, who reputedly floated between them on a rock.

The chapel here is unique in being hewn out of the stone cliff, and excavations have yielded pilgrims' badges and a sandstone statue which is possibly a representation of St Medana.

OBAN
Oban Cathedral *(above, right)*

There are two cathedrals in Oban, St Columba's Roman Catholic Cathedral and the Scottish Episcopal cathedral of St John the Divine, shown here.

St Columba's is built in pink granite and is one of the few cathedrals in the world built entirely of granite. Designed by Sir Giles Gilbert Scott, St Columba's is small, with a tall tower but without transepts.

The cathedral of St John dates from 1864, and has a sanctuary, choir, chapel, sacristy and aisle of red stone. While early building plans by James Chalmers were unfortunately never completed, a crossing and lantern were built in 1958, and considerable renovation work took place in the 1960s.

PAISLEY
Paisley Abbey *(below, right)*

A priory was founded here in 1163 by Walter Fitzalan, with monks from the Cluniac community at Wentlock. It became an abbey in 1245, although much of today's parish church is 15th C. This is due to destruction caused by the English in 1307 and subsequent re-buildings and restorations.

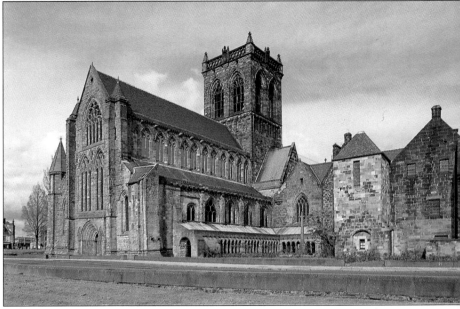

Paisley is one of the largest towns in Scotland and originally grew up around the 12th C monastic community. It is famous for its linen manufacture and the production of Paisley shawls (an imitation of Kashmir shawls). The Paisley pattern recurs in the stone work tracery of the abbey's stained-glass windows, and makes them one of the church's most interesting modern features.

Structurally, the west end and

doorway are impressive, and are in the first pointed style of the early 13th C. There is also an interesting processional doorway at the east end of the south wall of the nave.

A chapel in the church is dedicated to St Mirren, one of St Columba's friends and contemporaries, and Paisley's patron saint. It has a rare medieval sculptural frieze depicting the life of this little known Celtic monk. Marjorie, daughter of Robert the Bruce and mother of Robert II (the first Stewart King) is also thought to be buried here.

PERTH
St Matthew (below)
With its tall spire overlooking the River Tay, St Matthew's is one of this city's finest churches. Like many Scottish churches, it was built during the 19th C as a result of the 'disruption' in 1843 when the Free Church of Scotland was formed.

Fine stained glass is a feature of the church, which has a large gallery, and seats 900 people in all. An impressive suite of halls and rooms adjoins the building, used by the church and the local community. Not long ago, a convict escaped from the local prison,

and hid for some days under the hall floor before being recaptured.

RUTHWELL
Ruthwell Church
A pleasant church of classical design, it is particularly noted for the 'Ruthwell Cross', one of the foremost monuments of Dark Age Europe.

Standing 18 ft high, it was discovered under the church floor, placed there in the 17th C. Of 7th C date, there is inscribed upon it a runic text, a portion of the oldest poem in English literature, and numerous figure scenes. Now displayed in a specially designed apsidal annexe attached to the church.

ST ANDREWS
St Andrews Cathedral
Once the longest and greatest church in Scotland, this spectacular 12th C cathedral was largely destroyed after the Reformation.

The first church may have been 4th C, followed in the 8th C by another, built when Regulus brought holy relics of St Andrew to these shores from Greece. Scotland's only bishopric at that time was transferred here, not least to increase the already large numbers of pilgrims visiting the shrine.

Now a national monument, the cathedral grounds also contain extensive remains of Scotland's first Augustinian priory (c.1100), a museum, and St Regulus tower. A climb to the top of the tower affords a magnificent view of this small cliff-top city, including the beautiful St Salvator's chapel (c.1410) at the nearby University.

WIGTOWN
St Machutus
Of ancient origin, this church was rebuilt in 1730 and again in 1853. It has 10th C cross-shafts, and a remarkable memorial to the 'Wigtown Martyrs'—two women who were tied to a stake and drowned by the rising tide for their adherence to the faith of the Covenanters.

Glossary

Ambulatory, aisle around the chancel used for processions.

Ashlar, blocks of masonry with smoothed, squared surfaces. Also called 'dressed stone'.

Ambo, raised lectern, often used in medieval Italian churches, from which the Bible was read.

Apse, vaulted semi-circular east end of a chancel or chapel.

Aisle, side areas running parallel to the nave.

Altar, table or stone slab on supports used for celebration of the Eucharist.

Arch, structural support between two columns or piers made in an inverted curve.

Arcade, range of arches carried on columns or piers.

Aumbry, cupboard or recess used for storing cups and plates used in the Eucharist.

Bay, section of wall between pillars. Generally a nave consists of a succession of bays, each with the same combination of windows and columns.

Bema, raised platform in early churches, on which preacher stood to speak.

Blind (as in 'blind tracery', 'blind arcade', etc.), decorative feature applied to the surface of a wall rather than standing free.

Boss, ornamental knob covering the intersection of ribs in a vault or ceiling.

Baptistry, building or section of the church used for baptisms; or a baptism pool.

Basilica, early style of church, consisting of a nave and two or more lower, narrower aisles.

Buttress, brick or stonework built against a wall to give it support.

Capital, top crowning feature of a column or pier.

Carrel (or carol), niche in a cloister, designed for a monk to sit in and work.

Chancel, eastern end of a church, sometimes reserved for the clergy and choir.

Chevron, Romanesque decoration in form of a zig-zag.

Chapter house, assembly room in a monastery or cathedral used for discussion of business.

Choir, area of the church where the services are sung.

Churrigueresque, florid, highly-decorated, late Baroque style, found particularly in Spain and Mexico.

Clerestory, upper level of the nave wall, pierced by windows.

Cloisters, external quadrangle surrounded by a covered walkway.

Column, vertical, load-bearing shaft with circular cross-section, usually slightly tapered.

Compound pier, upright support comprised of a cluster of shafts, not necessarily attached to each other.

Corbel, projecting stone block which supports a beam.

Cornice, topmost decorative moulded section surmounting a column. Also any projecting moulding at the roof level of a building.

Corinthian order, see ORDER.

Crypt, space beneath the main floor of a church.

Diaperwork, ornamental pattern of repeated lozenges or squares.

Dogtooth, Early English and Norman ornamental pattern consisting of series of three-dimensional, star-like shapes.

Dome, vault built on a circular base.

Dressed stone, see ASHLAR.

Drum, round vertical wall supporting a dome.

Elevation, square-on 'flat' view of the back, front or side of a building.

Entablature, uppermost part of the 'order' surmounting a column. Consists of cornice, frieze and architrave.

Engaged shaft, see HALF SHAFT.

Facing, finish material applied to the outside of a building.

Fan vault, see VAULT.

Finial, ornament at the tip of a spire, pinnacle or canopy.

Flamboyant, late Gothic style in France, characterized by wavy lines of tracery.

Flying buttress, buttress in the form of an arch, supporting the upper portion of a wall.

Gallery (or tribune), upper storey inside a church, above the aisle, open to the nave.

Gargoyle, water spout projecting from a roof, often carved as a head or figure.

Groin vault, see VAULT.

Grisaille, stained glass with mostly white glass in small lozenge-shaped panes painted in decorative patterns.

Half shaft, shaft or column partially attached to or let into a wall. Also called 'engaged shaft'.

Hall church, church in which nave and aisles are about the same height.

Iconostasis, screen in a Byzantine church which separates the nave from the sanctuary, usually with three doors 187 and covered with images (icons).

Icon, image of a saint, apostle or ~~martyr used in and for worship of~~ God, especially in Eastern churches.

Iconoclasm, opposition to the veneration of religious images.

Ionic order, see ORDER.

Keystone, central stone in an arch or rib.

Lancet window, narrow window with a pointed arch.

Lady chapel, chapel dedicated to the Virgin Mary, often at the east end of the church.

Lantern, circular or polygonal tower topping a dome or roof.

Lights, openings between the mullions of a window.

Lintel, horizontal timber or stone beam.

Martyrion, memorial or church building constructed over the grave of a martyr.

Misericord, bracket on the underside of the hinged seat of the choir stall, provided for monks to lean against while standing through long services.

Mouldings, contoured shaping given to projecting elements such as arches, lintels, string courses, etc.

Mullion, wooden or stone framework within a window.

Narthex, vestibule across the west end of a church.

Nave, main middle section of the inside of a church running from the west end to the crossing.

Ogee arch, arch with two S-shaped curves meeting at the apex.

Order, combination of columns, base, capitals, and entablature developed in ancient ~~Rome and~~ Greece, and extensively copied in periods of classical revival. The most usual orders are the Doric, Ionic and Corinthian.

Pediment, gently pitched gable above a portico.

Pier, solid vertical masonry support with non-circular cross-section.

Pilaster, shallow pier or squared column attached to a wall.

Pinnacle, small tower-like top to a spire, buttress, etc.

Piscina, basin in a niche, for washing the vessels used in the Eucharist.

Plinth, projecting base of a wall.

Portico, entrance in the form of an open or partially-enclosed roofed space.

Pyx, container in which the bread consecrated for the Eucharist is kept. It is often elaborately carved or decorated.

Quoins, dressed stones at the corner of a building, often protruding slightly from the face of the wall.

Reredos, raised decorated screen behind the communion table.

Retro-choir, area behind the communion table in a cathedral.

Rib, projecting stone or brickwork on a ceiling or vault, usually load-bearing.

Rood, the old Saxon word for cross. Crucifix attached to a 'rood beam' and usually flanked by images of saints.

Rood screen, screen below the rood separating the chancel from the nave, sometimes substantial enough to carry a 'rood loft', or gallery.

Sanctuary, area around the communion table at the east end of a church.

Sedilia, seats for the clergy built into the south wall of the chancel.

Spire, tall conical or polygonal structure built on top of a tower.

Squinch, arches placed diagonally across the corner of an intersection of walls to carry a tower, drum, or dome.

Stalls, row of carved wooden or stone seats in the choir.

Steeple, combination of tower and spire.

Strainer arch, a reinforced arch, e.g. with bolts or canvas strapping.

String course, projecting moulded horizontal band of stonework.

Tabernacle, ornamental receptacle or recess for relics or the sacraments used in the Eucharist.

Transept, transverse arms of a cross-shaped church.

Tribune, gallery above the aisle in some cathedrals.

Triforium, middle level of nave between the arcade and clerestory.

Tracery, ornamental, shaped stone or woodwork in windows or screens.

Tympanum, area between the lintel of a doorway and the arch above it, usually decorated.

Vault, arched ceiling. There are several types of vault: the barrel (or tunnel) vault, the groin vault, the fan vault, the lierne vault and the quadripartite vault.